The Charlie Chan Films

The Charlie Chan Films

By James L. Neibaur

BearManor Media
2018

The Charlie Chan Films

© 2018 James L. Neibaur

All rights reserved.

No portion of this publication may be reproduced, stored, and/or copied electronically (except for academic use as a source), nor transmitted in any form or by any means without the prior written permission of the publisher and/or author.

Published in the United States of America by:

BearManor Media
P. O. Box 71426
Albany, GA 31708

BearManorMedia.com

Printed in the United States.

Typesetting and layout by John Teehan

ISBN—978-1-62933-314-4

This book is dedicated to the memory my grandmother, Josephine Rizzo (1911–1995) who used to love the Charlie Chan movies, and saw most of them first-run at the theater. Thanks Grandma.

I wish I could walk upstairs and watch movies with you again.

Contents

Acknowledgments xi

Introduction 1

The History of Charlie Chan 3

Charlie Chan Carries On 7

The Black Camel 13

Charlie Chan's Chance 21

Charlie Chan's Greatest Case 25

Charlie Chan's Courage 29

Charlie Chan In London 33

Charlie Chan In Paris 41

Charlie Chan In Egypt 47

Charlie Chan In Shanghai 53

Charlie Chan's Secret 59

Charlie Chan's At the Circus 65

Charlie Chan At the Race Track 71

Charlie Chan At the Opera 79

Charlie Chan At the Olympics 87

Charlie Chan On Broadway 95

Charlie Chan At Monte Carlo 103

Charlie Chan At the Ringside/Mr. Moto's Gamble 109

Charlie Chan In Honolulu 115

Charlie Chan In Reno 121

Charlie Chan At Treasure Island 127

City In Darkness 135

Charlie Chan In Panama 143

Charlie Chan's Murder Cruise 149

Charlie Chan At the Wax Museum 155

Murder Over New York 159

Dead Men Tell 165

Charlie Chan In Rio 169

Castle In the Desert 175

Charlie Chan In Transition 179

Charlie Chan In the Secret Service 183

The Chinese Cat 187

Black Magic 193

The Jade Mask 197

The Scarlet Clue 203

The Shanghai Cobra 209

The Red Dragon 213

Dark Alibi 217

Shadows Over Chinatown 223

Dangerous Money 229

The Trap 235

The Chinese Ring 241

Docks of New Orleans 247

The Shanghai Chest 253

The Golden Eye 259

The Feathered Serpent 265

The Sky Dragon 269

Charlie Chan After the Movies 275

Appendix A: Revealing the Murderer In Each Movie ... 281

Appendix B: Bibliography 287

Acknowledgements

SPECIAL THANKS to Katie Carter for continuing to live every book with me and offer her own suggestions and insights. Her contribution is always invaluable.

Another special thank you to Kelly Parmelee who helped so much with the research on this project, working tirelessly to find as much info as she could. Thanks Hero!

Richard Finegan offered a wealth of wonderful photos and graphics as well as other materials that assisted us in our research.

Thanks to Michael Blake, who shared his father's recollections of having appeared in Sidney Toler's final movie. Also thanks to Jeffrey Roberts who told of his friend Elena Verdugo's memories of working in what turned out to be the last Chan movie in the entire series.

So many thanks to Rush Glick and the wonderful Charlie Chan Family website that was such of an enormous help with our research. His hard work deserves special praise.

And, certainly, to the late Mantan Moreland, who took time out of his day to talk to a couple of fans that randomly phoned him way back in 1971. His vivid memories of working in the Charlie Chan films are seeing print for the first time in this book.

Further thanks is extended to Max Neibaur, Ted Okuda, Allie Schulz, Terri Lynch, Brian Taves, Steve Elliot, Jennie Lloyd, Micah Carey, and the late Ken Hanke,

Introduction

THE DETECTIVE DRAMAS featuring Chinese sleuth Charlie Chan solving crimes with shrewd patience and relaxed good humor have been popular in literature, on stage, in movies, the radio, television, even the Sunday comics. It is the film series for Fox (later Twentieth Century Fox), and Monogram that will be the focus of this text.

Based on the popular books by Earl Derr Biggers, the Charlie Chan films began with a couple of silent movies, and an early talkie, before beginning a continuing series featuring Warner Oland from 1931 until his death in 1938, then Sidney Toler until he died in 1947, and finally Roland Winters until the series concluded in 1949. While we will discuss the earlier films in a chapter on the character's history, it is the 44 films from 1931-1949 that this study will be specifically discussing.

Each film in the series will get its own chapter, and will offer credits, the plot, an assessment of the film, and information about its production, its reception, the actors, the director, and screenwriters. Along with the early silents, four of the films in the series proper are now lost, and those chapters will be based on what research can provide. There will be a concluding chapter on later presentations of the character. This will include the TV series featuring J.Carroll Naish, later features with Ross Martin and Peter Ustinov, and a cartoon with Charlie Chan voiced by noted number-one-son actor Keye Luke.

The book's intent is to offer an appreciation of a detective mystery series from the 1930s and 1940s that continues to be fresh and enjoyable as late as the 21st century, due to the appeal of its actors, writers, and directors. Whether it is a vintage production from the prestigious 20th Century Fox studios or a low budget quickie from the poverty row Monogram Pictures, the Charlie Chan films are always diverting and good humored.

The History of Charlie Chan

CHAN WAS CREATED by author Earl Derr Biggers, a Midwestern-born writer who had scored in 1913 with the popular novel *Seven Keys to Baldpate* which was adapted into a Broadway play by George M. Cohan, who also starred in the 1917 movie version. One of Derr Biggers' early novels, *Love Insurance* (1914), was later revamped into a musical comedy film entitled *One Night in the Tropics* (1940), which is notable as being the movie debut of Bud Abbott and Lou Costello.

Charlie Chan was conceived by Biggers while vacationing in Hawaii in 1919. The character was based on an actual Asian American detective in Hawaii by the name of Chang Apana (1871-1933). Pondering the possibility of a Chinese detective over several years, it was 1925, before the author's first Chan book, *House Without a Key*, was released. Biggers wrote six books featuring Chan, also including *The Chinese Parrot* (1926), *Behind That Curtain* (1928), *The Black Camel* (1929), *Charlie Chan Carries On* (1930), and *Keeper of the Keys* (1932). While he planned to continue the series, Biggers died of a sudden heart attack in 1933 at the age of only 48. He lived to see all of his books adapted into movies, except *Keeper of the Keys*, which was never made into a film (it was adapted into a Broadway play in 1933).

Biggers' presentation of Charlie Chan was said to be partly a reaction to how the Chinese were being portrayed as evil in such films as D.W. Griffith's *Broken Blossoms* (1919), or the Fu Manchu books and movies. He created Charlie Chan as a shrewdly deductive, patient, and good-humored sleuth who solved crimes on an international level. Biggers described Chan in the first novel as walking daintily "like a woman" and being "very fat indeed," emphasizing a non-threatening appearance.

This description was not carefully followed in subsequent movie versions.

The first time Charlie Chan appeared on film was in the 1926 movie adaption of the novel *The House Without a Key*, produced by the Pathé studios as a ten-chapter serial directed by Spencer Gordon Bennet. Chan is a supporting character, portrayed by Japanese actor George Kuwa (1885-1931). The popularity of the Charlie Chan novels, serialized in *The Saturday Evening Post*, sparked initial interest in the serial, with *Moving Picture World* reporting:[1]

> Pathé's newest mystery serial, *The House Without a Key*, is now proving in the number of advanced circuit bookings already consummated, to be one of the greatest Pathé serial box office attractions released to date. When Shown before special previewers representing the Loew Circuit, it was immediately contracted to run in twenty-two theaters. In addition to this contract, *The House Without a Key* has been booked for such important New York circuits as the Small-Straussbeg circuit, the Rosenwiecz and Katz, Meyer and Schneider, and the William Yost and Chrisedge Circuits.

The serial featured Allene Ray and Walter Miller in the leads, based on their popularity in previous Pathé serials like *The Green Archer* (1925) and *Snowed In* (1926), both also directed by Bennet. Frank Lackteen, the villain in *The Green Archer*, played such a role in this film as well.

While critics were dismissive, moviegoers enjoyed *The House Without a Key*, with one theater owner reporting to the *Exhibitor's Herald World*: "The best serial that I have run. Increased attendance by 15 percent and holding them." Chan's supporting role was not played by an actor who fit Biggers' dainty, rotund description. George Kuwa (born Keiichi Kuwahara in Japan), was slender and attractive. Kuwa was already a ten year veteran of movies when he took the Chan role, having already appeared with Rudolph Valentino in *Moran of the Lady Letty* (1922), and with Jackie Coogan in *Daddy* (1923). While *The House Without a Key* is a lost film, accounts at the time describe Kuwa's approach to the role as one of stern stoicism.

Kuwa also appeared in the second Charlie Chan film, *The Chinese Parrot*, based on Biggers' second Chan novel. However, Kuwa did not

---

1. "House Without a Key" review *Moving Picture World*. November 26, 1926

play Chan in this movie. That role was essayed by another Japanese actor, Sôjin Kamiyama (1884-1954). This Universal feature is also lost, which is a pity as it was helmed by German director Paul Leni, noted for the expressionist classic *The Cat and the Canary* (1927). His approach to the Biggers' material would likely offer a very interesting vision, Leni also having experience in art direction. Kamiyama's Chan character was also a supporting role, with Marian Nixon and Edmund Burns in the leads. In the studio's periodical *Universal Weekly*, a moviegoer from Saginaw, Michigan wrote in to state:[2]

> It gives me great pleasure to pronounce a 100 percent rating for Paul Leni's *The Chinese Parrot*. I am very fond of Edmund Burns, and have seen him in several films. Hobart Bosworth is without question a might fine actor who played his part with earnestness and sincerity. But Sôjin Kamiyama took away all the honors in this picture. He surely is a fine actor.

It was 1929 before another Charlie Chan feature was produced, this time a talkie, *Behind That Curtain*, for the Fox studios. A pre-release ad in *Exhibitors Herald-World* indicated: "A private screening recently of *Behind That Curtain* brought 200 branch managers and salesmen to their feet cheering." The film was chosen to open the new Fox Theater in San Francisco in June of 1929.

Behind That Curtain, based on the Biggers novel, is only interesting as being the first Fox film to feature the detective, to be the third and final time Chan was played by an Asian actor in an American film, and featuring such notables as Warner Baxter, Lois Moran, and Boris Karloff (in his first sound movie). E. L. Park (1876-1948), who played Chan, was American born, but of Korean descent. His daughters Bo Ling and Bo Chung were also actresses and can be spotted in the Paramount musical comedy feature *International House* (1932), featuring W.C. Fields, George Burns and Gracie Allen, Bela Lugosi, Rudy Vallee, and Cab Calloway. Bo Ling would briefly show up in a couple of the Charlie Chan movies during the 1930s.

Behind That Screen gives little footage to the Chan character, and not until toward the end of the movie, and offers little of Biggers' original concept. Rather than focus on the story involving Chan, the movie instead

---

2. "The Chinese Parrot." *Universal Weekly*. September 17, 1927

focuses on the book's tangential sub-plot of a runaway wife. This early melodrama does not hold up nearly as well as any of the ensuing Charlie Chan films, with the sort of affected delivery of dialog that hampers many early talkies. Its historical significance would be nil if not for it being Karloff's talkie debut as well as the first sound film in which the Charlie Chan character appears at all.

It was 1931 when Fox produced a film version of Biggers' novel *Charlie Chan Carries On* featuring Swedish-born Warner Oland as Chan, and the first to feature Charlie Chan as the central character. Warner Oland's approach to the role is also noted as the quintessential interpretation of Chan, on which his successors would base their portrayals. Claiming to have some Mongolian in his heritage, Oland reportedly exhibited the look of a Chinese man by merely combing his mustache downward and his eyebrows upward. Taking the role seriously, Oland studied the Chinese language and its culture in order to properly convey his idea of the character. It is this film that is considered the first of the series.

Charlie Chan Carries On

Director: Hamilton MacFadden
Screenplay and Dialogue: Philip Klein; Barry Conners
Based on the novel *Charlie Chan Carries On* by Earl Derr Biggers
Cinematography: George Schneiderman
Film Editor: Al DeGaetano

Cast:
Warner Oland: Charlie Chan,
Marguerite Churchill: Pamela Potter
John Garrick: Mark Kennaway
Warren Hymer: Max Minchin
Marjorie White: Sadie Minchin
C. Henry Gordon: John Ross
William Holden: Patrick Tait
George Brent: Captain Ronald Keane
Peter Gawthorne: Inspector Duff
John T. Murray: Doctor Lofton
John Swor: Elmer Benbow
Goodee Montgomery: Mrs. Benbow
Jason Robards, Sr.: Walter Honywood
Lumsden Hare: Inspector Hayley
Zeffie Tillbury: Mrs. Luce
Betty Francisco: Sybil Conway
Harry Beresford: Kent
John Rogers: Martin
J.G. Davis: Eben

Shooting days: December 26, 1930 to January 29, 1931
Released April 12, 1931 by the Fox Film Corporation
Running Time: 69 minutes, black and white

AS THIS IS THE FILM that introduced the movie Charlie Chan as we know him, it is especially maddening that *Charlie Chan Carries On* is a lost film. This prevents us from assessing the director's vision, the impact of the screenplay, and the effectiveness of the actors. Our information as to what happens in the movie comes from an examination of the script.

In this film, a man named Hugh Morris Drake is murdered while on world tour, and Inspector Duff of Scotland Yard is contacted. It is discovered that Drake was murdered with a strap from luggage belonging to the head of the tour, Dr. Lofton. There is not enough evidence to hold the other tourists, but the man with the room next to Drake, Walter Honywood, is questioned. It is later found that Honywood and Drake had changed rooms the night that Drake was murdered. Honywood is then also murdered, with a gun that is found in his own hand. Duff contacts Honywood's estranged wife, who identifies the murderer as her ex-husband Jim Everhard, a jewel thief, as revenge for her having run away with Honywood and taking two bags of jewels. In Hong Kong, an attempt is made on the life of Pamela Potter, Drake's granddaughter, who has continued on the world tour in an attempt to uncover her grandfather's killer.

Charlie Chan gets involved when Inspector Duff travels to Honolulu prior to the tour's arriving there. Duff visits Chan, who is a friend, and is shot in the back. At that point Chan joins the tour as it heads to San Francisco. When they are gathered, he states that Everhard had planned to murder Honywood, but mistakenly killed Drake after the two men changed rooms. Chan continues that he has written a letter to the Everhard, who is traveling on the tour undercover, when in fact he has written identical e to all the suspects. He states that the note indicates he will not arrest Everhard until they dock. Chan then puts out a dummy to represent himself, and when one of the suspects attempts to shoot it, he reveals himself to be the murderer and is arrested (see Appendix A).

Charlie Chan Carries On is based on Earl Derr Biggers' novel of the same name that had been serialized in *The Saturday Evening Post* from August 9 through September 13, 1930. Warner Oland's vision, his approach to the character, was to define it for movie audiences and continue

Trade ad for *Charlie Chan Carries On*

to be the blueprint from which later actors would work. It is unfortunate that a four minute trailer is all the exists of his performance in this film. Along with the script, a Spanish version of this film, *Eran Trece*, with Manuel Arbó as Charlie Chan, is available. This allows us to see how the Biggers material plays out as a film, and this version does contain stock footage from the English speaking one, but it still gives us no indication as to Oland's initial performance as Chan. We can garner, through criticism, as to how well it was received.

In the July 31, 1931 issue of *Motion Picture Magazine* its critic singled out Oland's performance as the reason why *Charlie Chan Carries On* was effective:[1]

> Warner Oland is perfect as the smooth-tongued Oriental. His performance demands a continuance of the Chan character in further adventures of the humorous fellow. Others in the cast are likewise capable, but the laurel wreath goes, as it should, to Oland. It is to be regretted that his entrance into the story occurs so late in the footage. At any rate, let's have more of Charlie Chan. He is a welcome change from our drawing-room problem dramas.

---

1. "Charlie Chan Carries On" *Motion Picture Magazine.* July 31, 1931

The Swedish-born Oland came to America as a child, and became fluent in both English and Swedish, helping to translate the work of August Strindberg. He and his wife, whom he married in 1907, published a book of translated Strindberg plays in 1912. Oland's film career began deep into the silent movie era, and he played Asians in many movies prior to taking on the Chan role, including the title role in *The Mysterious Dr. Fu Manchu*, being the first film portrayal of that character. He would portray Fu Manchu in three more movies. Oland would play Asian characters in other films even after debuting as Chan, including *Shanghai Express* (1932) and *Werewolf of London* (1935). He needed no special makeup to play the Charlie Chan character. Oland also, notably, played the cantor father in *The Jazz Singer* (1927) with Al Jolson, a milestone for being the first feature with spoken dialog.

Charlie Chan Carries On is also the first Chan movie to present the character using astute observations such as "Only very brave mouse make nest in cat's ear," "all mischief begins with opening of mouth, "man seldom scratches where he does not itch," and "talk will not cook rice." Oland's delivery of such lines would continue to improve with each subsequent movie, and became among the most anticipated aspects of his performance.

Marguerite Churchill and John Garrick in *Charlie Chan Carries On*

Along with our inability to see Oland's first crack at the Chan character in movies, the lost status of *Charlie Chan Carries On* prevents us from enjoying the supporting performances by Marguerite Churchill and John Garrick, two noted stars of screen drama during the pre-code era, as well as the comic relief of Warren Hymer and Marjorie White, two appealing comedy performers whose careers were cut short by early death. Hymer continued to bolster every movie in which he appeared until off-screen alcoholism led to his passing at only 42. Marjorie White, perhaps best known for appearing with The Three Stooges in their first Columbia short, *Woman Haters* (1934) died from injuries suffered in a car accident in 1935. As Max and Sadie, the two offered dialog exchanges to lighten up the heaviness of the mystery:

> MAX: The first thing to remember if anybody here done it, don't say nothin' until you seen a lawyer.
>
> SADIE: Come on, Maxie, it's no use nursing a grudge, nobody's accusin' you.
>
> MAX: Patrol your own beat, I'm takin' no info from a skirt!
>
> MRS. LUCE: What language is he speaking?

C. Henry Gordon would appear in several more Charlie Chan features, while Zeffie Tilbury is perhaps best known for her role in *The Grapes of Wrath* (1940). It should be noted that the William Holden who appears in this film is not the Oscar winning actor who stars in such films as *Stalag 17* (1952), *Sunset Boulevard* (1950), *The Bridge on the River Kwai* (1957), *Network* (1976), etc.. This William Holden died in 1932, while the more famous one did not enter films until 1939.

The fact that *Charlie Chan Carries On* was popular enough to ignite a successful series makes it significant on the most basic level, along with other milestones regarding Warner Oland, et. al. In 1940, Twentieth Century-Fox would revisit the story *Charlie Chan Carries On* under the title *Charlie Chan's Murder Cruise*.

Bela Lugosi and Warner Oland

The Black Camel

Producer and Director: Hamilton MacFadden
Screenplay: Barry Conners; Philip Klein
Original Story: Earl Derr Biggers
Adapted by: Hugh Strange
Cinematography: Joseph August; Daniel Clark
Film Editor: Al DeGaetano

Cast:
Warner Oland: Charlie Chan
Sally Eilers: Julie O'Neill
Bela Lugosi: Tarneverro
Dorothy Revier: Shelah Fane
Victor Varconi: Robert Fyfe
Murray Kinnell: Smith
William Post, Jr.: Alan Jaynes
Robert Young: Jimmy Bradshaw
Violet Dunn: Anna
J.M. Kerrigan: Thomas MacMasters
Mary Gordon: Mrs. MacMasters
Rita Rozelle: Luana
Otto Yamaoka: Kashimo
Dwight Frye: Jessop
Richard Tucker: Wilkie Ballou
Marjorie White: Rita Ballou
C. Henry Gordon: Huntley Van Horn
Robert Homans: Chief of Police
Louise Mackintosh: Librarian
Hamilton MacFadden: Val Martino

James Wang: Wong
Melvin Paoa: Hawaiian Beach Boy
Bo Ling: Number One Chan Daughter

Shooting days: Early April to early May, 1931
Released July 1931 by the Fox Film Corporation
Running Time: 71 minutes. Black and white

EARL DER BIGGERS' *The Black Camel* had originally published serially in *The Saturday Evening Post* between May 18 and June 22, 1929. Of the five films based specifically on novels by Biggers, *The Black Camel* is the only one that currently survives. The others are all lost films. It is also the only Charlie Chan movie to be shot on location.

While working on a movie in Honolulu, actress Shelah Fayne (Dorothy Revier) arranges for a mystic named Tarneverro (Bela Lugosi) to fly in from Hollywood and stay near the filming location. Shelah has been using Tarneverro as an advisor and has come to depend upon him. When she tells her friend Julie (Sally Eilers) that she will be asking the mystic's advice on whether to marry her wealthy boyfriend Alan Jaynes, Julie expresses concern over Tarneverro's influence. Honolulu detective Charlie Chan is investigating the unsolved murder of film star Denny Mayo, who was killed years earlier and meets Tarneverro at his hotel to discuss it with him.

With the film's opening, director Hamilton MacFadden creates a scene that details Shelah's trip to Hawaii for filming and the escalation of her affair with Jaynes through newspaper headlines. It is an effective way of introducing the characters and setting the scene without a lot of unnecessary exposition.

Julie and her boyfriend, the film's publicity agent Jimmy Bradshaw (Robert Young), find Shelah dead in her hotel room. Julie has Jimmy remove Shelah's emerald ring before notifying the police. Chan is called upon to investigate and asks Tarneverro to accompany him. Tarneverro informs Chan that Shelah confessed to having murdered Denny.

At this point in the film, the audience knows more than the characters in the film. There is a pivotal scene between Tarneverro and Shelah where the mystic questions her repeatedly about the murder and her emotional level gradually rises as the interrogation becomes louder and more heated. Director Hamilton MacFadden shoots this scene in the dark, with a

Dwight Frye, Bela Lugosi, C. Henry Gordon, Warner Oland, Richard Tucker, William Post, Jr.

large crystal ball illuminating the faces of Tarneverro and Shelah. The scene is effectively staged, with MacFadden cutting from medium shots to close-ups as the emotional state of the characters increases.

Dorothy Revier, a veteran actress of ten years in movies by this time, has little to do in this film, as she is murdered during the early scenes. Her strongest impact occurs during this sequence with Bela Lugosi, who exhibits a powerful command. Lugosi plays Tarneverro as very grounded and stately, someone who appears as secure and in control as he does mysterious. The fact that the audience is more aware than the characters in the film creates a heightened feeling of suspense, and wonderment as to when and how Chan will piece together all these little snippets that cast suspicion on virtually every character.

A bit of ominous foreshadowing occurs when Shelah returns to her room and tears up a photo of Denny Mayo. The photo is autographed and the hotel servant, Anna, sees the ripped piece featuring the actor's name, and reacts in a startled manner as she back out of the room after making a delivery.

The dynamic between Warner Oland and Bela Lugosi is an interesting one. Of course Chan is equally grounded and controlled, the steadiness of his appearance occasionally being disrupted by the sudden appearances of his helper, Kashimo (Otto Yamaoka), who frequently interrupts the action by running in and shouting "Clue!" and offering his attempts to assist in the investigation. However, his scenes with Lugosi offer almost a teaming-up of sorts as the two men discover clues (e.g. that a bouquet of flowers has been stomped on), discuss their significance, and come to joint, but tentative, conclusions.

When Chan gathers all of the suspects and indicates they are not to leave, he fields the varying protests and insists the killer is among them. In these scenes Oland controls the footage while Lugosi stands apart, mingling among the suspects and assisting the proceedings in his own way. Kashimo had earlier delivered the ripped photograph of Denny Mayo from Shelah's room, but as Chan is piecing it together, Kashimo enters and the wind from the open door blows the photo pieces off the table. Chan reacts in anger, pounding the table, in an outburst that seems jarring to the character's usual solid patience and calm.

The tangential characters that surround the story add to its atmosphere. The wealthy, entitled Wilkie Ballou and his attractive blonde wife Rita, who is much too young and too pretty to not have married for money, offer a neat contrast in character. Ballou is impatient and feels that the entire proceedings are an inconvenience. His wife exhibits starry-eyed fascination with each new development. The equally inconvenienced McMasters adds weight to the Ballou character, and both are offset by Alan Jaynes (William Post, jr.) who had wanted to marry Shelah, and the appearance of Shelah's ex-husband Robert Fyfe (Victor Varconi), a red herring who confesses to Shelah's murder. It is part of another plot tangent where Smith (Murray Kinnell), an artist, is found outside the pavilion and upon his entrance, Fyfe impulsively confesses. However, Chan realizes Fyfe's whereabouts when the murder takes place and indicates the he is the only one of the gathered suspects who could not possibly have murdered Shelah.

Smith's involvement becomes more layered as he indicates he overheard Shelah's confession to murdering Denny Mayo, and will reveal this and destroy the actress's legacy. He tries to blackmail Fyfe into buying one of his paintings, but is shot in the dark woods. He makes his way back to his hut, where his wife, Luana (Rita Rozelle) summons Chan and accuses Fyfe. A dying Smith reveals that Shelah killed Mayo and Fyfe corroborates his story, admitting he confessed to protect his ex-wife's memory. Chan places him under arrest.

This plot tangent moves away from the central mystery but does not distract from it. It does have a connection and further allows Chan's deeper understanding of the Shelah's backstory. The protectiveness over Shelah's legacy extends to Julie, who, after Jimmy's urging, admits to Chan that she removed an emerald ring from Shelah that has an inscription from Mayo.

When Chan discovers the stomped-upon bouquet of orchids has a missing pin, he realizes the pin is in the shoe of the murderer and it is this clue that reveals who killed Shelah (see Appendix A). When the murderer is revealed, that person's lover pulls a gun, but is disarmed. Furthermore, Tarneverro is discovered to be Mayo's brother, and was posing as a mystic to get close to Shelah and find out who murdered his brother.

The film ends on a gag. Kashimo rushes in to announce he has another clue, but since this case is solved, Charlie Chan advises him to save it for their next one.

The Black Camel was filmed in April and May of 1931, and Universal had released *Dracula*, featuring Bela Lugosi in the title role, the previous February. As a result, Lugosi had achieved a powerful mainstream popularity and had some level of clout while working on *The Black Camel*. He suggested Dwight Frye, so brilliant as Renfield in *Dracula*, for the part of a strange, jittery servant who figures prominently at the conclusion of the film.

The eeriness of the film is somehow bolstered by the fact that this early talkie offers no background music during the non-verbal scenes. The sensitive microphones pick up the wind during the outdoor location shooting, and it is this noise that backs up the dialog. The romantic leads, typical for this era, are fresh-faced and attractive. Robert Young, in his first credited role in a feature film, would enjoy a successful career in films and television, while Sally Eilers would enjoy a career that had her working with the likes of Buster Keaton, Spencer Tracy, and Randolph Scott, albeit most of her movies were B's. Similarly, Dorothy Revier would be known as "queen of poverty row," and even the great Lugosi would move to low budget movies as his career continued. Of course the Charlie Chan series itself would follow this same trajectory.

Sally Eilers didn't want to appear in this film, solely due to the fact that it was to be shot on location. She didn't want to leave her husband, western star Hoot Gibson, back in Hollywood. She and Gibson had married a year earlier. The studio convinced her to remain with the project by allowing Gibson to accompany her on location in Hawaii.

Comic relief would eventually become a central part of any Charlie Chan movie, but this was Otto Yamaoka's only appearance as Kashimo. The actor appeared pretty regularly throughout the 1930s, but did not extend into the next decade. Although Yamaoka was born in Seattle, Washington, he was still placed in an interment camp during World War Two. After being released from the camp in August of 1943, Otto Yamaoka did not return to the film industry. He died in New York in 1967. Yamaoka also had a sister, Iris, who was in some films during the thirties, who also was interred, never returned to films, and relocated to New York where she died in 1960.

Along with Kashimo, the heaviness of the murder mystery is lightened up by a short scene with Chan, at home, having dinner with his wife and many children, all of whom offer typical American slang as a counterpart to their father's tentative English.

None of the dialogue in *The Black Camel* is stilted as is sometimes the case in early talkies, and all of the actors do a fine job. It is also a plus that the film was shot on location in Hawaii, and the use of native music. It's very atmospheric—beautiful, but also dark and creepy when the occasion calls for it, like some of the nighttime scenes by the beach.

The Black Camel was a big hit for the Fox corporation. *The Motion Picture Herald* stated:[1]

> Warner Oland has never given a better performance than that of Charlie Chan in this production. He shares the honors with Bela Lugosi whose portrayal of Tarneverro is masterly. Dorothy Revier is convincing in the role of Shelah Fane, although her is but a brief appearance. Sally Eilers, also, is pleasing as the devoted secretary who finds romance during the unhappy hours following the star's death. Hamilton MacFadden deserves great credit for the direction. There are some clever touches of comedy introduced to lighten the drama. On the whole, an unusually good offering.

There is one charming anecdote to *The Black Camel*. Chang Apana, the actual detective on which the Charlie Chan character is based, was on the

---

1. "The Black Camel" *Motion Picture Herald*. May 16, 1931

set for most of the location shooting in Honolulu. According to a story in *The New Yorker*:[2]

> Chang Apana, now in his sixties, was invited to watch the filming. He and Oland met, on Kailua Beach, and posed for a photograph together. Chang looks amused. Oland is grinning. Oland inscribed the back of the photograph, "To my dear friend, Charlie Chang, 'The bravest of all,' with best of luck, from the new 'Charlie Chan,' Warner Oland."
>
> Chang missed hardly a day of shooting. In one scene, someone tells Charlie Chan that he ought to have a lie detector. "Lie detector?" Chan asks. "Ah, I see! You mean wife. I got one." Chang laughed and laughed.

The success of this film caused Fox executives to arrange for another Charlie Chan mystery to be produced. This time, their source material would again be *Behind That Curtain*, which had been filmed a few years earlier, but relegated the Chan character to a supporting role. This would not be the case with *Charlie Chan's Chance*.

---

2. LePore, Jill. *Chan The Man*. The New Yorker. August 20, 2010.

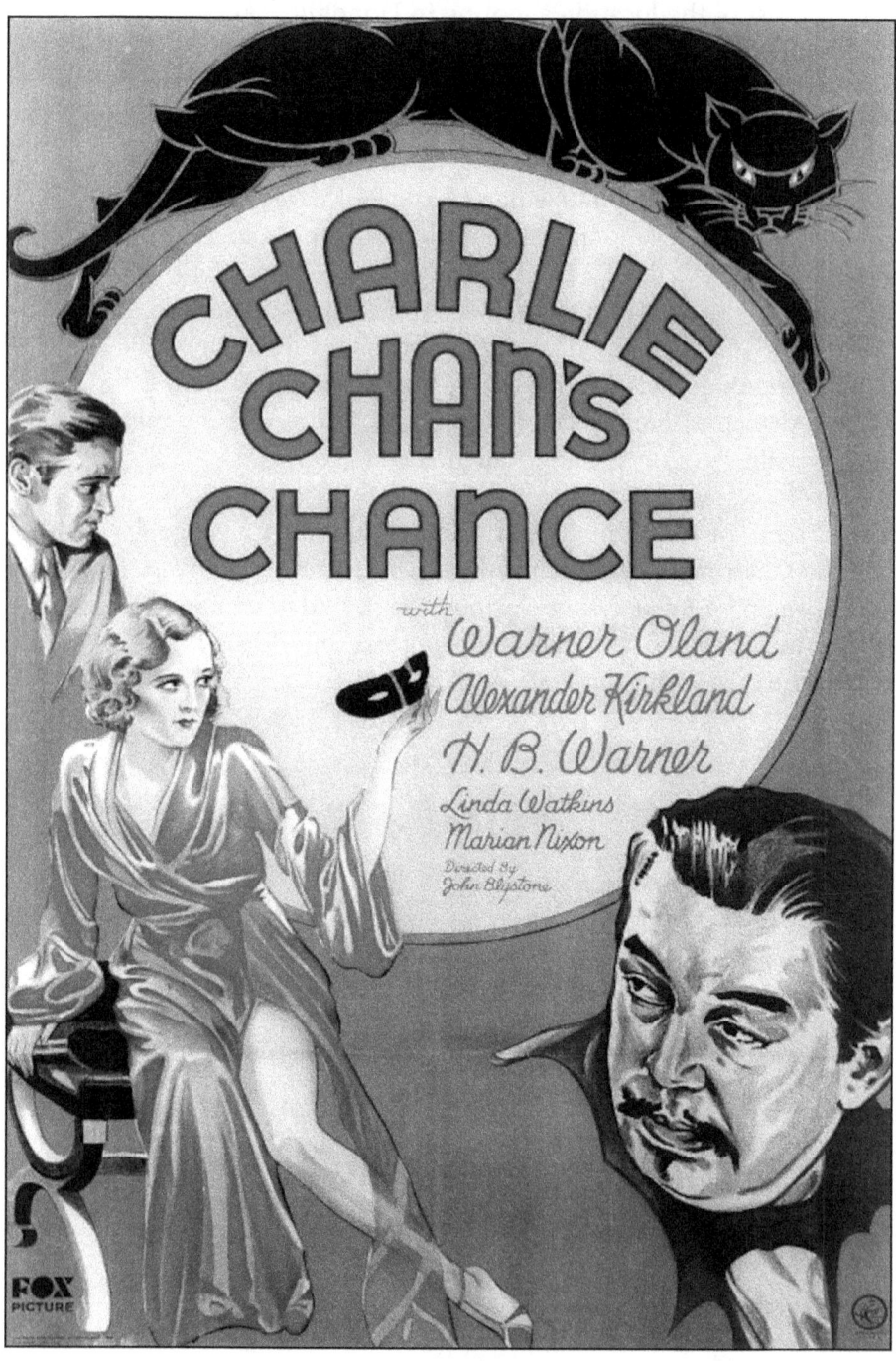

Poster for *Charlie Chan's Chance*

Charlie Chan's Chance

Director: John Blystone
Assistant Director: Jasper Blystone
Screenplay: Barry Conners; Philip Klein
Based on the novel *Behind That Curtain* by Earl Derr Biggers
Cinematography: Joseph August
Film Editor: Alex Troffey

Cast:
Warner Oland: Charlie Chan
Alexander Kirkland: John R. Douglas
H. B. Warner: Inspector Fife
Marian Nixon: Shirley Marlowe
Linda Watkins: Gloria Garland
James Kirkwood: Inspector Flannery
Ralph Morgan: Barry Kirk
James Todd: Kenneth Dunwood
Herbert Bunston: Garrick Enderby
James Wang: Kee Lin
Charles McNaughton: Paradise
Edward Peil, Sr.: Li Gung
Joe Brown: Doctor
Tom Kennedy: Hawkins
Puzzums the cat: Cat in Li Gung's Apartment
William P. Carleton, Thomas A. Curran: bit parts

Shooting days: November 16 to early December 1931
Released January 24, 1932 by the Fox Film Corporation
Running Time: 73 minutes, Black and white

ANOTHER LOST FILM, this one based on the Earl Derr Biggers novel *Behind That Curtain*, which had already been filmed in 1929. However, this 1931 version presents Chan as the central figure and is closer to the novel's concept. It is unfortunate that no screening print is available (a fire at the Fox warehouse in 1937 destroyed a lot of important films), but based on our research, including taking a look at the script, we can get an idea of how the film played out.

Sir Lionel Grey, former Scotland Yard chief, is in the process of solving a crime that had baffled the yard for years. All suspects were gathered, when Grey takes a phone call in a Wall Street office and his mysteriously murdered. Inspector Fife of Scotland Yard and Charlie Chan or Honolulu are both in New York at the time of this murder, to learn more about the methods used by that cities police department. They receive the news about Grey while at lunch, and investigate, Chan staying in New York rather than returning to Honolulu for the birth of his eleventh child.

A doctor insists Grey's death was natural, but a dead cat in the same room arouses Chan's suspicion. The guests that had been gathered by Grey are questioned, and all seem suspicious as well. The subsequent mystery involves a vaudeville dancer named Shirley, who is connected to a John Raleigh, who presents himself to Chan as Dunwood, Raleigh's servant, Li Gung, attempts to kill Charlie Chan, but a cat bumps the contraption set up to fire gun at the detective, saving his life and killing Li Gung.

The film concludes with Charlie Chan, Inspector Fife, and New York detective Flannery waiting for the man who is revealed to the killer. Charlie pretends to sneeze and drop his gun, the suspect picks it up and confesses to the murder while holding the others at gunpoint. However when Charlie goes to capture him, the suspect realizes the gun is not loaded. Chan reveals that he never loads his gun, as a safety measure regarding his children.

It is unfortunate that any of the Charlie Chan films are inaccessible to our study, but this one has the added measure of being the only Chan film that featured Biggers' involvement in contributing to the screenplay. The impressive supporting cast includes veteran actor H.B. Warner (now best known for playing Mr. Gower the druggist in *It's a Wonderful Life*, in which he'd appear 15 years after this movie), and Marian Nixon, whose career dates back to silent comedy (she appeared in such films as *The Shiek of Araby* with Ben Turpin and *Hands Up* with Raymond Griffith). Ms. Nixon had also appeared in the silent Charlie Chan feature *The Chinese Parrot*, which is also lost.

In their review of *Charlie Chan's Chance,* the Hollywood trade paper *Variety* seemed reasonably impressed:[1]

> Previous chapters of Fox's Charlie Chan series are bound to bring comparisons, but this latest won't suffer. A compact, frequently suspenseful and sufficiently convincing detective feature, it rates with its predecessors as entertainment and should equal the fair grosses they registered. Because Fox isn't overdoing the Charlie Chan character with too frequent repetition, the Oriental detective is still on his pins as a reliable screen character, with the quality of *Charlie Chan's Chance* setting things up for a future return. As long as they don't kill Charles with more than bi-annual release, Warner Oland and Fox can probably continue along the same lines indef. Earl Derr Biggers' magazine and novel yarns on the subject provide the structure for this chapter, like the others. It has Biggers also - absence of billing for a dialoguer discounts the possibility of another author - who provided the constant philosophical sayings which are delivered through the principal character as a means of sewing the action together and maintaining a regular pace. Chan rolls them off his proverbial knife, giving Oland the pushover job of sounding like a resident of Mott street by simply dropping his prepositions like "Some heads, like hard nuts, much better if well cracked." The killing of Li Gung, though arriving some time ahead of the climax, is the most exciting sequence. He's killed by a bullet intended for Chan, with the stage set and death contraption rigged up for Chan's benefit before he arrives. A black cat walks across the table, pointing the gun at Li Gung and away from Chan. Li is destroyed by his own creation. Chan is sitting in the hot seat while the audience waits for the trigger to snap. This talker's production is good-looking without denoting undue extravagance. The principal location, a penthouse, is neat, and a helpful attitude of realism is gained through the skyline background which looks like New York from the Empire State building tower. Another standout tech-

---

1. "Charlie Chan's Chance. *Variety.* January 26, 1932

nical detail is the studio version of the East River at night, whose scenic excellence lends importance to an otherwise unimportant situation that under less expert handling might have been mere padding.

While there are few Chan features that are lost, the fact that they are grouped together at the outset of the series disrupts our ability to fully appreciate the evolution of the character, and the trajectory of each film, as they are still responding more directly to the actual Earl Derr Biggers novels.

The next film in the series, *Charlie Chan's Greatest Case* is another lost film. It is another version of *House Without a Key*, which had been made as a 10 chapter silent serial in 1926, and which is also lost.

Charlie Chan's Greatest Case

Director: Hamilton MacFadden
Assistant Director: Percy Ikerd
Screenplay: Lester Cole; Marion Orth
Based on the novel *The House Without a Key* by Earl Derr Biggers (Indianapolis, 1925)
Producer: Sol M. Wurtzel
Cinematography: Ernest Palmer
Editor: Alex Troffey

Cast:
Warner Oland: Charlie Chan
Heather Angel: Carlotta Eagan
Roger Imhoff: The Beachcomber
John Warburton: John Quincy Winterslip
Walter Byron: Harry Jennison
Ivan Simpson: T. M. Brade
Virginia Cherrill: Barbara Winterslip
Francis Ford: Captain Hallett
Robert Warwick: Dan Winterslip
Frank McGlynn: Amos Winterslip
Clara Blandick: Minerva Winterslip
Claude King: Captain Arthur Temple Cope
William Stack: James Eagan
Gloria Roy: Arlene Compton
Cornelius Keefe: Steve Leatherbee
Dorothy Hoo: Number One Daughter
Mabel Hoo: Number Two Daughter
Frances Chan: Number Three Daughter

Ellen Tim: Number Four Daughter
Frank Tang: Oswald Chan, number one son
Frank Dong: Herbert Chan , number two son
Alan Dong: Number Three Son
Harry Dong: Number Four Son
David Dong: Number Five Son

Shooting days: mid-July to mid-August 1933
Released September 15, 1933 by the Fox Film Corporation
Running Time: 71 minutes. Black and white

IDEALLY IT WOULD BE GREAT if we could see the silent movie serial *House Without a Key* and do a comparison/contrast with this sound remake, but both films are lost. It is significant that Charlie Chan is a supporting character in the earlier film, and is the central figure in this talkie. But otherwise, all that research presents us is the fact that moviegoers were less enthused with *Charlie Chan's Greatest Case* than they had been with the other films featuring Warner Oland as the detective.

When wealthy Dan Winterslip receives a telegram that his daughter is about to marry his lawyer, he responds to his lawyer threatening to expose information about his nefarious past if the engagement is called off. Dan is later found stabbed to death in Honolulu, police captain Hallett is called and he immediately contacts Charlie Chan. On the scene, the crime doctor reveals Dan's arm was also broken. Chan questions Dan's sister, Minerva, and she indicates hotel man James Eagan had been calling repeatedly a day earlier. She also points out that she saw a prowler in the bushes wearing a glow-in-the-dark wristwatch with its 2 faded. Eagan is questioned and it is discovered that he and Dan had not seen each other in decades, but did meet that day. The nature of their meeting is not revealed. Eagan is taken into police custody and his daughter must now run the hotel. Later, Dan's brother Amos is found dead. Chan assembles all of the suspects at Dan's home with the intention of revealing the murderer. A new suspect, named Berkeley, is brought in and revealed as the murderer. When he makes a run for it, one of the suspects stops him and breaks his arm the same way Dan's arm had been broken. It is then revealed who the killer is (see Appendix A).

Because this film, like *The Black Camel*, is set in Honolulu, the Chan family home is depicted with Charlie attempting to enjoy some peace and

Charlie Chan and the Chan kids in *Charlie Chan's Greatest Case*

quiet before being called onto the case, and despite the tumult of eleven children in the house. While a helpful son would soon become a consistent part of the screen dynamic, presentations of the large Chan family were rarely shown in the series.

Of course if one's reads the script for *Charlie Chan's Greatest Case*, there are more details to the mystery, but our inability to see how it plays as a film precludes us from making a deeper assessment. Mordaunt Hall in the *New York Times* stated:[1]

> As far as the mystery of these particular murders is concerned it is not difficult for the audience to decide on the identity of the slayer, but the manner in which Chan makes his deductions is always interesting. When something is said about his easygoing manner this wise Chinese declares that haste is only necessary when withdrawing one's hand from a tiger's mouth or when catching a flea. He hazards that theories are like fingerprints—"everybody

---

1. "Charlie Chan's Greatest Case" *The New York Times.* October 7, 1931

has them. Only facts and motives lead to a murderer." He also says he cannot hasten and adds that a cat which tries to catch two mice at one time goes without supper.

This opposes the fact that our research indicates audiences were less enthusiastic. But exhibitors reported to the *Motion Picture Herald* that the film was "a little tiresome" and "not as amusing in dialog as the others in the series."

Another article in the *Motion Picture Herald* discussed some promotional methods used by theaters, including several of Charlie Chan's sayings printed on 5x16 sheets and placed in merchants' windows as teasers. Other theaters had a six-foot cut-out of Warner Oland as Chan centered in the lobby. Perhaps the most elaborate promotional idea was a one act playlet performed before the trailer was screened. A boy and girl are in dimly lit phone booths on opposite sides of the stage. The boy throws a scare into the girl by impersonating Chan and telling a bit of the story by asking questions relating to the characters in the movie. The boy then discloses his identity as the lights come up, with the girl accepting a date to see the movie. This is followed by the film's trailer.

The standard way to assess a series of films is to examine how each movie allows the central character to develop and how each production expands its scope. When a block of films is inaccessible, this is not possible. Any information is merely historical, with no real discussion of the cinematic process. Unfortunately, the next film, *Charlie Chan's Courage*, is also lost. Fortunately, it is the last of the lost films in this series.

It is worth noting that around the time this movie was being filmed, there was a very short-lived Broadway play of the Earl Derr Biggers novel *Keeper of the Keys* with William Harrigan as Charlie Chan and Dwight Frye playing his Chinese sidekick Ah Sing.

Before beginning production on his next Charlie Chan film, Warner Oland became one of the founding members of the Screen Actor's Guild, which was established in October of 1933. Oland was particularly supportive of actors in bit roles getting proper compensation and recognition.

Charlie Chan's Courage

Director: George Hadden
Screenplay: Seton I. Miller, Based on the novel *The Chinese Parrot* by Earl Derr Biggers
Producer: John Stone
Cinematography: Hal Mohr
Film Editor: Alex Troffey

Cast:
Warner Oland: Charlie Chan
Drue Leyton: Paula Graham
Donald Woods: Bob Crawford
Paul Harvey: P. J. Madden
Murray Kinnell: Martin Thorne
Reginald Mason: Alexander Crawford
Virginia Hammond: Sally Jordan
Si Jenks: Will Holley
Harvey Clark: Professor Gamble
Jerry Jerome: Maydorf
Jack Carter: Victor Jordan
James Wang: Louie Wong
DeWitt C. Jennings: Constable Brackett [Sergeant Brackett]
Francis Ford: Hewitt
Lucille Miller: Stenographer
Mary McLaren: Mother
Gail Kaye: Child
Larry Fisher: Taxi Driver
Sam McDaniel: Porter
Carl Stockdale: Train Station Lounger

Lita Chevret: Chorus Girl
Susan Fleming: Chorus Girl
Caryl Lincoln: Leading Lady
John David Horsley: Leading Man
George Magrill: Heavy
Frank Mills: Prop Man
Sherry Hall: Assistant Director
James P. Burtis: Eddie Boston
Paul McVey: Movie Director
Wade Boteler: Bliss
Teru Shimada: Jiu Jitsu Man
Frank Rice: Prospector
Paul Hurst: Bit Role

Shooting days: April 23 to May 27, 1934
Released: July 6, 1934 by the Fox Film Corporation,
Running Time: 74 minutes. Black and White

THE LAST OF THE LOST CHARLIE CHAN FILMS, this one a remake of the equally lost silent feature *The Chinese Parrot*. Sally Jordan, a friend of Charlie Chan, has sold a valuable necklace to P.J. Madden, a wealthy businessman. The jewelry broker is Alexander Crawford, a family friend. Because of its value, detective Charlie Chan agrees to deliver the necklace from Honolulu to San Francisco, at a ranch located in a remote area of the desert. Crawford's son Bob also travels to the ranch to help ensure the success of the sale. He is accompanied by Paula Graham, a film agent who wants to ask Madden about shooting some location scenes at his ranch.

When Chan arrives, he goes undercover and claims to be an out-of-work cook, and is hired by Madden's secretary, Martin Thorne, to work at the ranch. There had been conflicting destinations as to where to deliver the pearls, and Chan has become suspicious. The mystery involves murder at the ranch, and a talking parrot who communicates in the Chinese language, offering helpful clues to Chan's case. When the parrot is found poisoned the mystery becomes deeper and more serious. Kidnappings and doubles complicate things even further until Charlie Chan's deductive reasoning solves the crime (see Appendix A).

Our inability to offer more in-depth details limits our ability to better understand how effectively *Charlie Chan's Courage* fits into the Chan

Poster for *Charlie Chan's Courage*

filmography. It was well received by audiences at the time and appears to have allowed the series to successfully progress.

The promotional ideas include one theater that got permission to start a chain letter stating that a murderer was on the loose, and the receiver of the chain letter must forward it to a friend so that it eventually finds its way into the hands of Charlie Chan. A theater ad accompanied the chain letter. In another amusing promotional idea, a theter owner got hold of a rickshaw, placed a pretty young woman in it, dressed in stereotyped Chinese garb and pulled her through the streets, handing out advertising copy promoting the Charlie Chan feature.

By the time he starred in *Charlie Chan's Courage*, Warner Oland had comfortably established himself as the screen's Charlie Chan. The increasing popularity of the movies allowed Oland to enjoy a level of stardom that matched his importance as a stage actor. Even Roscoe Fawcett's "Screen Oddities" cartoon featured a large drawing of Chan in its July, 1934 syndicated comic. The info given was that Oland wears a large Buddha ring as a good luck charm, which he'd been given as a birthday present by his wife 20 years earlier. The claim was that she bought it with the

Warner Oland and his dog relax between scenes

substantial she acquired during her only time ever playing poker. While most of these bits of trivia were apocryphal, they do indicate Oland's increasing popularity.

The supporting cast for *Charlie Chan's Courage* included such welcome veterans as Paul Harvey, Donald Woods, Murray Kinnell, and Drue Leyton, all of whom would appear in other Chan movies. Ms. Leyton would only make then films and three are Charlie Chan pictures. After leaving movies in 1939, Ms. Leyton spent World War Two broadcasting a Voice of American program from Paris, where she would be captured by Nazis, escape from a concentration camp and join the French resistance. She lived until 1997.

Fortunately the remainder of the Charlie Chan films are available and accessible, allowing us to carefully assess them as they expand their scope, make use of their formidable supporting casts, and allow Oland the actor to add more layers to the character.

Charlie Chan In London

Director: Eugene Forde
Assistant Director: Ed O'Fearna
Original Screenplay: Philip MacDonald
Dialog: Stuart Anthony and Lester Cole
Based on the character "Charlie Chan" created by Earl Derr Biggers
Producer: John Stone
Cinematography: L.W. O'Connell
Assistant Camera: John Schmitz; Robert Surtees
Wardrobe: Sam Benson

Cast:
Warner Oland: Inspector Charlie Chan
Drue Leyton: Pamela Gray
Ray Milland: Neil Howard
Mona Barrie: Lady Mary Bristol
Alan Mowbray: Geoffrey Richmond
Murray Kinnell: Phillips
Douglas Walton: Paul Gray[1]
Walter Johnson: Jerry Garton
E. E. Clive: Detective Sergeant Thacker
George Barraud: Major Jardine
Madge Bellamy: Betty Fothergill
David Torrence: Sir Lionel Bashford
John Rogers: Lake
Paul England: Bunny Fothergill

---

1. Incorrectly billed as Hugh Gray

Elsa Buchanan: Alice Perkins
Perry Ivans: Kemp
Claude King: RAF Commandant
Reginald Sheffield: Commander King
Helena Grant: Miss Judson
Montague Shaw: Doctor
Arthur Clayton: Warden
Mary Gordon: Prison Matron
Phillis Coghlan: Nurse
Margarett Mann: Housemaid
Carlie Taylor: Manor Guest
Doris Stone: Manor Guest
Ann Doran (stand-in for Drue Leyton)

Released September 12, 1934 by the Fox Film Corporation
Shooting days: July 9 to early August 3, 1934
Running time: 79 minutes, Black and white

BY THE TIME *CHARLIE CHAN IN LONDON* was filmed, Detective Chan was firmly established in cinema, and audiences were conditioned well enough to know what to expect from the character and the proceedings. The trick, then, was to create mysteries that were absorbing, but still not too easy for the average moviegoer to figure out. It is unfortunate that there are three feature films immediately previous to this one that are lost. This limits us from understanding the complete trajectory that led to this sixth film, and it really leaves a gap as to Oland's early development of the character. In the time from *The Black Camel* to *Charlie Chan in London*, the Chan character grew into the calm, secure persona and had diffused the occasional bursts of anger that were seen several movies earlier. Just how that evolved is lost to us.

The plot of *Charlie Chan in London* deals with Paul Gray, in prison and sentenced to be hanged in a matter of days for having committed a murder. Gray insists he is innocent, but only his sister Pamela and her friend Geoffrey Richmond believe him. Even Pamela's fiancée admits he thinks Paul is guilty, causing her to angrily end their relationship. After a court of appeals upholds the verdict, Pamela goes to see Charlie Chan, whom she hears is visiting London. Chan is packing to return home, but after hearing a few details, believes there is enough evidence for him to investigate further.

Poster for *Charlie Chan in London*

Invited to the manor where Pamela is also staying, Chan interviews suspects, but subsequent murder of a groomsman and a near-fatal accident involving Richmond's fiancée while on a fox hunt, further complicate the case. Chan, working against time, goes to the Aereodome where the murdered man was stationed while in the air force. He discovers that the murdered man was an inventor who was nearing completion on a method that would silence war planes. Chan gathers some suspects at the manor and reveals that he will know the murderer's identity once he finds the plans for that invention, which are currently missing. Chan has one of the suspects whom he pretends to trust, to accompany him to a room where the plans are laid upon a desk. He gives the suspect a gun to guard him while he makes his discovery. The suspect shoots Chan, and police quickly enter the room and capture the murderer. Chan gets up and smiles, indicating the gun was filled with blanks. Paul Gray is released from prison only hours before his scheduled execution.

Eugene Forde was a noted director at Fox's B unit for many years and helmed a few of the Charlie Chan films. This was not his first Chan movie, as he directed the previous *Charlie Chan's Courage*. But because that is a lost film, this is the first one for which we can assess his approach to the material. Ford responds well to the fact that this movie is set in London. Older buildings offer a lot of vast negative space as the director frames each scene. The ceilings are high, the walls are imposing, and the castle-like structures offer an eeriness that is further enhanced in the more dimly lit scenes.

The aforementioned calmness in the Chan character is immediately evident upon his first entrance. He walks in slowly, quietly, and smiles warmly. He does not have the noisy charisma of then-popular actors like James Cagney or Edward G. Robinson, but somehow commands the scene every bit as much as either. However, his demeanor is tested especially when he arrives at the manor to see Pamela, who has given orders not to be disturbed. Unmoved by Chan's quiet insistence, Phillips the butler slams the door on him, causing him to slightly stumble backward. He smiles and finds another way in. Contrast this with the scene in *The Black Camel* when Chan is assembling the pieces of a ripped photograph, and his assistant impulsively opens a door and allows a wind to blow the pieces off the table. In that scene, Chan's anger is palpable. In this one, there is calm and no rage. Without the three previous films, we can not discern how Warner Oland's approach to Chan evolved from that point to this one, but the difference shows that the actor continued to hone the character.

Because Chan has so little time to solve this murder, the film is briskly paced despite his centered manner. Some cleverness on the part of the screenwriters is evident in each subsequent murder. When the groomsman who tends the manor horses is found dead, it is ruled a suicide. Chan discovers the dead man's finger is on the trigger but the fatal wound is in the middle of his brow. He concludes that such a self-inflicted wound would have to have been triggered by the man's thumb. When he examines the horse that is killed in the accident involving Richmond's fiancée, he sees dried tears and wipes them away. An analyst determines pepper was used to blind the horse, causing it to go over a fenced embankment and fall to its death, seriously injuring the rider.

One of the strongest sequences, directorially, is when Forde crosscuts between the fox hunt and a car racing to the scene after Chan receives a note from Richmond's fiancée indicating she has information important to the case. They realize she is in danger, but are too late. Forde cuts in what is likely authentic footage of a fox hunt, along with the actors on horses, and includes the car containing Charlie racing to the scene. It is perhaps the most exciting sequence in the movie and a good example of the director's ability to economically stage a location action scene effectively.

Warner Oland, Ray Milland, Drue Leyton

When the murderer is revealed (see Appendix A) it is further discovered that the individual is not English, but a foreign spy. It is then that Phillips reveals he is undercover military and has been trailing the murderer for other matters. A neat touch as the film concludes reverts back to an earlier scene in the movie. When Pamela breaks up with her fiancée upon hearing he believes her brother is guilty, she removes her diamond engagement ring and throws it to the floor. Chan picks it up, and, at the end of the movie when all is resolved, returns it to Pamela so that she can now resume her engagement (apparently forgiving her intended for believing her brother, now proven innocent, was guilty).

The supporting cast includes Ray Milland as Pamela's fiancée, appearing fairly early in his long career that would eventually include an Oscar for his performance in *The Lost Weekend* (1945). Drue Leyton appears in her second Chan film, and Murray Kinnell is in his third of four movies featuring the detective. Alan Mowbray had a long, distinguished career in films and later television, lasting until his sudden death in 1969. The cast is rounded out by a smattering of familiar veterans such as Mona Barrie, Madge Bellamy and E.E. Clive (delightfully off-kilter as usual, addressing Charlie Chan as "Chang").

Douglas Walton was also quite good as Paul. There's a noteworthy scene between him and Ms. Leyton where she visits him in prison and they both become hysterical over the apparent hopelessness of his case. It could have been over-the-top but instead reinforced everything that was at stake in this case.

For comic relief, soon to be handled by the introduction of Chan's number one son in the next film, *Charlie Chan in London* features Elsa Buchanan as a hysterical maid who insists Charlie Chan is a murderous foreigner, and loudly flees every time she sees him. Elsa Buchanan was known for having the biggest eyes and smallest waist in movies. Ms. Buchanan married nobility and left movies in the later 1930s after appearing in only 18 features, usually in small, uncredited roles. However, she lived to be 95 years old, dying in 2004. There is a scene in the 2001 Robert Altman movie *Gosford Park* in which a character discusses casting a hysterical maid in *Charlie Chan in London*. Ms. Buchanan reportedly saw the film and was delighted by the reference.

Charlie Chan in London was the first movie to not be drawn from one of Earl Derr Biggers' books. Biggers had planned to continue writing Chan novels, from which movies could be produced, but he died in 1933. The films initially attempted to be faithful to his vision, but eventually expanded to include other characters and different ideas, especially when responding to the prevailing culture of the times.

The Motion Picture Herald praised the "showmanship" of *Charlie Chan in London*, and stating that despite its not being a cinematic version of an actual Biggers' novel, it "carries the same colorful plot structure and offers the same opportunities for Warner Oland's performance." [2] A writer for *Silver Screen* magazine reported visiting the set and noted the "library with a huge carved desk" and surmised "apparently nothing ever happens except in rich circles."[3]

Charlie Chan in London was well received by audiences, but some found the London setting a bit too remote in this less global era. As the series continued, the filmmakers would augment the character, and the settings. But first, detective Chan makes his way to Paris for the next film.

---

2. "Charlie Chan in London." *Motion Picture Herald.* September 22, 1934
3. Studio News: At Fox's Western Avenue Studio. *Silver Screen.* October 1934

Poster for *Charlie Chan in Paris*

Charlie Chan In Paris

Director: Lewis Seiler (Original Director: Hamilton MacFadden)
Producer: John Stone
Assistant Director: Eli Dunn
Screenplay: Edward T. Lowe; Stuart Anthony
Story: Philip MacDonald
Contributor on Special Sequences: William Allen Johnston
Cinematography: Ernest Palmer (replacing Dan Clark)

Cast:
Warner Oland: Charlie Chan
Mary Brian: Yvette Lamartine
Thomas Beck: Victor Descartes
Erik Rhodes: Max Corday
Keye Luke: Lee Chan
John Miljan: Albert Dufresne
Murray Kinnell: Henri Latouche
Minor Watson: Inspector Renard
John Qualen: Concierge
Henry Kolker: M. Paul Lamartine
Dorothy Appleby: Nardi
Ruth Peterson: Renee Jacquard
Perry Ivans: Bedell
George Davis: Roberts
Auguste Tollaire: Concierge
Louis Nartheaux: Reporter
Ed Cecil: Customs Officer
Marty Faust: Taxicab Driver
Landers Stevens: Bank Attendant

John Dilson: Information Clerk
Samuel T. Godfrey: Cashier
Rolfe Sedan: Bank Teller
Gino Corrado: Pierre
Wilfred Lucas: Doorman
Richard Kipling: Master of Ceremonies
Eddie Vitch: Sketch Artist
Paul McVey: Detective
Moore & Allen: Apache Dancers
Harry Cording, Robert Graves: Gendarmes
Lynn Bari, Gloria Roy: Nightclub Patrons

Shooting days: November 12 to December 18, 1934
Released January 25, 1935 by the Fox Film Corporation
Running time: 70 minutes. Black and white

AN IMPORTANT ENTRY in the Charlie Chan filmography, *Charlie Chan in Paris* was, for years, among the lost films until a print turned up in the 1970s. It was then put into circulation on TV among the other films and eventually released on DVD. Since it features the first appearance of Keye Luke as Charlie's number-one-son Lee Chan, it has significance beyond also being one of the most briskly paced films in the Warner Oland period of the series.

Picking up where the previous film left off, Chan travels to Paris allegedly on vacation, but actually investigating a case of forged bank bonds for a London banking house. Upon his arrival, Chan is approached by a panhandler to whom he gives a few coins, then goes to the phone and calls his contact, Nardi, who is performing as a dancer at a café while working under cover. He visits Victor Descartes, who works as a clerk at the Lamartine Bank where his father is the director. His fiancée is Yvette LaMartine, daughter of the bank's president. When Yvette arrives, she is accompanied by two friends – Max Corday, a drunken free-spirited artist, and his girl, Renee Jacquard. They go to the café together. As they get into the cab, Max is approached by the same beggar to whom Charlie had given change earlier. Charlie notices.

At this point in the film, the characters are quickly introduced and established. There is a fresh innocence to Yvette, and a determined inherent heroism to Victor. Max comes off as offbeat, playing the sort of upper

Warner Oland reads about Australia on the set between scenes

class drunk that permeated 1930s-era drawing room settings centering on privileged people. Max mimics Chan's accent, exaggerating it in an effort to be amusing, but comes off as insulting. Chan does not extend beyond his usual relaxed demeanor, and responds to Max with the same affected delivery as if to intellectually overcome the other man's childish behavior. It should be noted, in the wake of later controversy that a white man played the Chinese detective, that actions such as what Max displays are only used in a manner that presented the character as off-putting and dislikable.

The others believe Chan is merely on vacation and going to the café to enjoy the apache dance, not realizing the woman, Nardi, is an accomplice. The dance is performed, concluding with Nardi thrown offstage. When back stage, she is confronted by a man with a knife. Responding to her screams, Chan goes back stage and finds her dying in her dance partner's arms. She tries to tell him some info, but perishes before finishing.

This scene offers a area of Chan's personality that is rarely displayed. Chan, always grounded and relaxed, responds with a more aggressive, perhaps even frantic, manner as he pushes through the crowd to get back stage upon hearing the scream. Yelling, rather than speaking in his quiet manner, Charlie pushes his way to the back. His scene with the dying Nardi shows an emotional tenderness that is also usually more subdued. It is one of the strongest sequences in this film. Dorothy Appleby, playing Nardi, makes an impact in her very short screen time.

The little that Nardi is able to say while dying leads Charlie to her apartment. He finds a diary that contains some valuable information. As he leaves, the strange panhandler drops a rock on Charlie from the roof, but misses. Chan does not see who it is. When Charlie returns to his hotel, he enters cautiously, realizing someone is there. He is ready to confront the intruder until a pajama-clad man comes out of the bathroom wiping his hair, the towel covering his face. He lifts it to reveal himself as Lee Chan, Charlie's eldest son.

In one of the most moving scenes in the entire Chan series, Charlie expresses delight at seeing his son, who exudes youthful vitality and an American voice without a trace of an accent. The young vibrant man seems even more carefree than the drunken artist, but his serious side is displayed as soon as his father reveals the real reason he is in Paris, that his accomplice was murdered, and that an attempt had just been made on his life. Lee's concern is such that he insists on helping his father with the case. During the dialog of this sequence, Lee helps his father on with his robe and his slippers, and the men embrace more than once. The very real affection they show each other presents yet another side of Charlie and for the first time.

Lee poses as his father's chauffeur and drives him to the bank where he meets with office manager Henri Latouche and once again sees the mysterious panhandler, this time being escorted from the bank for creating a disruption. Chan is told that the man is Marcel Xavier, a shell-shocked war veteran. Charlie asks Lee to follow him. He also shows bank president Lamartine and his assistant Albert Dufresne to show them the forged documents. Neither Chan nor the bank president are aware that Dufresne is currently blackmailing Lamartine's daughter by threatening to show her fiancée some love letters she'd sent the assistant.

While Charlie is distracted by a social engagement with Inspector Renaud, Lee follows Xavier who is spying on Dufresne. Yvette goes to see Dufresne to get the letters, when he is shot by a hidden Xavier, who then tosses the gun into the room. Yvette retrieves the letters, picks up the gun as people break into the room, and is accused of murdering Dufresne. Chan and the Inspector are alerted and hurry to the home. Yvette is arrested, but, beforehand, gives the letters to Charlie. He realizes she is innocent and sets out to prove it by finding the real killer. With the information Lee brings to his father that connects Xavier, and the help of Victor, Chan discovers there are actually two murderers Each took turns putting on the panhandler uniform (complete with a realistic mask) when the other was present (see Appendix A).

Charlie Chan in Paris has a quicker pace than the previous films, and despite the complex set of circumstances that lead to the culprits, the ending that reveals two of them is a neat twist that effectively caps the story. The direction by Lewis Seiler is commendable, especially a dark climax that takes places in the Paris sewers. Hamliton MacFadden was originally signed as the film's director and actually started production for one week along with cinematographer Dan Clark. However, the merging of Fox with 20th Century studios, forming 20th Century Fox, occurred during filming, putting Darryl F. Zanuck in charge of production. Producers and directors from the previous regime were replaced as a result. So, after filming for only one week, Lewis Seiler was brought in to finish this production and Ernest Palmer replaced Dan Clark. MacFadden would continue to direct B movies for various studios and also work as an actor in small roles, until 1945. He died in 1977.

The supporting cast is good, with Erik Rhodes offering a sort of wry scoundrel as Max, much different than the characters he would play in later films. Mary Brian had already appeared with James Cagney in *Hard to Handle* (1933) and would, this same year, work with W.C. Fields in *Man on the Flying Trapeze*, one of the comedian's finest films. She is supported by welcome veterans in the cast like Thomas Beck, John Miljan, and Minor Watson. Watson's Inspector engages in a friendly competition with Chan, but respects and understands him, even when he alludes at the end of the film that the innocent Yvette was "working with me." They compare their discoveries with finding a hole in a donut. When the mystery is solved, the Inspector invites him for coffee and Charlie smiles and says "with donuts?" John Qualen is among the familiar faces who are given little opportunity to make much of an impact as they would in other films, but Ruth Peterson manages to resonate in a role that extends beyond the bit parts she'd usually play.

The dynamic between Charlie Chan and his number one son was planned for this movie only, but it truly resonated with critics and audiences. *Film Daily,* calling the movie, "Another excellent number in the Chan series," stated that "the picture introduced Keye Luke, Chan's son and assistant, who is quite an engaging character." *Motion Picture Herald* indicated that "several novel twists are to be found, one that should provide good showmanship material is the presentation of Chan's son, who helps in solving the mystery." *Variety* stated that "Warner Oland holds his own, and Keye Luke does a good job as his college bred son."

Keye Luke was an artist for Fox studios, working on the poster for the Chan pictures, when he was invited to act in one. Luke had already played a small role in the MGM Greta Garbo feature *The Painted Veil,* but considered acting something of a tangential lark to supplement his work as a studio artist. He certainly had no idea that he would end up acting in movies and on television for over 40 more years. It should be noted that the sketch Max is scene working on in this movie was actually drawn by Keye Luke.

Luke's performance belies the fact that he has almost no acting background. While being fresh and effervescent for the most part, his angry emotional response to his father's danger, and determined manner in wanting to help solve the crime while protecting Charlie, is one of the strongest elements of this film.

The series continued to be popular, and *Charlie Chan in Paris* did well at the box office. New studio head Zanuck understood the popularity of his lower budgeted features and even formed a B unit for the studio. He would continue to support the Charlie Chan series.

Charlie Chan In Egypt

Director: Louis King[1]
Original Screenplay: Robert Ellis and Helen Logan
Based on the character "Charlie Chan" created by Earl Derr Biggers
Produced by Edward T. Lowe jr.
Cinematography: Daniel B. Clark
Editing: Al De Gaetano

Cast:
Warner Oland: Charlie Chan
Pat Paterson: Carol Arnold
Thomas Beck: Tom Evans
Rita Cansino:[2] Nayda
Stepin Fetchit: Snowshoes
Jameson Thomas: Dr. Anton Racine
Frank Conroy: Professor John Thurston
Nigel de Brulier: Edfu Ahmad
James Eagles: Barry Arnold
Paul Porcasi: Fouad Soueida
Arthur Stone: Dragoman
Frank Reicher: Dr. Jaipur
George Irving: Professor Arnold
Anita Brown: Kitten
John Davidson: Atrash
John George: Ali
Gloria Roy: bit

1. Incorrectly billed as Luis King
2. Rita Hayworth was billed this way early in her career

Poster for *Charlie Chan in Egypt*

Shot during April 1935
Released June 21, 1935 by the Fox Film Corporation
Running Time: 72 minutes. Black and White

AT THIS POINT, Warner Oland was telling reporters that the Charlie Chan character had become a part of him. In a widely syndicated newspaper feature, Oland stated:[3]

> Charlie Chan is virtually a living person as far as I am concerned. I've played him so often, thought about him so much, that I feel I know him personally. I know how he reacts to any situation, how he sizes up people and events. I've build up in my mind a background for him, his family history, the kind of friends he has, everything about him. If I am able to pay him realistically on the

---

3. "Star Says Chan's Virtually Alive." *The Kane Republican* July 6, 1935

screen, that's the reason. It's something like knowing a foreign language well enough to think in that language.

Charlie Chan in Egypt has the detective traveling from Paris to Egypt when the French Archeological Society reports that the artifacts discovered by Professor Arnold are showing up in various museums, which contradicts an agreement he has with the society. When Chan arrives in Egypt, he discovers the Professor has been missing for several weeks. Arnold's daughter, Carol, is frantic with worry, suffering a breakdown and hallucinating that she is being haunted by the vengeful goddess Sekhmet, who guards the tomb of Ahmeti that Professor Arnold was excavating when he disappeared. Chan, Arnold's brother-in-law Professor Thurston, and Carol's fiancée Tom examine a mummy from the tomb and discover a bullet hole. When they unwrap the mummy, the discover Professor Arnold's corpse. Arnold's son, Barry, fears the entire family is cursed by Sekhmet. Late that knight, Chan, Tom, and a helper named Snowshoes go to the tomb and are confronted by a glowing image of Sekhmet in the darkness.

When Barry dies suddenly while plyaing his violin, Chan, Tom, and Snowshoes go back to the tomb. Discovering a watery passageway, Tom

Warner Oland, Rita Hayworth

swims to a secluded room discovers the tomb's treasures. He also finds a hat once owned by Professor Arnold. Shot by a hidden assailant, Tom falls onto a lever that opens a passageway, allowing Charlie and Snowshoes to enter the area. They find the wounded Tom and bring him back to the house. When a bullet is removed, Chan takes it and finds that it is the same that killed Arnold. When another attempt is made on Tom's life by the man who fired the gun, Chan reveals the murderer (see appendix). Tom recovers and is embraced by Carol.

Not as briskly paced as *Charlie Chan in Paris*, the mystery is still such that nearly every character is a suspect. The journey on which Chan goes to unravel the mystery is fraught with eerie imagery that further enhances the narrative. One interesting element to the story is that Chan's actions appear to be getting others into trouble, and it culminates with Carol asking him to leave the case. He accepts her decision and apologizes for his inability to solve the mystery, but soon offers evidence that further moves toward the conclusion. This is an especially great scene, because Chan's reaction to Carol's outburst is so subdued. He doesn't argue, but just requests that everyone hear him out on what he

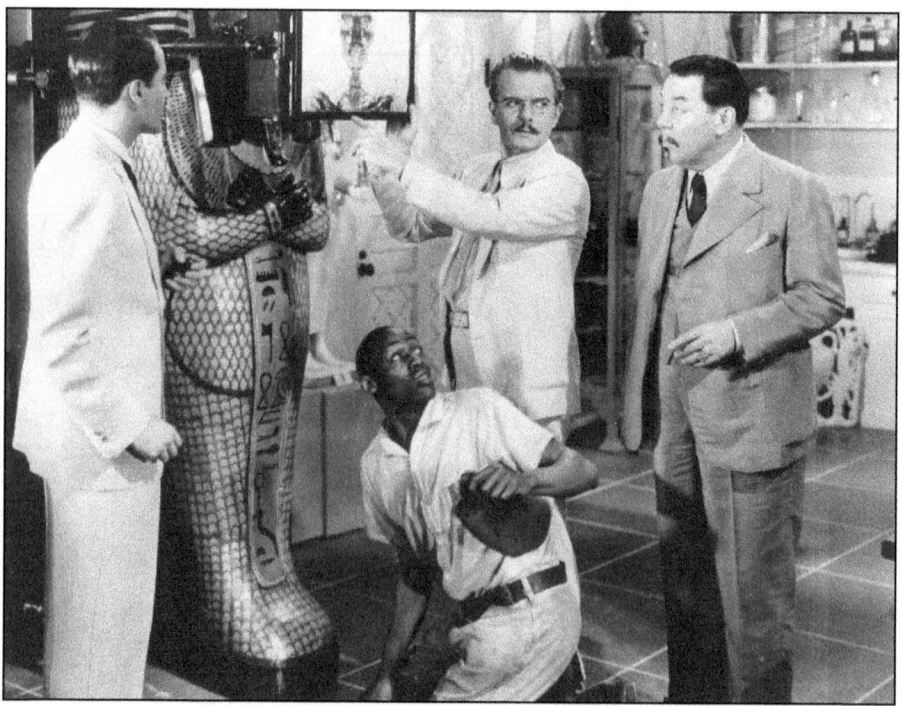

Thomas Beck, Stepin Fechit, Frank Conroy, Warner Oland

has discovered before he leaves. It reveals a lot about how his character reacts under pressure.

The comic element in these films has become inevitable by this point, and is this time presented by African American comedian Stepin Fetchit. Fetchit virtually invented the slow, stammering, shuffling black stereotype, and its success made him the first African American movie actor to receive star billing and the first to become a millionaire. As meek and servile as Fetchit was on screen, he was just the opposite in real life. Of West Indies descent, he considered himself superior to black Americans and delighted in the negative presentation. He'd fight with directors, not over the stereotype, but for more screen time. He'd spend money wildly, owning several residences and automobiles, and employed many servants. His reckless lifestyle included several dalliances with teenage girls that made negative headlines. By the end of the 1930s he had gone through his fortune and the negative publicity ended his success in movies, as he plummeted from featured parts in major studio productions to small roles in low budget indies. He lived until 1985, bitter that his portrayal was considered negative during the civil rights movement, but pleased that it began to receive greater recognition toward the end of his life. He was inducted into the Black Filmmakers Hall of Fame in 1978 and received the Special Image Award from the NAACP.

Other supporting players were stalwarts of the Fox B unit, most appearing in their first or only Charlie Chan movie with the notable exception of Thomas Beck. Rita Casino would later be billed as Rita Hayworth and become one of Hollywood's most glamorous stars. Here she registers only slightly with the screen time she is allotted.

Director Louis King (billed here as Luis and often billed Lewis) was a veteran B director but not a stylist, and his approach to this feature was merely to tell the story. As with many of the Charlie Chan films from this period, the visuals alternate from film noir to standard detective mystery, but do so without clashing.

When *Charlie Chan in Egypt* hit theaters, it was a popular movie, but resulted in some level of backlash. Many moviegoers wrote to Fox studios enquiring why Keye Luke's number one son character was not included. In fact, while Luke did return to the Fox art department, he began taking on small roles in films since his appearance in *Charlie Chan in Paris* including a rather good supporting part as Dr. Wong in the Peter Lorre film *Mad Love*, directed by cinematographer Karl Freund for MGM. It was agreed that Keye Luke would return for the next Charlie Chan film, this one taking him to Shanghai.

Number one son Lee comes to his father Charlie's rescue

Charlie Chan In Shanghai

Director: James Tinling
Assistant Director: Aaron Rosenberg
Original Story and Screenplay: Edward T. Lowe and Gerard Fairlie
Based on the character "Charlie Chan" created by Earl Derr Biggers
Produced by John Stone (associate producer)
Cinematography: Barney McGill
Film Editor: Nick De Maggio

Cast:
Warner Oland: Charlie Chan
Irene Hervey: Diana Woodland
Keye Luke: Lee Chan
Charles Locher: Philip Nash
Russell Hicks: James Andrews
Halliwell Hobbes: Colonel Watkins
Frederick Vogeding: Burke
Neil Fitzgerald: Dakin
Max Wagner: Taxi Driver
David Torrence: Sir Stanley Woodland
Bo Ling: Lee Chan's Girlfriend
Joan Woodbury: Exotic Dancer
Charles Haefeli: Crook on Boat
Gladden James: Forrest
Harry Strang: Chauffeur
Pat O'Malley: Beldon
James B. Leong: Shanghai Police Telephone Operator
Jockey Haefeli: Crook on Boat
Torben Meyer: French Diplomat

Guy Usher: Shanghai Chamber of Commerce President
Moy Ming: Mr. Sun Wong
Jehim Wong: Rickshaw Boy
Eddie Lee: Servant
William Kum: Porter
Pat Somerset, Phil Tead, Jimmy Philips, , Jack Chefe, Collin Kenny: Reporters
Sammee Tong, Willie Wong, Walter Wong, Luke Chan, Beal Wong: group that captures disguised Lee
Ed Hart, Russel Hopton: G-men
Frank Darien, Harrison Greene: Tourists
Lynn Bari: Second Hotel Switchboard Operator
Regina Rambeau: bit

Shooting days: July 11 to August 3, 1935
Released October 11, 1935 by Twentieth Century-Fox Film Corporation
Running time: 70 minutes. Black and White

CHARLIE CHAN IN SHANGHAI shows the series continuing to evolve, not only further defining Charlie, but re-introducing the dynamic between him and number one son Lee Chan. This relationship would progress over the next several films.

This time Charlie Chan is on assignment from the US government. He travels to Shanghai to investigate opium smuggling ring. Upon his arrival he is met by his number one son who arranged to be there on business, out of concern for his father's well being. He also meets Phillip Nash and Diana Woodland. Nash is the secretary of Sir Stanly Woodland who is hosting a banquet for Charlie that night. Diana is Woodland's niece. At a banquet that night, Charlie meets Sir Stanley Woodland. Woodland opens a box containing a scroll he wants to give to Charlie, but the box is rigged to fire a bullet, which kills Woodland. Charlie agrees to investigate this murder.

The set-up here is a bit more complicated, but not in a way that is difficult. It just presents a case that was originally about smuggling and has extended to another layer by including murder. Charlie's job is to balance the proceedings and discover clues that pertain to both, while keeping himself out of danger.

Later that night an attempt is made on Charlie's life by an unknown assailant while the detective lies sleeping. Lee hears the shot and runs to phone police, but Charlie walks into the room and turns on the light. A further definition of Lee's character is offered here. His concern for his father is more emotional than cerebral, and he responds more with worry than with anger. When Charlie turns on the light, Lee panics and raises his arms. This comical reaction would be explore further with subsequent films, but it is in this movie where the humor element inherent in the Lee character is first introduced.

Charlie is later is summoned to meet Colonel Watkins, but after he leaves, Watkins phones Charlie. Lee answers and states that his father is on his way in answer to the message. Watkins who states that he sent no such message. Lee, realizing Charlie is walking into a trap set by the men who attempted to kill him the night before, hurries out of the hotel in an attempt to stop his father. Charlie is captured and held by a man with a Russian accent who sits in the shadows and questions him.

The effect of the man sitting in darkness was noted in the January, 1936 issue of *Movie Makers* which stated:[1]

> The criminal, using police methods, is seated between two brilliant lights which are reflected on Charlie Chan's face, but which make it impossible for him to see the mystery man behind the lights. One well handled shot, taken from Charlie's viewpoint, shows the lights glaring directly into the camera (with no halanation, however), and reveals that Chan cannot see his questioner.

Lee, attempting to stop his father, is taken to the same hideout by phony cab. Charlie tricks the men by stating two beggars standing in the street below are undercover police. Lee goes along with his father, stating that he phoned the police before arriving. As the men look out the window, Lee kicks the gun out of the man guarding him, and punches him. He and Charlie escape, Lee fighting off other guards on the way.

The strong, adventurous element of Lee Chan, the presentation of his ability to fight when necessary, is helpful to the Charlie Chan character, who is presented as older and more quietly grounded. Thus, the more forceful personality Lee exhibits in this movie is extended to his willing-

---

1. "Critical Focusing." *Movie Makers* January, 1936

Keye Luke, Warner Oland

ness to resort to violence as needed. It is another aspect of the character's continued development. Lee acts quickly, kicking the gun away from the guard as he turns away, punching him, and hitting him with a chair. As he and Charlie make their way down the stairs, Lee subdues the next guard by leaping from the staircase onto the man, knocking him to the floor. It is one of the more exciting sequences in the film.

Charlie visits James Andrews, an agent from Washington. As they discuss the case, Nash goes through Andrews' things in another room. Charlie looks toward a mirror and sees a gun point from the door. He ducks in time before being shot. He slams the door shut on the gun, retrieves it, and the thumb print of Nash is found on the weapon. Nash is arrested. Chan gets hold of a letter Nash stole from Andrews' things. Holding a light to the letter reveals a secret message revealing the Russian as Marloff.

That night Charlie and Andrews meet with Colonel Watkins and Nash who is in custody. Diana is invited to join them in hopes she can get Nash to talk. But she slips Nash a gun and helps him escape. Back at the hotel, Lee Chan tells Charlie he trailed their kidnapper, Marloff, to the

Café Versailles. Later Andrews phones Charlie and states he has cracked the case. Charlie goes to Andrews and finds that the agent has a suspect tied up and is beating information out of him. The suspect reveals that they are to go to the Café Versailles. When they leave, we see Andrews' valet releasing the suspect, who comments on how rough Andrews had been in pulling off this ruse.

Nash is undercover at the Café, sees Marloff and some of his men, and follows them to the basement, where he is captured. Chan and Andrews also head to the basement upon their arrival later and discover opium hidden in wine bottles. The police soon arrive by waterboat and capture the Marloff gang. Charlie then pulls off a capture of his own, with Lee's help, to everyone's surprise (see Appendix A).

Charlie Chan in Shanghai was one of the most popular Chan films to date, and is perhaps the first one that truly ushers in the series as we understand it. Charlie will work most frequently for the American government. His locales will switch from exotic places to venues in the states. He will continue to travel throughout the duration of the series, but as the films continue, the focus will be less expansive.

The other elements regarding character of Charlie Chan are presented in this film. The opening has him playing leap frog with a group of children on the ship taking him to Shanghai. He also sings them a folk song, much to their delight. During the sequence where he is captured by Marloff, Chan's cleverness crowds his concern, and, unlike what would happen in future movies, Charlie seems pleased and comforted once Lee is also captured, ostensibly believing he has a better shot at escaping (which turns out to be true). When Charlie reveals the killer, he pulls out a gun and demands the suspect put up his hands, in a more serious, forceful manner than the pleasant detective usually exhibits. The Chan character continued to expand, as did the series.

The supporting cast is benefited by tall, imposing Russell Hicks as Andrews, and Halliwell Hobbes in the role of Watkins. Each was established in films by this time. Irene Hervey, who stars as Diana, had already made several movies, but this was only the third feature for Charles Locher. Locher would achieve greater success after changing his name to Jon Hall and appearing in the hit film *The Hurricane* (1937). Hall's career would include several B movies (including two in Universal's *Invisible Man* series), as well as a stint on TV as *Ramar of the Jungle* in the early 1950s. Bo Ling, the daughter of former Chan actor E.L. Park (*Behind That Curtian*) makes a brief appearance as Lee's girlfriend.

Keye Luke's performance as Lee Chan added a great deal to this film, as he had *Charlie Chan in Paris*, and reviewers noticed. *The Motion Picture Herald* stated:[2]

> While Warner Oland naturally is the outstanding interest-creating factor in connection with the character he has created over several years, the idea of the Keye Luke son relationship is one that commands more than usual showmanship attention.

Lee is presented as intelligent and resourceful in this film, dressing up as a beggar to follow suspects, and being accurately suspicious of circumstances, sometimes even moreso than his seasoned detective father. The comical aspects of his character, and his stumbling into trouble due to his attempts to be helpful, would be added in later films. It is worth noting that a cartoon of Lee and his girl friend was drawn by Keye himself.

The success of *Charlie Chan in Shanghai* pleased 20th Century Fox executives, and plans were made to step up production on the series and attempt to do more films per year. They were inexpensive, efficiently produced, and were good training vehicles for up and coming actors (like Robert Young, Rita Hayworth, Jon Hall, and Ray Milland, all of whom had appeared in Charlie Chan movies by this time). The plan was to produce four Charlie Chan features for release in 1936. The first would be *Charlie Chan's Secret*.

---

2. "Charlie Chan in Shanghai" *Motion Picture Herald.* September 14, 1935

Charlie Chan's Secret

Director: Gordon Wiles
Screenplay: Robert Ellis and Helen Logan, in collaboration with
    Joseph Hoffman
Original Story: Robert Ellis and Helen Logan
Based on the character "Charlie Chan" created by Earl Derr Biggers
Producer: John Stone
Cinematography: Rudolph Maté
Film Editor: Nick DeMaggio

Cast:
Warner Oland: Charlie Chan
Rosina Lawrence: Alice Lowell
Charles Quigley: Dick Williams
Henrietta Crosman: Henrietta Lowell
Edward Trevor: Fred Gage
Astrid Allwyn: Janice Gage
Herbert Mundin: Baxter
Jonathan Hale: Warren T. Phelps
Egon Brecher: Ulrich
Gloria Roy: Carlotta
Ivan Miller: Morton
Arthur Edmund Carew: Professor Bowan
Jerry Miley: Allen Colby
William Norton Bailey: Harris
James T. Mack: Fingerprint Man
Landers Stevens: Coroner
Francis Ford: Salvage Boat Captain
Charles Ernest: Salvage Diver

Bud Geary: Police Officer
Chuck Hamilton: Police Officer
Brick Sullivan: Police Officer

Shooting days: August 26 to September 21, 1935
Released: January 10, 1936 by Twentieth Century-Fox Film Corporation
Running Time: 71 minutes   Black and white

PERHAPS IT IS DUE to other responsibilities at the studio, or maybe the script had been written without his character in mind, but Keye Luke is sorely missing from *Charlie Chan's Secret*. The on-screen relationship between Charlie Chan and number one son Lee had settled into a firm niche with *Charlie Chan in Shanghai* and it is manages to leave a gap in the character makeup for this film. This is not to say that *Charlie Chan's Secret* is a bad film, however. In fact, its dealing with macabre and superstition refers back to *The Black Camel* as the occult is once again central to the narrative.

Alan Colby, a man from a wealthy family, has been missing for seven years, but returns to claim a fortune that has been left to him. However, Colby is murdered before he can collect. Charlie Chan conducts an investigation, digging through the backstory of Alan's running away, and how his being alive meant that he would inherit funds that would go elsewhere if he were dead. Thus, there are several linking suspects for Charlie to investigate.

Colby comes from a family that is fascinated by the occult, believing in Ouija boards and séances to reveal facts about those living or dead. They claim he left due to his conflicting views about such things. Charlie spends the night in the spooky Colby house, filled with secret passages, and reconstructs the crime. He discovers a speaker set that creates séance music and that the corpse's face was covered with a solution that caused it to glow in the dark. Henrietta Lowell, the family matriarch, realizes the séances were staged. She also realizes that Professor Bowen, conductor of the séances, would likely stand to lose her donations toward his research once Alan returned and claimed the inheritance. Seeing a gun in a mirror reflection, Charlie pushes Mrs. Lowell out of harm's way. Soon afterward, Fred Gage, husband of Henrietta's daughter, arrives offering concern for Mrs. Lowell.

Warner Oland, Herbert Mundin

Chan's investigation takes him to the cottage of Ulrich the caretaker where he finds a radio transmitter being used by Carlotta, the Professor's accomplice, who conducts the séances. He further inspects a receiver at Carlotta's and Professor Bowen's residence. As Charlie handles the coiled wires, Bowen turns on the current, shocking Chan into unconsciousness. The police arrive and arrest Carlotta, while Bowen escapes to safety. He is considered the culprit and is later caught by police.

Mrs. Lowell plans to rewrite her will. It is being delivered at 8:30pm. As she sits waiting, a bullet comes through the window and hits her in the head. Chan discovers a high powered rifle at in the bell tower that was automatically set to fire at 8:30pm. A new séance is held and the image of Mrs. Lowell is revealed indicating she will name the murderer. A knife is thrown, and it is discovered that Mrs. Lowell's image was a mirror reflection, and that she was never shot in the head as others were informed. She is alive. Gage and Ulrich get into a fight when Charlie opens the hand of one of them which shows the dark carbon Chan had put on the knife that was thrown, revealing the culprit. (see Appendix A). All other suspects are released.

Despite missing Keye Luke's presence, *Charlie Chan's Secret* is one of the stronger mysteries during the Warner Oland era. *Variety* stated:[1]

> Warner Oland's new Charlie Chan story is easily the best of his recent screen efforts. It should more than please the Chan clientele and get satisfactory box office returns. Director and writers never overlooked bet in story development, with Henrietta Crosman and Herbert Mundin heading a well-balanced supporting cast. As with all detective yarns framed around Earl Derr Biggers' Oriental sleuth, Chan in this instance sets out to solve a baffling murder and to protect others from threatening doom. It all hinges on the settlement of an estate, with virtually every person in the cast excepting the police and master detective suspected. That's a highly familiar film formula, but here it is made plausible through faithfulness to detail. Customary feigned dumbness of Charlie Chan is never forced, though this characteristic is intelligently maintained here. In fact, it is this apparent weakness that brings about the eventual downfall of the murderer. After an apparently ponderous beginning, Chan soon is at work attempting to put his finger on one of several who might have slain the son of a wealthy family. Anti-climax of picture is the most powerful to be concocted for Charlie Chan story in some time. Figures as a hair-raiser but logical follow to the main climax. Warner Oland turns in his customary skillful interpretation of the shrewd detective, but is not permitted to clutter up the action too much with Chinese-American proverbs. Whole film is strengthened by grand trooping job by Henrietta Cros-

---

1. "Charlie Chan's Secret" *Variety* January 22, 1936

Henrietta Crossman and Warner Oland go over the script

man, Herbert Mundin again is butler. As the frightened involuntary assistant to the super sleuth, he provides his usual quota of rare comedy scenes.

The February 5, 1936 issue of *Film Bulletin,* a trade magazine for exhibitors, singled out Warner Oland's performance, stating:[2]

> Without Oland, the Chan series would have faded from the public taste long ago, but with him there is no reason why it should not remain one of the most definite box office attractions for lovers of the mystery film. *Charlie Chan's Secret* is one of the better Chans.

As with most Charlie Chan features, there are elements of film noir blending the detective drama. Without Lee Chan's effusive action, it is up the Charlie Chan to carry the film, beset by skeptical detectives and a myriad of suspects. Henrietta Crosman, as Mrs Lowell, was a former

---

2. "Charlie Chan's Secret" *Film Bulletin* February 5, 1936

theater actress who entered films in 1914. She adds a firm presence to her important supporting role. Herbert Mundin, as a bumbling butler, adds the film's comic element. There is a very funny bit where the frightened butler goes to climb the bookshelves to escape violence, and ends up merely pulling the books down on top of him. Mundin would continue to offer such amusing performances in films like *The Adventures of Robin Hood* (1939), which was released the same year Mundin was killed in a car crash at age 40.

Arthur Edmund Carewe, who plays Professor Bowen, is seen here in his final film before a stroke left him incapacitated and led to his suicide in 1937. Charles Quigley as the love interest for Rosina Lawrence, who plays Lowell's daughter Alice, is given little to do. Ms. Lawrence is best known for the Laurel and Hardy feature *Way Out West* (1937). She would leave movies in 1939 to marry a man to whom she'd remain wed until his death in 1973. She would remarry Laurel and Hardy biographer John McCabe in 1987 and remain with him until her death ten years later.

Charlie Chan's Secret would be the last of Warner Oland's films not to feature Keye Luke as Lee Chan. Once again moviegoers, though they liked the film, sent letters that asked that Luke return. He would with the next film, *Charlie Chan at the Circus*.

Charlie Chan At the Circus

Director: Harry Lachman
Original Screenplay: Robert Ellis and Helen Logan
Based on the character "Charlie Chan" created by Earl Derr Biggers
Producer: John Stone (associate producer)
Cinematography: Daniel B. Clark
Film Editor: Alex Troffey

Cast:
Warner Oland: Charlie Chan
Keye Luke: Lee Chan
George Brasno: Tim
Olive Brasno: Tiny
Francis Ford: John Gaines
John McGuire: Hal Blake
Maxine Reiner: Marie
Shirley Deane: Louise
Paul Stanton: Joe Kinney
J. Carrol Naish: Tom Holt
Boothe Howard: Dan Farrell
Drue Leyton: Nellie Farrell
Wade Boteler: Lieutenant Macy
Shia Jung: Su Toy
John Dilson: Doctor
Franklyn Farnum: Mike
Anna Mar: Mrs. Charlie Chan
Florence Ung: Number One Chan Daughter
Richard Ung: Number Two Chan Son
Frances Hoo: Number Two Chan Daughter

Mae Jean Quon: Number Three Chan Daughter
Gene Hoo: Number Three Chan Son
Stanton Mui: Number Four Chan Son
Helen Quon: Number Four Chan Daughter
Faye Hee: Number Five Chan Daughter
Hippie Hoo: Number Five Chan Son
Lily Mui: Number Six Chan Daughter
Eunice Soo Hoo: Infant Chan Daughter
Paul McVey: Ringmaster
Esther Brodelet: Circus Performer
Anita Thompson: Circus Performer
John Aasen: Circus Giant
Charles Gemora: Caesar the Ape

Shooting days: January 6, 1936 – February 3, 1936
Released March 27, 1936 by Twentieth Century-Fox Film
    Corporation
Running Time: 72 minutes.   Black and white

AFTER VISITING A VARIETY of exotic locales, the series shifted with *Charlie Chan's Secret* to investigating murders within the odd realm of the occult. Thereafter, the series continued to present Charlie Chan in different unusual settings, beginning with *Charlie Chan at the Circus* and subsequent visits to a race track, an opera, the Olympics, and Broadway.

The circus provides an especially interesting setup for one of Charlie's investigations, as it is filled with various unusual performers, some of whom come off as oddly mysterious. Having the crime transpire as Charlie attends the circus with his wife and large family purely for some fun and relaxing entertainment is a good way to offer a jarring shift in focus, forcing the detective to approach the event with seriousness. Allowing for the (permanent) return of number one son Lee Chan extends the entertainment value further. In fact, *Charlie Chan at the Circus*, is more humorous than previous Chan films and is something of a harbinger for all subsequent movies of the series. Humor will, hereafter, be used more consistently to enhance to heaviness of the murder mysteries.

While vacationing, Charlie and his large family arrive at the circus, due to free passes from one of the co-owners, Joe Kinney, who is a personal friend of the detective. Joe mentions to Charlie that he has been

Olive and George Brasno, Drue Leyton, Wade Boteler, Warner Oland

receiving threatening letters and would like to meet him later to explain more fully. Chan ponders this as his children enjoy such acts as a dancing midget couple and an pretty Asian contortionist to whom Lee is especially attracted. Kinney is shown arguing with the other co-owner, John Gaines, about financial matters, the tension causing a gorilla from one of the acts to react violently in its cage. Kinney responds by taking a whip from the ape's handler and attacking the ape. Gaines goes back to his girlfriend Louise, whose sister Marie, a trapeze artist, is engaged to Kinney, and expresses concern about Joe's volatile temper.

Later, when Chan goes to meet with Kinney, he discovers that Joe has been killed. Since his office was locked from the inside and animal hairs are found near the body, the obvious conclusion is that the gorilla entered through a window and killed Kinney. The culprit is whomever let the ape out of its cage. Chan turns the case over to Macy of the local police and returns to his family. Colonel Tim, one of the dancing midgets, and John Gaines are held on suspicion.

That night, as the Chans are packing to continue their vacation, Tim's partner Tiny comes to see them and begs Charlie to take the case and prove the innocence of her partner and Gaines. The Chan family supports Tiny's plea and Charlie agrees to take the case, bringing Lee along to assist him. He then convinces local police to release Gaines and Tim so the circus can move on and the killer eventually reveal himself. Among the other suspects are snake charmer Tom Holt, especially when Charlie narrowly escapes death from the bite of a cobra while traveling on the circus train, Nellie Farrell, the circus wardrobe lady who claims to have married Kinney in Juarez, and Marie, who Joe had named his beneficiary. When the ape attempts another attack, it is shot dead, and it is discovered the gorilla is not really an ape at all (see Appendix A).

There is a great deal of visual interest offered in *Charlie Chan at the Circus*. Director Harry Lachman was primarily an artist who specialized in well mounted productions that featured impressive sets. The circus setting allows for such footage as an elephant pushing a lion's cage car, imposing camels taking up the foreground in transition scenes, and establishing shots where Lachman shoots from overhead, making the central characters in the foreground appear surrounded by the location's visuals. Unusual characters like the circus giant, playing an early scene with the two little people, and the composition offered when Charlie sits for breakfast with the two midgets, further present visual imagery that enhances the production. Lachman would lend his talents to a later Charlie Chan film as well.

George and Olive Brasno, a brother and sister midget act that was popular during this time, add an authenticity to their roles, and are able to act convincingly as well. The quiet, sinister presence of J. Carroll Naish as the snake charmer is noteworthy in that he would later, on television, play the character on Charlie Chan for a weekly episodic series. Shirley

Deane, given little to do here in her first speaking role on screen, would never rise much above small roles in B movies, but is noted as being originally cast in the title role of the Blondie series a couple of years later. "I thought she was really good," Arthur Lake, who played Dagwood in that series, recalled for the author in a 1980 interview, "but the producers felt she seemed to harsh when she scolded Dagwood. So they hired Penny Singleton. When she scolded Dagwood it seemed more "cute-mad."

Also of interest is the appearance of Francis Ford as John Gaines. Ford was a director in the silent era from 1912 until the end of the 1920s when he switched to acting. He was the mentor of his younger brother John Ford. When Francis was head of Universal's short films during the silent era, he hired John to work in actor Harry Carey's unit, thus beginning his directing career, which eventually led to such classic films as *The Informer* (1935), *The Grapes of Wrath* (1940), *How Green Was My Valley* (1941), *The Searchers* (1956), and *The Man Who Shot Liberty Valance* (1962), among many other timeless classics.

The biggest change in the series dynamic is Keye Luke as number one son Lee Chan. While more dramatically cerebral and something of an action hero in his two previous appearance in the series, *Charlie Chan in the Circus* presents him as the film's comic relief. His reactions are more comically manic. He acts loftily beyond his capacity. And Charlie seems more patronizing than respectful. He has some strong scenes, such as when he pulls off a bulls-eye when shooting the cobra that is attacking Charlie, and when he outsmarts detective Macy as his father looks on with smiling approval. But a lot of his scenes are played for laughs, such as his attempting to save the pretty contortionist from the escaped ape by locking her in an empty tiger cage. When he goes to set her free, she turns the tables and locks him in a monkey cage. This is the way the character would be presented from this point on. It is this film that establishes Charlie's offspring as a well-meaning bumbler who is smart enough to be helpful at times, but often gets in the way or ends up in trouble, which distracts Charlie from the case at hand. This would be explored further in subsequent films as the series progresses.

Featuring the large Chan family, the return of Lee Chan as Charlie's helper, and offering a fascinating series of visuals within the big top backdrop, *Charlie Chan at the Circus* is one of the best films from this period of the series. *Modern Screen* magazine stated:[1]

---

1. "Charlie Chan at the Circus" *Modern Screen* June, 1936

You won't want to miss the Chan family as they all have the Chan charm. We counted eleven of them, from the eldest son, Keye Luke, to the youngest Tai Wo Kung[2]. This time it's the gruesome murder of a circus manager. There are plenty of suspects this time too, for it develops that said unfortunate was cordially loathed by almost everyone at the circus, including the apes and the elephants. It's all so baffling that you'll suspect everyone in the crowd, including Tai Wo Kung. Warner Oland, as always, gives a flawless performance, and is ably supported by Keye Luke and the circus folks, most notably George and Olive Brasno.

With *Charlie Chan at the Circus* the series has fully established itself with all of its elements intact. It is this structure that would continue to be utilized as the films continued to be produced. And, with its gamblers, bookies, and touts, the idea of making the next film seemed like a natural progression.

---

2. It should be noted that no actor by that name appears in the cast – perhaps the reviewer was simply making up a name to be cheeky as that is the tone of his review.

Charlie Chan At the Race Track

Director: H. Bruce Humberstone
Screenplay: Robert Ellis, Helen Logan, and Edward T. Lowe
Story: Lou Breslow and Saul Elkins
Based on the character "Charlie Chan" created by Earl Derr Biggers
Producer: John Stone (Associate Producer)
Cinematography: Harry Jackson
Film Editor: Nick DeMaggio

Cast:
Warner Oland: Charlie Chan
Keye Luke: Lee Chan
Helen Wood: Alice Fenton
Thomas Beck: Bruce Rogers
Alan Dinehart: George Chester
Gavin Muir: Bagley
Gloria Roy: Catherine Chester
Jonathan Hale: Warren Fenton
G.P. Huntley, Jr.: Denny Barton
George Irving: Major Kent
Frank Coghlan, Jr.: Eddie Brill
Frankie Darro: "Tip" Collins
John Rogers: Mooney
John H. Allen: "Streamline" Jones
Harry Jans: Al Meers
Robert Warwick: Honolulu Police Chief Inspector
Billy Wayne: Smithers
Sam Flint: Captain Blake

Selmer Jackson: J.L. Lansing
Ivan "Dusty" Miller: Captain Wade
Ed Hart: Detective
Boothe Howard: Ship's Doctor [Dr. Johnson]
Sidney Bracey: Waiter
Jack Mulhall: Second Purser
Charles Williams: Reporter #1
Eddie Fetherston: Reporter #2
Max Wagner: Joe
Jerry Jerome: Chuck
Paul Fix: Lefty
Holmes Herbert: Melbourne Cup Chief Steward
Colin Kenny: Judge
Robert E. Homans: Judge
H. Bruce Humberstone: Gambler
Lew Hicks: Policeman
Bob Ellsworth: Policeman
Lucille Miller: Secretary
James Eagles: Chick Patton
Bobby Tanzel: Gilroy
Bruce Mitchell: Gateman
Clyde McAtee: "Blackton" man
Jack Green: "Blackton" man
Pat O'Malley: Track Official
Tom McGuire: Track Official
David Thursby: Steward
Forrest Taylor: Photo Booth Worker
Ray Hanson: Third Officer
Sam Hayes: Track Announcer
Cyril Ring: Race Track Extra
Larry Steers: Railbird
Harlan Tucker, Sammy Finn, Wilbur Mack, Norman Willis: Gangsters
George Magrill, David Worth, James Flavin, Harry Strang, Al Kirkune: Detectives
William Wayne, Lee Srechley: Seamen
Josephine the monkey: Lollipop

Shooting days: May 18 to June 16, 1936

Released August 7, 1936 by Twentieth Century-Fox Film Corporation
Running Time: 70 minutes. Black and White

CHARLIE CHAN IS SUMMONED by his friend Major Gordon Kent when Kent believes a major gambling ring is controlling horse racing, due to a situation that occurred at a Melbourne race where Kent had a horse entered. Charlie meets Kent's boat in Honolulu and boards it when he discovers that en route, Kent was kicked to death by his own horse. Chan believes the direction of splattered blood in the stall, as well as a missing winch shoe that would leave the same impression as a horse shoe, points to murder rather than an accidental death. Along with solving the murder, Charlie also wants to uncover the gambling ring that is likely responsible. There is a fire in the stalls, allowing the crooks to switch horses, which would change the odds for the gamblers. When a horse who had been skittish around a pet monkey that is kept in the stalls offers no reaction, Chan discovers the ruse. He and his number one son Lee are kidnapped to be held until the race is over, but manage to escape, make it to the race, and reveal the man behind everything (see Appendix A).

Horse racing offers a great backdrop for a Charlie Chan mystery, the first of several where specific venues, rather than exotic locales, are used as settings. The film opens with Charlie offering lessons to some would-be detective students when Lee comes bursting in with odds on a horse race that causes the students to hover around the radio. Charlie takes him by the ear and brings him to the door to eject him when Lee explains that the horse in question is owned by a friend of the Chans.

The relationship between Charlie and Lee has now been established as the stern-yet-understanding patriarch and the earnest-but-bumbling offspring, a comic dynamic that will remain with the character for the duration of the series. Guiding him by the ear, slapping his behind as he Bends over, Charlie is the disciplinarian. However, despite Lee's enthusiasm becoming a bit two blatant for incidents that need to be shrouded in secrecy, Charlie appears to still respect his son's intelligence and gives him responsibilities that he handles nicely.

Lee's heroics are not overshadowed by his more comical aspects, however. In the scene where he and Charlie are kidnapped by gangsters, the detective asks his guard for materials to roll a cigarette. Director H.

Warner Oland

Bruce Humberstone does a nice job of cross-cutting between close-ups of a pondering Lee and a determined Charlie, displaying that the son is aware of what his father is planning to do. Charlie blows the tobacco through the rolling paper in the guard's eyes, giving Lee enough time to punch him and break a bottle over his head. This allows the two of them to escape.

To create a diversion at the race track so that Charlie can go back and investigate further matters, Lee Chan starts setting of fireworks that he brought in with a laundry truck, and, using an affected Chinese accent, pretends to not realize what's going on our why. This distraction is effective and Charlie gets into the guarded area. Director Humberstone shoots this with an effective medium shot, the fireworks exploding in the background with Keye Luke, his back turned, in the foreground, jumping up and down as if reacting to a surprising situation.

Humberstone would go on to direct several more Charlie Chan films, and while he never stuck to a specific genre (comedies, dramas, westerns, and thrillers were all helmed by him), he was particularly adept at mysteries and settled into a comfortable niche with the Chan features. Keye Luke in a 1985 interview recalled, "I think we had the most fun with Humberstone."

Keye Luke, Warner Oland

Among the fun Luke and Warner Oland had on the set of *Charlie Chan at the Race Track* was reported in *Silver Screen* magazine:[1]

> Children accept Warner Oland as a contemporary – a compliment which he appreciates. While *Charlie Chan at the Race Track* was being filmed, the company was on location and had seeral scenes to shoot without Warner, who promptly disappeared. Presently an intermittent popping and cracking somewhere in the distance began ruining sound tracks and the sound engineer's temper. Investigation disclosed Warner and Keye Luke, with a collection of children mysterious assembled, out in back of the grandstand shooting off firecrackers. They had raided the laundry truck full of fireworks, which you remember in the picture, and were giving the kids, and themselves, a swell Fourth of July, even if the date was wrong.

---

1. Rankin, Ruth "Charlie Chan Reveals" *Silver Screen* July, 1937

Charlie Chan at the Race Track boasts a particularly strong cast. Returning to the series are Thomas Beck and Jonathan Hale, with the welcome appearance of such veteran character actors as Alan Dinehart, Selmer Jackson, and juvenile performers Frankie Darro and Frank "Junior" Coghlan. Darro, especially, is perfectly cast as a jockey willing to commit fouls on the track for a payoff from the gamblers. Darro was already beginning to specialize in such roles, and his tough-talking character fits nicely within the proceedings.

Two of this film's screenwriters, Robert Ellis and Helen Logan, wrote several of the Chan features during this period, and while they had a good understanding of the mystery structure, they also were the ones responsible for developing Keye Luke's character of Lee Chan from his original heroics into more of a comic bumbler with the occasional good idea. They would continue to provide screenplays, and use that character structure, after the series was being done with different actors. Edward T. Lowe also contributed to the screenplay for *Charlie Chan at the Race Track*, having worked on *Charlie Chan in Paris*.

One interesting aspect of the Charlie Chan character is how he will suddenly go from "your humble servant" to a man of action and forcefulness. This is evident in his switching demeanor at the end of *Charlie Chan in Shanghai* as he commands the criminal to put up his hands while holding a gun on him. Here he is even more forceful as Charlie hauls off and punches out a guard coming around the corner, so the detective and venture further and proceed with the investigation.

Curiously enough, *Charlie Chan at the Race Track* concludes the same way as *The Black Camel* had. In the earlier film, there is a running gag with Charlie's comical accomplice running in and announcing "Clue!" and then offering whatever evidence he has uncovered. At the end of *The Black Camel*, he rushes in after the crime has been solved and is told to keep his clue for their next crime. In this film, Lee Chan rushes in after the case is wrapped up and makes the announcement that he has a clue and is given the same advice as the film concludes.

Charlie Chan at the Race Track was another popular entry in the Charlie Chan series, and remains among the most entertaining. One theater owner in Illinois went so far as to promote the movie playing in his theater by presenting a display of famous horse shoes. The shoes had been worn by horses owned by the likes of Rudolph Valentino, Will Rogers, General Pershing, even King George.

Working with the man that he recalled as his favorite director of the Chans, having a lot of fun scenes, and continuing to believe Warner

Oland was "a marvelous man," Keye Luke particularly enjoyed this entry in the series. But in later years he would admit that the next film, *Charlie Chan at the Opera*, is the best Charlie Chan movie in which he appeared.

Trade ad for *Charlie Chan at the Opera*

Charlie Chan At the Opera

Director: H. Bruce Humberstone
Assistant Director: Sol Michaels
Screenplay: Scott Darling and Charles S. Belden
Story: Bess Meredyth
Based on the character "Charlie Chan" created by Earl Derr Biggers
Associate Producer: John Stone
Cinematography: Lucien Androit
Film Editor: Alex Troffey

Cast:
Warner Oland: Charlie Chan
Boris Karloff: Gravelle
Keye Luke: Lee Chan
Charlotte Henry: Mademoiselle Kitty
Thomas Beck: Phil Childers
Margaret Irving: Madame Lilli Rochelle
Gregory Gaye: Enrico Barelli
Nedda Harrigan: Madame Anita Barelli
Frank Conroy: Mr. Whitley
Guy Usher: Inspector Regan
William Demarest: Sergeant Kelly
Maurice Cass: Mr. Arnold
Tom McGuire: Morris
Hilda Vaughn: Agnes
Fred A. Kelsey: Dugan
Selmer Jackson: Hudson
Emmett Vogan: Smitty
John Bleifer: Orderly

Lee Shumway: Sanitarium Guard
Gladden, James: Secretary
Stanley Blystone: Police Officer
Benson Fong, Sammee Tong: Soldiers in opera
Joan Woodbury: Opera Dancer
Tudor Williams: Boris Karloff's operatic singing voice

Songs: "March Funebre," "Ah, Romantic Love Dream," "King and Country Call,"
"Carnival Marche," and "Then Farewell" from the opera Carnival, Music by Oscar Levant, Libretto by William Kernell, Orchestrations by Charles Maxwell

Released January 8, 1937 by Twentieth Century-Fox Film Corporation
Running time: 68 minutes. Black and White

FOR THE FIRST TIME since taking on the role of detective Charlie Chan, Warner Oland shares above the title billing with another actor. Boris Karloff, having achieved major stardom with *Frankenstein* and *Bride of Frankenstein* takes on the role of a crazed opera singer who escapes confinement and is suspected of a series of murders. It is considered by many, including Keye Luke, to be the best of the Charlie Chan pictures during Warner Oland's time in the role.

After being kept in an insane asylum for seven years, opera star Gravelle escapes and finds his way to an opera house where his wife, who tried to murder him with the help of her lover, is performing. Hiding in various areas of the building, he is eventually discovered after several murders take place. Charlie Chan investigates but believes the case is more complicated than to simply pin the murders on Gravelle.

There are a few elements that add depth to the narrative. First, Gravelle is initially presented as an amnesiac whose memory suddenly returns when he sees his wife's picture in the newspaper, advertising the opera in which she is performing. Also, while Chan is usually respected by the accompanying detective on the case, this time he has to deal with the skeptical Sergeant Kelly who derisively refers to Charlie Chan as "chop suey" and through his irascibility, refuses to respect that Chan might have clues that extend beyond his own conclusions. Both the Chan character and

Warner Oland, Keye Luke

Kelly (played by William Demarest) offer sharp contrasts to the frivolous pretentions of the opera prima donna types, each played for their stereotypes.

There are a lot of layers to the murders due to the actions of the characters. Prima donna Lilli Rochelle is having an affair with baritone Enrico Barelli, but is married to Mr. Whitely, as Enrico is married to soprano Anita Barelli. There are jealousies abounding. Meanwhile, Phil Childers wants to marry Kitty, the daughter of Lilli Rochelle, whom she does not acknowledge. These in-and-outs among the characters help confuse the mystery. Lee Chan, Charlie's number one son, wants to become involved in investigation so he puts on a knight's suit and blends in with extras in the opera. Just as Gravelle's image is discovered by a screaming woman, attracting Kelly and most of the opera company, Lee is spotted sneaking around and is suspected to be the culprit.

The characters each have their own respective situations, but it never becomes too convoluted to keep the narrative from effectively flowing. There is some fun backstage when Kelly chases down Lee, who hides with a group of knight extras, all of whom are Chinese. The harried stage manager is upset by the intrusions on his opera's performance, and finally states "This show is going on even if the Frankenstein monster himself shows up," which is a cheeky reference to Boris Karloff's most famous role.

There is a scene in which Gravelle takes Barrelli's place on stage and begins singing thrilling those watching backstage who have never heard Barelli sing so well, but former wife Lilli's reaction is one of fear without dropping character. It really is a nice balance that the actors, and director, pull off flawlessly. Karloff's other strong scene occurs when he confronts Kitty, who is his daughter, and who believes him to be dead. He wants to approach her with warmth and gentleness but cannot help coming off as creepy and threatening. His frustration is palpable as he tries hard to convey he means no harm. She faints, Charlie enters, and discovers Gravelle. Chan's instinctive wiles manage to charm the unsettled singer.

Charlie arranges for the opera to be staged with Gravelle in his old role, much to the chagrin of Kelly and the other detectives. He believes that the ensuing production will result in revealing the culprit. Of course he is correct (see Appendix A).

As *Charlie Chan at the Opera* was in post-production being readied for release, producer John Stone told the press how each film was created:[1]

> First of all, the crime that Charlie Chan is to be called upon to solve in each picture should involve murder. That's really serious business. We go into a protracted huddle – the writers and myself – months before our picture is to go into production and we devise an unsolvable murder. Logical, yes, but with no clues that even the smartest detective in the world could use to track down the killer. Having done that, we solve our own crime. *Charlie Chan at the Opera*, which we have just completed, is a good example of our mode of operation. I doubt very much if anyone will be many guesses ahead of Detective Chan in this picture, yet we place before our audience each clue available to Chan. It's a lot of work, but it's a lot of fun too, and the steadily increasingly popularity of the Chan pictures indicates it's a pretty practical system as well.

Director H. Bruce Humberstone did not want to continue making B movies, so he chose to make *Charlie Chan at the Opera* look more like an A-

---

1. Syndicated article in newspapers to promote *Charlie Chan at the Opera*

level movie by utilizing the beautiful sets being used by *Café Metropole*, an expensive production being shot around the same time. Studio head Darryl Zanuck stated that Humberstone's B movie put the Fox A directors to shame. With his consistent penchant for science and gadgetry, Humberstone presents how to send a wire photo in this film. While the material is archaic in the 21st century, it was fascinating for 1930s audiences.

Oscar Levant took the time to compose an entire opera for this film, but only some of his work is used in the film. Still, his contribution adds greater authenticity to those scenes in which Karloff is singing (dubbed by Tudor Williams).

There are a few points of significance regarding *Charlie Chan at the Opera* aside from its status as perhaps the best Chan feature of its time. This was the first American film to use the new DeBrie camera for its cinematography. Lighter and quieter than other models, it carried 1000 foot reels, requiring less time to load. *Charlie Chan at the Opera* was also the first American film to be forbidden by the Third Reich, by special order of the Reich censor. No specific reason was announced but it was assumed

Boris Karloff and Warner Oland go over the script

that the theme, and the role being played by a Chinese detective, was contrary to the Propaganda Minister's film policy.

Charlie Chan at the Opera increased the series popularity by almost double the amount. Theater owners reported that the films had been popular, but now each showing filled the house and had people standing. Part of the reason was the box office pull of Boris Karloff. Made for only $125,000, *Charlie Chan at the Opera* grossed over $500,000 *Film Daily* called it "One of the best of the Chan series." *Motion Picture Daily* said it was "probably the best Chan story to date." *The Motion Picture Herald* stated:[2]

> The axiom that age improves things is very well demonstrated here. Of the long Charlie Chan series, practically all of which have found a ready market with legions of theater goers, this latest member stacks up as the best. It is desirable entertainment, the field for which is not limited strictly to the Chan followers. It holds much to engage the attention of rank and file audiences.

William Demarest as Detective Kelly is his delightfully irascible self, engaging in the politically incorrect practice of dismissing Charlie Chan as "chop suey" or "egg fu yung." Detective Kelly is another instance of racism being negatively presented in the series, with Kelly realizing in the end that he was wrong to hold those stereotypes.

Thomas Beck is making yet another appearance in a Chan film, while the fresh faced innocence of Charlotte Henry is also commendable. Of course Keye Luke as Lee Chan is delightful support as usual, but given comparatively less to do here. He is amusing throughout but does not have a truly big scene of his own.

Boris Karloff chews the scenery with gusto as Gravelle, his sinister manner working nicely opposite Detective Chan. During a period where he was doing some of his best work, Karloff turns in one of the finest performances of his career. Technically, this is his second appearance in a Charlie Chan movie, Karloff having appeared in *Behind That Curtain* (1929) in which Chan is merely a peripheral character and not played by Warner Oland.

It is impressive how the writers took what could have been a very straightforward film about chasing down the supposed killer in the opera

---

2. "Charlie Chan at the Opera" *Motion Picture Herald* October 17, 1936

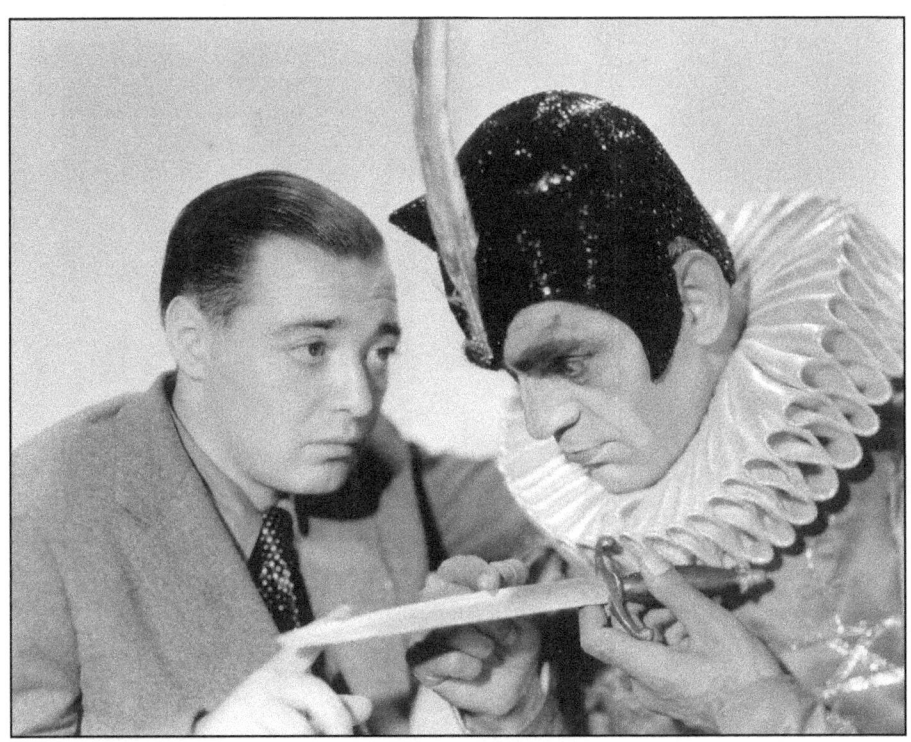

Peter Lorre, during a break while filming *Crack Up* visits the set for a gag photo with his friend Boris Karloff

house and turned it into a very complex mystery with a surprise ending by introducing all of these various characters. And it does all of that in a manner that isn't too complicated in just a little over an hour.

From this point the Charlie Chan movies increased in popularity, extending beyond the parameters of their initial audience. Production continued to explore areas where there was good potential for the detective to conduct an interesting and entertaining investigation. For his next film, Charlie Chan's on-screen family dynamic extends beyond number one son Lee.

Charlie Chan At the Olympics

Director: H. Bruce Humberstone
Screenplay: Robert Ellis and Helen Logan
Original Story: Paul Burger
Based on the character "Charlie Chan" created by Earl Derr Biggers
Producer: John Stone (Associate Producer)
Cinematography: Daniel B. Clark
Film Editor: Fred Allen

Cast:
Warner Oland: Charlie Chan
Katherine De Mille: Yvonne Roland
Keye Luke: Lee Chan
Pauline Moore: Betty Adams
Allan Lane: Dick Masters
Layne Tom, Jr.: Charlie Chan, Jr.
C. Henry Gordon: Arthur Hughes
John Eldredge: Cartwright
Jonathan Hale: Hopkins
Morgan Wallace: Honorable Charles Zaraka
Fredrick Vogeding: Captain Strasser
Andrew Tombes: Police Chief Scott
Howard Hickman: Dr. Burton
Selmer Jackson: Navy Commander Wright
Edward Keane: Colonel Webster
Arno Frey: Carlos
Caroline Rankin: Hotel Landlady
O.G. "Dutch" Hendrian: Miller
David Horsley: Edwards

Frank Bruno: Footman
Billy Wayne: Ship's Steward
Al Kikume: Honolulu Police Officer
Emmett Vogan: Ship's Officer
George Chandler: Ship's Radio Operator
William von Brincken: Berlin Police Officer Posted as a Guard
Brooks Benedict: Henchman
Ferdinand Schumann-Heink: Officer on the Hindenberg
John Peters, Hans Fuerberg: Berlin Police Radio Officers
Minerva Urecal: Olympics Matron
Constant Franke: Attendant
Paul W. Panzer: Berlin Police Officer Posing as a Vendor
Perry E. Seeley, Virgil B. Nover: Sign Language Experts
Tommy Klein: Page Boy
Ben Hendricks: Coast Guard Officer
Don Brody: Navy Commentator
Phillip Morris, Lee Shumway, Stanley Blystone: New York Police Officers
Walter Bonn, Glen Cavender: Berlin Police Radio Car Officers

Shooting days: January 28 to February 15, 1937
Released May 21, 1937 by Twentieth Century-Fox Film Corp.
Running Time: 71 minutes. Black and White

THERE ARE A LOT OF ELEMENTS within *Charlie Chan at the Olympics* that make it among the better films in the series. The Chan family is expanded here, with Charlie Chan jr. introduced. Lee Chan's role is given separate attention away from his "Pop." Director H. Bruce Humberstone's interest in science and electronics is evident. And, coming off the heightened success of *Charlie Chan at the Opera*, this film manages to maintain its increased audience with a good mystery, some action and comedy, and a number of appealing characters.

When an airplane is set up with a new remote control device to be used in the military, a stowaway hijacks the aircraft, murders the pilot and steals the device. Charlie Chan is called in to investigate, and signs point to just who that stowaway is. Accompanied by police, Charlie goes to the man's hotel room and discovers his dead body. When several potential suspects leave for Germany on a steamship, Charlie Chan joins

Charlie Chan At the Olympics • 89

Layne Tom Jr., Warner Oland, Keye Luke

two accomplices, Mr. Hopkins and the remote control's inventor, Cartwright, and travels to Germany by way of the Hindenburg. The steamship also contains the Olympic team on which number one son Lee Chan is a member, competing in the swimming competition.

With Lee separated from Charlie and given his own scenes with a different group, the writers apparently felt compelled to have another offspring play off of the detective. Child actor Layne Tom, jr. appears as Charlie Chan, jr. Much younger than older brother Lee, Charlie jr. has every bit as much effervescence and enthusiasm for the finding of clues that move toward the crime. He only appears in the opening scenes, and is no longer in the movie once dad Charlie heads to Germany. But he is there when his detective father discovers the downed airplane that leads to further investigation. He witnesses some of the techniques used to reach the conclusion that a trip to Germany is necessary. He offers advice, wise beyond his years.

Lee Chan, traveling on the ship with the Olympic team, notices suspicious activity between Yvette Roland and Mr Hughes, an older man sneaking around her. Yvette is also seen frequently with Dick Masters, who was originally going to be the pilot that tests the remote control device, but backed out of the job when he qualified for the Olympics. Dick's girlfriend, Betty, confides in Lee that she's keeping an eye on the two of them.

This sets up a separate situation for Lee Chan. He has no idea his father is headed to Germany, but he has a natural curiosity when he sees what he believes to be suspicious activity. The older man is Mr. Hughes, who has been established earlier in the film as someone interested in the remote control. Lee is unaware of this, and simply sees a telegram placed in a book that is left on a step, and removed by Hughes. Lee runs past Hughes, bumps into him, apologizes in Chinese while brushing him off, and gets ahold of the telegram.

When Charlie arrives and boards the ship, he and his party are joined by a German inspector. They search Ms. Roland's stateroom and find it ransacked. As Charlie continues his investigation alone, curious Lee comes in through the porthole to do some snooping on his own, and is pleasantly surprised to see his detective Pop. When Charlie explains why he is on board ship, Lee turns over the material he has and gives him all the information he has observed. As the two travel to Berlin by train, they narrowly escape being shot by a car driving alongside the train. It is Hughes who pushes them out of the way, seeing the gun pointing out of the passing car.

Once at the hotel, Charlie and company enter Betty's room to search through her things as there is evidence the remote has been stashed in her luggage unbeknownst to her. They enter just as the Olympics Matron is trying to steal the remote control, which is hidden in a box of candy. They confiscate the device, then she goes to the window and yells to a car down below that the police are here. The car drives off and the maid is taken into custody. While this is going on, Charlie quietly replaces the remote control with a book in the candy box and returns it to the luggage. Later, Charlie and a policeman hear a gunshot coming from Hopkins' room and find a dazed Cartwright, who claims Hopkins took a shot at him and ran out with the invention after Hughes accused him of planning to gyp the stockholders.

At the Olympic games, Lee is kidnapped and held for ransom by criminals who believe Chan has the device. Charlie is sent a note to be somewhere with the device to trade it for his son. He asks police to allow him to act alone for Lee's safety. Charlie shows up, but with a phony remote control that is actually a radio transmitter that allows police to identify his location. The criminals are fooled into believing they now have the actual device, and plan to dispose of Charlie and Lee. Hughes comes in with two accomplices and interrupts the proceedings, wanting the device himself. He sees that it is a phony, tosses it aside, it breaks open, and the transmitter is discovered. Hughes threatens to kill Lee if Charlie does not come up with the device, but the police arrive in time. Hopkins is shot, but not killed. One man is blamed, but Charlie realizes another man is the culprit (see Appendix A). Once the case is wrapped up, Lee is shown winning the 100 meter swim at the Olympics, stating that he learned to swim fast when he was a child and his father chased him with a paddle. Coming up to congratulate his son for his victory, Charlie pulls out a large paddle and states, "I was ready just in case," as both men laugh.

At this point the Charlie Chan series has all of its elements worked out and each series entry looks polished. The screenwriters for this entry had written *Charlie Chan at the Circus* and *Charlie Chan at the Race Track*, so their ability to develop the characters and understand how to guide the mystery is sufficiently presented in *Charlie Chan at the Olympics.*

The separation of the Lee Chan character allows Keye Luke to command his own scenes with other supporting actors. It shows him laughing and carrying on with people his own age, while also confiding in Betty that he is suspiciously watching what is going on with Yvette. When he attempts to copy his father's penchant for proverbs, he doesn't come off quite as effectively, usually laughing at the end and adding "....or something...." This gives actor Luke another dynamic to work within, and he succeeds admirably.

Adding 9 year old Layne Tom Jr. as Charlie Chan Jr. gives us the dynamic of the detective responding to one of his younger offspring. Exhibitors had been stating that the Charlie Chan series was attracting essentially an older demographic, The addition of Charlie jr., plus Lee being connected with other young people in his own scenes, were attempts to expand that audience. Responding to the increased popularity of the series, his appearance extends the Chan family's immediate connection to the story and widens the film's demographic to the family trade. Layne Tom Jr. would later appear with Sidney Toler as Chan in two other films after Oland died.

Director Humberstone was attracted to the scientific element of the film. It features a remote control device for aircraft that would assist military operations as its major plot point. The case is solved partially by the use of an electronic transmitter that allowed Charlie to venture alone into the dangerous hideout where Lee was being held, while still remaining connected to police. There is also some historical significance of Charlie and company traveling on the Hindenburg. This film was shot in early 1937 before the tragic explosion that destroyed the Zeppelin on May 6. The movie was released on May 21, a full two weeks afterward.

The Hindenburg was shown via stock footage from Fox's newsreel library (its Movietone News shorts being a staple of theaters for some time). Humberstone makes good use of this in a nice cutaway from the ship scenes with Lee, and later does a good job incorporating footage of Jesse Owens from the most recent (1936) Olympic games, which were indeed held in Germany. Thus, *Charlie Chan at the Olympics* has topical elements that have become interesting historical ones.

Warner Oland had, by now, fully enveloped himself with the Charlie Chan character. Keye Luke would call him Pop off screen as well as on. In a 2006 interview on the DVD of this film, Layne Tom Jr. recalled: "I would look into Warner Oland's eyes, and I would see a Chinese man. Mr. Oland really looked Oriental. I couldn't believe he was a Swede. He represented what Chinese men were like back then. When he said a proverb, he did it so well." The scenes during which Lee was being held by kidnappers offered another emotional level to Charlie that had not been seen in earlier films. The usually unflappable detective shows real concern, even worry, as he thinks of a way to rescue his number one son. It's also a struggle for Charlie because he doesn't want his personal feelings to intervene with the investigation and cause the device to fall into the wrong hands, but as a father he also as a responsibility to save his son. It offers some of Oland's best acting in the series.

The supporting cast features solid B movie stalwarts like Allan Lane, who would eventually star in his own western series and later provide the voice of talking horse Mr. Ed on TV, and Katherine DeMille, adopted daughter of Cecil B. DeMille, as well as Pauline Moore and C. Henry Gordon, both of whom would appear in more Chan pictures. This was the third and final appearance in a Charlie Chan movie for Jonathan Hale, who would later find a comfortable niche as Mr. Dithers in the Blondie movie series at Columbia. Despondent over failing health and his wife's recent death, Hale shot himself to death at the Motion Picture Home in 1966.

Both critics and audiences enjoyed *Charlie Chan at the Olympics* as the series was now firmly established. The review in *Silver Screen* magazine stated:[1]

---

1. "Charlie Chan at the Olympics" *Silver Screen* June, 1937

> Another swell impression by Warner Oland of the lovable Chinese detective. This time we meet him at the German Olympics and are introduced to another son of his, but Keye Luke is present also, for which we offer thanks. The plot moves quickly and is as exciting as its predecessors.

At least one amusing even occurred during the filming of *Charlie Chan at the Olympics*. Warner Oland, while on a trip to the Orient the previous year, had misplaced his cigarette case. While working on this movie, a package arrived at the studio and it was brought to the set. It was his lost cigarette case, which had been found by a rubber planter in Singapore. Apparently the cigarette case had slipped down between the cushions of a chair in the lounge of the Peninsula Hotel in Hong Kong and, after many months, the initials W.O. were traced to their owner. Oland told the press: "I'm very grateful for the return of the case but it sort of upsets things. I manage to lose at least on cigarette case a year and that has always made it easy for Mrs. Oland to select a Christmas present."

For his next film, the writers would take Charlie Chan to the Great White Way, and Warner Oland would revisit his theater roots.

Ad for *Charlie Chan on Broadway*

Charlie Chan On Broadway

Director: Eugene Forde
Screenplay: Charles Belden and Jerry Cady
Original Story: Art Arthur, Robert Ellis, and Helen Logan
Based on the character "created by Earl Derr Biggers
Associate Producer: John Stone
Cinematography: Harry Jackson
Film Editor: Al DeGaetano

Cast:
Warner Oland: Charlie Chan
Keye Luke: Lee Chan
Joan Marsh: Joan Wendall
J. Edward Bromberg: Murdock
Douglas Fowley: Johnny Burke
Harold Huber: Inspector Nelson
Donald Woods: Speed Patten
Louise Henry: Billie Bronson
Joan Woodbury: Marie Collins
Leon Ames: Buzz Moran
Marc Lawrence: Thomas Mitchell
Toshia Mori: Ling Tse
Charles Williams: Meeker
Eugene Borden: Louie
William Jeffrey: Coroner
Sidney Fields: Porter
Norman Ainsley: Steward
Philip Morris: Customs Officer
George Regas: Hindu

Allen Wood: Bellhop
George Guhl: Smitty
Billy O'Brian: Copyboy
Lon Chaney, Jr.: Desk Clerk
Beulah Hutton: Telephone Operator
Harry Depp: Candid Camera Snapper
Kenner G. Kemp: Candid Camera Photograher at Hottentot Club
Cyril Ring: Candid Camera Photographer at Hottentot Club
Gloria Roy: Hat Check Girl
Sam Ash: Waiter
Blue Washington: Doorman at Hottentot Club
Allan Cavan: Doorman
Art Miles: Porter
Charles Haefeli: Pickpocket
Victor Adams: Gangster
Edwin Stanley: Laboratory Expert
Robert Middlemass: Police Official
Robert Lowery, Franklin Parker. Don Brodie. Billy Wayne, Sherry Hall, Creighton Hale, Allen Fox: Reporters
Henry Otho, James Blaine, Monte Vandergrif, Jack Clifford, James Flavin: Detectives
Paddy O'Flynn and Lester Dorr: Photographers
Jack Dougherty, Eddie Dunn, Harry Strang, Don Rowan, Carly Faulkner, Chuck Hamilton, Lee Shumway, Harry Burns: Police Officers

Shooting days: June 10 to July 16, 1937
Released October 8, 1937 by the Twentieth Century-Fox Film Corporation
Running Time: 65 minutes. Black and white

EUGENE FORDE RETURNS as director with *Charlie Chan on Broadway*, having helmed both *Charlie Chan in London* and the lost *Charlie Chan's Chance*. Forde was a stalwart of the Fox studios, whose penchant for keeping things moving and under budget, offers an unremarkable, but very entertaining effort. The fifteenth Chan movie featuring Warner Oland, *Charlie Chan on Broadway* shows the series settling so firmly into a niche, it has become a bit too easy to pull off an effective production.

While this film is quite competent as a Chan vehicle, it offers nothing beyond its immediate parameters.

Charlie Chan on Broadway takes up where *Charlie Chan at the Olympics* leaves off, with Charlie and Number One Son Lee sailing from Germany to New York. The film opens the enthusiastic Lee going over the "swell" dinner he just had, much to the chagrin of his seasick father, offering what appear to be some light and amusing moments, but there was a more serious reason for doing so. Warner Oland notably liked to drink on the set while filming the movies, but his performance remained strong until later in the day when it got to the point that he was too inebriated to continue working. By the time *Charlie Chan on Broadway* was being filmed, personal problems, including difficulties in his marriage, were plaguing the actor. His drinking increased and scenes like this opening were written to work around this problem.

Charlie and Lee encounter Billie Bronson yelling from her bathroom, having been locked in. She tries to explain she must have accidentally

Keye Luke and Toshia Mori

Keye Luke and Warner Oland

locked herself in, but a chair against the door on the other side reveals otherwise. She later slips a package in with the Chan's luggage because a mysterious man on board ship has tried to steal it from her. Once in New York, the Chans are met by Inspector Nelson and two reporters – Joan Wendall and Speed Patton. When Billie is spotted, Speed gets in a car with her and it is revealed that she had left New York abruptly one year earlier to avoid being a witness in a murder trial. Her return to the city is big news, but she has a past with Speed and asks him to keep quiet and she will meet with him later that night.

Billie then tries to get into the Chans' room to retrieve her package but is caught by Lee. She indicates her room is just above theirs, and she got off on the wrong floor by mistake. Lee chuckles at the error, but still follows her to a nightclub owned by her former lover Johnny Burke. Speed and Joan are there as well, looking for a story. Billie is warned by racketeer Buzz Moran to get back out of town by morning, then goes to Burke's room. She confronts Burke, accuses him of an affair with dancer Marie Collins, and pulls a gun on him.

Chan and the Inspector are at a banquet when they receive word that Billie has been shot and Lee Chan has been accused. They arrive at the club, Lee is freed, while Speed, Joan, Burke, and Marie are questioned. The lights go out, and when they come back on, Charlie discovers a key is missing, based on a photograph Joan had taken shortly after Billie's murder. It is Charlie's room key, so they return to his hotel room but can't get in, because the door is blocked by a dead body. The dead man turns out to be the same mysterious person who tried to steal the package from Billie on the ship. Lee remembers Billie stating her room was directly above theirs. They go upstairs and find Murdock, editor of the newspaper Speed and Joan work at. He admits he was trying to find Billie's diary, believing it reveals a lot of secret info about New York racketeers that he would like his newspaper to expose.

The next day, Burke turns himself in after a confrontation with Buzz Moran, but a test to reveal gunpowder on his hands proves negative, so he is released. When he returns to his office, Lee is discovered going over the case with an attractive Asian girl who works at the club. Burke hits Lee, who punches back before he is removed from the premises by security. Lee returns to the hotel room with a black eye.

All of the suspects are rounded up by Charlie Chan who goes over the case, and reveals the murderer (see Appendix A). The murderer than pulls a gun as he confesses to the crimes, but Lee jumps him before he can shoot Charlie. As the film ends, Lee, wearing sunglasses, wants to remain in New York and enjoy the sites, which the case never allowed him and Charlie to see. As he removes his sunglasses, it is revealed that he now has two black eyes. "Broadway, hard on the eyes," his father quips and the film ends.

It is interesting that this film is called *Charlie Chan on Broadway*, considering that the story has nothing to do with either Broadway or the theatre. However, the New York setting made for a nice, gritty backdrop to the action. Keye Luke is given more time in this film than the others, allowing for comical bungling as well as courageous action. At one point he loses, to a pickpocket, the $20 bill his father just gave him, and then later he is saving his father's life with his heroics. Warner Oland, despite his personal struggles and his on-set drinking, remains consistent and steady throughout the proceedings, but Luke carries as much of the movie as he does. About a month after this film wrapped, Edith Oland was reported as serving husband Warner with divorce papers, citing his alcoholism as a contributing factor to her decision. Wanting separate maintenance and lawyer's fees, her decision was certainly being readied while *Charlie Chan on Broadway* was being filmed, thus distracting Oland and affecting his work. It did not, however, affect his performance. Oland may not exhibit the same enthusiasm he might have in earlier movies, and his response to Lee might be a bit abrupt and gruff at times (especially when the son is caught stealing towels from the ship's stateroom, and it is discovered he had been doing this from hotels for some time). But overall he is still grounded in the shots used for the movie.

Thomas Beck was originally slated to play Speed Patton, but this Fox contact player, who'd already appeared in four previous Charlie Chan movies, was just too busy to take the role. Beck would appear in eight features during 1937, including two entries in the new Fox detective series Mr. Moto, with Peter Lorre as a Japanese sleuth. Beck left movies at the end of the 1930s, because the studio reduced his wages, but he would live until 1995. Donald Woods took the role of Patton, appearing in his first Chan picture since *Charlie Chan's Courage* in 1934. Joan Marsh, who plays the Speed's partner Joan Wendell would work with everyone from W.C. Fields, to Bob Hope, to The East Side Kids before leaving films in the early 1940s, but this is her only Chan movie. She would live until 1998. The rest of the cast is rounded out with welcome veterans like J. Edward Bromberg, Harold Huber, Douglas Fowley, and Leon Ames. Marc Lawrence registers effectively as the mysterious stranger whose dead body is found in the Chans' room.

Charlie Chan on Broadway would continue the series' popularity with moviegoers who became connected to the clichés of the series by now and were uncritical if nothing particularly impressive was going on past surface entertainment. *Variety* stated in its review:[1]

---

1. "Charlie Chan on Broadway" *Variety* September 22, 1937

Newest entry into the Charlie Chan Chinese sleuth series fits alongside of the better ones. It holds more than usual for the metropolitan audiences because of having a New York locale and concerned with graft in the big town. Film provides an opportunity for the Oriental Sherlock to perform his deductions while a guest of the N.Y. police force. Good for locations where others in this series played. Running through the clever detective manipulations of Charlie Chan are bright situations, subtle and roughshod comedy, and pointed action. Chan uncovers the least suspected scandal column writer as the killer of two people mixed up in the big city's mob. Writers have permitted several in the cast to be placed under the cloud of suspicion without closing all doors to the entrance of other suspects. Producers have wisely kept Chan's son in the series, making him a foil for his father's shrewd nifties. But at the end, it is the aspiring offspring who is equal to the emergency and thwarts a third murder. Chan is again faithfully personified by Warner Oland, with just

Warner Oland's brother (center) visited the set and met actress Joan Marsh

as much interest as ever being shown to his clever portrayal. Keye Luke again is the effervescent son, with the lad even better than before if only because he does more things in his usual enthusiastic style. Production values are plenty in evidence, with even the nitery entertainment having some semblance of naturalness. Eugene Forde has directed with intelligence, and never lets up on the early fast tempo.

Box Office was even more enthusiastic, indicating in its review:[2]

Ace-high in ever production department, this is a worthy contribution to the well-established Charlie Chan series. In addition to satisfying the detective's followers, it should gain new friends for Earl Derr Biggers character through logical plot development, snappy dialogue, and a whirlwind finish in the best Chan manner.

The fact that Warner Oland was plagued by personal struggles was not just a situation here, but would also be a problem on his next film, *Charlie Chan at Monte Carlo*. Sadly, that would also be the actor's last completed film.

---

2. "Charlie Chan on Broadway" *Box Office* August 7, 1937

Charlie Chan At Monte Carlo

Director: Eugene Forde
Screenplay: Charles Belden and Jerry Cady
Original Story: Robert Ellis and Helen Logan
Based on the character "Charlie Chan" created by Earl Derr Biggers.
Producer: John Stone (associate producer)
Cinematography: Daniel B. Clark
Film Editor: Nick DeMaggio

Cast:
Warner Oland: Charlie Chan
Keye Luke: Lee Chan
Virginia Field: Evelyn Grey
Sidney Blackmer: Victor Karnoff
Harold Huber: Inspector Jules Joubert
Kay Linaker: Joan Karnoff
Robert Kent: Gordon Chase
Edward Raquello: Paul Savarin
George Lynn: Al Rogers
Louis Mercier: Taxi Driver
Eugene Borden: Hotel Clerk
George Davis: Pepite
John Bleifer: Ludwig Krauss
Georges Renavent: Renault
Sherry Hall: Bartender
Marcelle Corday: Concierge
Leo White: French Butler
Constant Frank, André Cheron: Croupiers
Joseph Romantini, Albert Pollet: Attachés

Victor Delinsky, Alphonse Martell, Louis Lubitch, Robert Graves, George Sorel, Jean Perry: Gendarmes
Jean De Briac:, Manuel Paris: Doormen
Gennaro Curci, Antonio Filauri, John Picorri: Waiters

Shooting days: September 20 to October 18, 1937
Released January 21, 1938 by Twentieth Century-Fox Film Corporation
Running Time: 71 minutes. Black and white

NOBODY REALIZED THAT *Charlie Chan at Monte Carlo* would be Warner Oland's final film. The announcement in the press that his wife was suing for divorce and separate maintenance was weighing heavily on the actor's mind, just as the troubles leading up to that point were a distraction on the previous film, *Charlie Chan on Broadway*. As with the other movie, *Charlie Chan at Monte Carlo* gives Keye Luke more footage, as Oland's on-set drinking became a problem. Actress Kay Linaker recalled in the documentary *Charlie Chan is Missing: The Last Days of Warner Oland* that the actor, "would come in early and they would shoot all of his close-ups first. Because by eleven o'clock, he might as well just go home." Director Eugene Forde, kept things moving efficiently and frugally, and Oland exhibits the usual grounded performance despite his off screen troubles. These traits were also a part of *Charlie Chan on Broadway*, and they were factors that the studio felt they could work with, as the films did get made and continued to be successful.

Oland was not difficult on the set. He was merely troubled, and his stoicism didn't allow a lot of sharing. Keye Luke recalled in an interview:[1]

> He'd miss a line and say, "Oh, so sorry. Honorable feet not in proper place," you know. Then, he'd say, "all right, we'll start again." Then he'll blow a line and say, "Oh, rustle of doves in rafters," you know, because we had doves flying around in those big stages and never could get them out. So then, another time he'd blow a line, and he'd look up and say, "Alex! Why did you rustle that paper just on my

---

1. Keye Luke interview conducted for Canadian television (TV Ontario) in Hollywood, California, circa 1985

Warner Oland, Keye Luke, Harold Huber

line?" Alex wasn't even on the set. Alex was his stand-in. I don't think that there was anything about him that a little rest wouldn't have helped. I knew that he drank heavily and all that, but he could maintain a level. And, as far as his health was concerned, he wasn't that sick.

Charlie Chan in Monte Carlo features Charlie and son stopping at the titular city on their way to an art show in Paris where Lee has a painting on display. When their taxi breaks down, they set out on foot and come upon a car containing a dead body. They flag down a police car, and Lee tries to communicate with them in French. He bungles the language to the point where he and Charlie end up arrested for the murder. Upon returning to Monte Carlo, Charlie and Lee are cleared and join Inspector Joubert in the investigation. The dead man was delivering a million dollars in bonds belonging to Victor Karnoff, and of course the money is gone.

The car belongs to Evelyn, who is staying at the same hotel. She is questioned and it is discovered she's connected with Paul Savarin who is Karnoff's enemy. She is also connected to Karnoff's secretary, Gordon Chase, who is in love with her.

Sadly, *Charlie Chan at Monte Carlo* was Warner Oland's final film

At about this time, an American bartender named Rogers attempts to sell some bonds to the bank, so he is questioned, but cleared. Later, Karnoff confronts the Rogers, insisting the bonds he tried to sell were among the attempted delivery. Rogers is later found dead, appearing to the French inspector to be suicide, but Charlie believes differently. It is found that Karnoff's wife Joan, to whom the bartender had been married, was being blackmailed by him, and she becomes one of the suspects. At Karnoff's house, a valise containing the bonds is presented while all of the suspects are gathered. The suspect is revealed upon producing a key and indicating the type of gun used in the murder. (see Appendix A).

Perhaps the least interesting of the extant Charlie Chan films featuring Warner Oland, *Charlie Chan at Monte Carlo* is more lightly comical in its isolated scenes rather than investigating elements of film noir like some of the other efforts. Some of the comic relief is indeed amusing. Charlie, attempting to order waffles for breakfast, makes a sketch to communicate with the French waiter, and is given a book of crossword puzzles. Lee walks down the hallway with a large painting covering his face, in order to look inconspicuous. There is even a scene where the seat of his pants are set on fire and he reacts comically while the blaze is extinguished at point blank range. But the comic relief isn't relief as much as it is a separate faction of the movie that is distracting in a positive way. The mystery is complex but less involving, while the comedy is lightweight fun.

In an effort to be authentic to the locale, much of the dialog is in French. Sometimes this can be disconcerting, except when Lee's fractured Gallic gets him into trouble. Veteran actor Harold Huber, who plays an inspector, was fluent in the language, and fluctuates from being comical to serious with equal aplomb.

Much of what sustains the narrative and concludes the mystery are elements that have now become clichés, including Charlie outsmarting the misguided police and Lee bungling about but occasionally helping the case much to his father's consternation and pride. However, the idea that Charlie and Lee are headed to a Paris art show where Lee has a painting being shown is a neat touch. Lee is presented throughout the series as having a variety of talents, but Keye Luke truly was an artist even moreso than he was an actor. It is Luke's scenes that are the most entertaining in Oland's swan song.

Again, it was not known during shooting that it would be Warner Oland's final film. Several future projects were mentioned in the trades, including *Charlie Chan at College* and *Charlie Chan in Radio City*. The next film to begin shooting in January of 1938 was *Charlie Chan at the Ringside*. But Warner Oland would not complete the movie.

Charlie Chan at the Ringside became a Mr. Moto film when Warner Oland left the production. Keye Luke with Peter Lorre in *Mr. Moto's Gamble*

Charlie Chan At the Ringside/ Mr. Moto's Gamble

THIS FILM STARTED SHOOTING on January 12, 1938 during which Warner Oland was still plagued by personal problems, but was seeking a reconciliation with his wife. He agreed to do something about his drinking, and work out other issues that hampered the couple's marriage. His wife, however, was initially not very receptive to his promises, and this further hampered his emotional state.

Production was underway when on January 17, 1938, Warner Oland left the shooting to get a drink of water and, without telling anyone, walked off the set. When he did not return the next day, production was called off and Oland was suspended by the studio. Production was suspended and the cast was paid off and sent home after $100,000 worth of footage had been shot. Various reports surfaced, indicating everything from a conflict with the studio to personal problems. It is likely that both were contributing factors.

Mr. Moto's Gamble

Not wanting to take a loss on the footage already shot, *Charlie Chan at the Ringside* was rewritten as a Mr. Moto mystery, taking advantage of the other detective series Fox had launched a year earlier. Peter Lorre, who played Moto, did not particularly like his dialog filled with Chanesque aphorisms but he was under contract to Fox and did what he could with the assignment. Keye Luke played Lee Chan, allowing the studio to use the footage of him already shot. Lee was a student visiting his father's colleague Moto, and getting caught up in an inevitable murder mystery. The resulting film, *Mr. Moto's Gamble*, turned out to be one of the best films of its series.

A boxer dies in the ring, poison is the culprit, and Moto (along with a police detective played by the reliable Harold Huber) is on the case. As with most of the Charlie Chan mysteries, the narrative unfolds, the clues are consistent but guarded, and everyone looks suspicious at some level. Luke and Maxie Rosenbloom provide tangential comic relief while still being integral to the plot (there is a fun running gag with Maxie as a hapless kleptomaniac). And while director James Tinling's job is to simply allow the narrative to unfold, he has some pretty creative ideas during the fight sequences, with close-ups of the fighters, key audience members, and medium shots intercut to maintain the action. A report in the Motion Picture Herald at the time stated that at the film's preview, audiences swayed as if watching an actual boxing match.

In a short 72 minutes everything is revealed. There is no unnecessary character development to slow down the action, no distracting subplots, and the entire enterprise is most delightfully entertaining in the best B-movie manner. The cast is rounded out by Dick Baldwin, Lynn Bari, Douglas Fowley, John Hamilton, George E. Stone, and Ward Bond. It is characters that sustain this entry, which was the third in the Moto series. Even the National Board of Review admitted at the time that "the atmosphere and the minor characters are more interesting than the solution of the mystery." Of course, in the end, the killer ends up revealing his own guilt due to a trap set by the clever Moto.

Keye Luke, Harold Huber, Peter Lorre

Comparing this to other films in the Moto series, it is easy to tell that this was originally a Chan movie, with Moto being a carbon copy of that character. Even his interactions with Lee are the same as Chan's, which just feels a bit awkward since theirs is a teacher/student relationship, not father/son. *Mr. Moto's Gamble* was released on April 7, 1938. By that time, Warner Oland had left for Europe, and according to Keye Luke:

> Well, he went to Europe. Everywhere he went, they wined and dined him, and he sent back these headlines and newspaper clippings to me. And, so, it was just like a triumphant tour - all through Europe. And then he finally got up to Sweden to Stockholm to the ancestral home. He got bronchial pneumonia, and he died in his mother's bed. First time he had been back to his home in forty years or so.

Oland falls ill

Warner Oland patched up whatever differences he had with the studio, who either forgave him for leaving the set of a film, worked out better arrangements for him, or both. But it was announced that he was slated to return to the Charlie Chan series with *Charlie Chan and the Clipper Ship* later changed to *Charlie Chan in Honolulu*. An article in *Film Daily* stated:

> Warner Oland, the cinema's Charlie Chan, will be back at work on the 20th Century Fox lot shortly. The actor, forced by illness to quit work during the production of *Charlie Chan at the Ringside* is nearing complete recovery, according to his physician, Dr. Eugene Czuckor.

However, this is merely studio publicity. Dr. Czuckor was an American holistic (naturopathic) doctor who worked in psychotherapy and helped many Hollywood stars (he would later marry one, actress Barbara Britton, with whom he'd share a happy life with children until her death in 1980). He was based in California, not in Sweden where Oland was at the time. A short time later, *Motion Picture Herald* reported that Warner Oland was ready to start work on this next film.

Warner Oland dies

Warner Oland died in his native Sweden on August 6, 1938. His estate, based on a will from May of 1937, left $50,000 to his estranged wife, including a farm in Massachusetts and 1000 acres in Mazatian, Mexico. He also bequeathed some cash legacies to relatives. Mrs. Oland sailed for Stockholm to attend her husband's funeral. He was buried in Southborough, Massachusetts where the Olands hoped to someday retire.

Keye Luke recalls being on the set of a film when it was announced that Warner Oland died. He was given permission to go home for the day. Luke stated:[1]

> He was the type of actor who could obliterate his own personality and create a believable character right before your eyes. Of course I had the great good fortune to work with him, and I observed how he worked. He was so thorough. If you watch him, he's as smooth as skating on ice. Never a break in there - one thing flowed into another. The words matched the looks, the looks matched the words, and the actions matched everything. He was amazing. He was a very lovable man, and fun. Always with a twinkle in his eye.

Oland's funeral was held in his native Sweden, with over 20 wreaths sent from his Hollywood friends.

A New Charlie Chan

Three days after Oland died, *Variety* announced that Fox planned to continue the Charlie Chan series with a new actor:

> No successor to Warner Oland in the Charlie Chan series will be picked by 20th-Fox execs until exhibitor reaction on a choice is studied. Studio denied that Keye Luke, who played Oland's son in the series, would be elevated to the part until exhibs have been consulted and a canvass made of all possibilities. J. Edward Bromberg is rated having the best chance as the new Chan. When

---

1. Keye Luke interview conducted for Canadian television (TV Ontario) in Hollywood, California, circa 1985

Warner Oland first fell ill, the studio cast about for a substitute, and Bromberg's tests reportedly showed up best.

Bromberg was a working actor who had appeared in Charlie Chan films. He would not get the role of the detective, but remained active until the Hollywood blacklist halted his career after he refused to name names for the House UnAmerican Activities Committee. The stress of the blacklist led to his fatal heart attack in 1951. Other actors to be considered for the role were Walter Connolly and Cy Kendall, both of whom played Charlie Chan on radio.

Sidney Toler, another working character actor who appeared in films with the likes of William Powell, Laurel and Hardy, and Clark Gable, landed the role of Charlie Chan. He was the 35th actor to be tested for the part. Toler secured the right to approve his co-stars, and indicated he wanted Keye Luke to remain with the series as Lee Chan. Luke, however, turned the role down. The actor would always indicate it was in loyalty to the late Warner Oland, but other reports claim it was a contract dispute with the studio. After what has been described as a "frantic" search that extended to Asian-American students at Universities, an American born actor of Chinese ancestry, Victor Sen Yung, was cast as Charlie's number two son, Jimmy Chan. *Charlie Chan in Honolulu* began shooting on October 31,1938

There was one last homage. During production of the Fox film *Mr. Moto's Last Warning*, Warner Oland's death was announced. The filmmakers included a passing shot of a theater with the marquee stating "*Charlie Chan in Honolulu* starring Warner Oland" along with a banner that states, "Last Day."

Trade ad for *Charlie Chan in Honolulu*, the first film with Sidney Toler in the role.

Charlie Chan In Honolulu

Director: H. Bruce Humberstone
Assistant Director: Saul Wurtzel
Original Screenplay: Charles Belden
Contributing Writer: Chandler Sprague
Based on the character created by Earl Derr Biggers
Producer: Sol M. Wurtzel
Associate Producer: John Stone
Cinematography: Charles Clarke
Film Editor: Nick DeMaggio

Cast:
Sidney Toler: Charlie Chan
Phyllis Brooks: Judy Hayes
Sen Yung: Jimmy Chan
Eddie Collins: Al Hogan
John King: Randolph
Claire Dodd: Mrs. Carol Wayne
George Zucco: Dr. Cardigan
Robert Barrat: Captain Johnson
Marc Lawrence: Johnny McCoy
Richard Lane: Mike Flannigan (posing as Joe Arnold)
Layne Tom, Jr.: Tommy Chan
Philip Ahn: Wing Foo
Paul Harvey: Inspector Rawlins
Grace Key: Mrs. Chan
Florence Ung: Ling
Al Kikume: Police Officer
Arthur Loft: Peabody

Grace Hayle: Stout Woman
Shirley Louie: Telephone Operator
James Pierce: Police Officer
Constantine Romanoff: Stanislav Usepopokovski
James Spencer: Hawaiian Peddler
Richard Alexander: Tough Sailor with Cigar
James Flavin: Desk Officer
Iris Wong: Number Two Chan Daughter
Barbara Jean Wong: Number Three Chan Daughter
Faye Lee: Number Four Chan Daughter
Margie Lee: Number Five Chan Daughter
Sinclair Yip: Older Chan Son
David Dong: Chan Son
Frank Dong: Chan Son
Allan Hoo: Chan Son
Blue Washington, Billy Wayne: Sailors

Shooting days: October 31 to November 29, 1938
Released January 13, 1939 by Twentieth Century-Fox Film Corporation
Running Time: 68 minutes. Black and white

THERE WAS A LOT RIDING on *Charlie Chan in Honolulu*. Twentieth Century Fox studios did not want to lose one of its most lucrative film series with the death of its beloved star. They were hoping Sidney Toler, his replacement, would be convincing enough to please the series' many fans. Also losing the equally beloved Keye Luke was another hit the series took, and Victor Sen Yung was entrusted to fill those shoes. Fortunately, the results were positive at every level. *Charlie Chan in Honolulu* pleased the critics, pleased moviegoers, and its box office receipts pleased the studio.

This time Charlie Chan and his large family are excited about an impending grandchild. Charlie goes to the hospital where his daughter is ready to give birth, but is called away to solver a murder that has taken place on board a ship. However, he does not get this information right away. The call comes to his home and is intercepted by his number five son Tommy. His number two son Jimmy has an interest in becoming a detective, just like older brother Lee had, so he decides to take the case himself and Tommy tags along. Jimmy is already starting to bungle things in his attempts to investigate when Charlie finally does get the message and shows up on the ship.

The opening scenes effectively establish the new actors playing Charlie and son. The screenplay indicates that number one son Lee is away at art school, and now number two son Jimmy is eager to take his place in helping his father solve crimes. Jimmy has the same enthusiasm as Lee, but is less talented and more comical. When he exhibits his passion, his siblings giggle. However when Tommy gives Jimmy the message about the shipboard murder, he shares his older brothers excitement.

The dynamic between the two brothers has some potential but it isn't explored too well. On ship, Tommy spends most of the time hiding in the closet, and when Charlie arrives he is sent back ashore. Jimmy, however, inspects the body and questions a few suspects, but the film presents him as a more comical character than Lee had been. There is an unsettling comic scene with Jimmy bumbling about a baggage room containing caged wild animals further hindered by a bombastic performance by Eddie Collins as the baggage room manager.

The relationship between Charlie and Jimmy utilizes only one aspect of the Charlie-Lee pairing, that being the stern father containing the enthusiastic behavior of the son. Unlike when Lee is given his own scenes to solve part of the crime on his own, Jimmy's opening sequence on the ship shows a comical ineptitude that means well, but has no real effect. His father, however, does support his potential and occasionally gives him duties to perform help the investigation. It is good that Victor Sen Yung does not simply replace Keye Luke in the role of Lee Chan, and is given his own separate character.

Charlie Chan in Honolulu features a mystery that is typically layered, with more than one murder, a tangential situation involving killers in a separate case traveling as a cop and his prisoner, stolen money, a firearm that is passed around, at least one red herring (played by the reliably creepy George Zucco), and an ending that reveals a suspect that truly is a surprise (see Appendix A). But the most significant aspect of this movie is its effective transition from a beloved actor who defined the character for films being replaced by one who had to embrace what had been established while adding his own delineation of the role. Sidney Toler plays Charlie with this same smiling patience and calm, but with a discernible edge that lapses into sarcasm as much as he uses aphorisms.

It is also interesting how this film is less of a noirish mystery and more of a family outing with as much light comedy as there is heavy mys-

Victor Sen Yung, Sidney Toler, and Layne Tom, Jr.

tery. Chan cleverly challenges the Zucco character on a couple of occasions, proving he is not deaf by throwing a coin which causes him to turn and look as it lands, and tricking him into putting his fingerprints on a gun. But at the same time, Jimmy reacts in comic fright to a roaming pet lion, and flails in equal comic fashion when the crew prepares to throw him overboard. This blending of clever mystery and silly comedy never seems to clash. There is some fun, clever comedy surrounding the impending birth of the first Chan grandchild, with his son-in-law occasionally interrupting the proceedings to provide Charlie with seemingly trivial updates. And the dialog between Charlie, the son-in-law, and Paul Harvey as a harried police inspector when they all end up on the same phone line is one of the movie's comic highlights.

Perhaps as a sort of insurance, *Charlie Chan in Honolulu* is filled with top drawer character actors, including, along with Zucco, such familiar B movie stalwarts as Richard Lane, Robert Barrat, Claire Dodd, Marc Lawrence, Paul Harvey, Phillip Ahn, and Phyllis Brooks. Each helps bolster the proceedings effectively. H. Bruce Humberstone was assigned to direct, his experience with previous Chan films further helping the transition.

Taking on the characters for the first time, Sidney Toler and Victor Sen Yung settle into the roles so quickly, it is surprising that they hadn't been playing the characters for years. The transition was seamless and the series would continue to enjoy consistent success for many more years. In fact, Sidney Toler would end up making more movies as the character than Warner Oland had. And, like Oland, he would play the role until his death.

Years later, Victor Sen Yung told newspapers,[1] "It was an easy role for me, a wise-cracking kid, because that's what I was then. Toler taught me everything I know about acting, and I had a ball in Hollywood. My house was the rendezvous for all the Chinese bachelors." He also addressed his opinion about a Caucasian actor playing the Chinese detective.[2] "I would prefer the qualified actor. Motion Pictures are entertainment and not there to protect national identity. There really wasn't a Chinese actor at the time to play Charlie Chan. I was making $250 per week with a 40 week guarantee. In 1938 that was good money for a kid just out of college."

The magazine *Modern Screen* was enthusiastic in their review of *Charlie Chan in Honolulu*: "Best news in regard to this picture is that Charlie Chan, as played by Sidney Toler, is as convincing a sleuth as was Warner Oland, with many ingratiating qualities which should endear him to Charlie Chan fans." *Photoplay* stated: "The witty detective's newest adventures deserve special mention as there is a new Charlie Chan, Sidney Toler. He does not copy the late Warner Oland, but the result is startlingly good." *Variety* stated:[3]

> Adventures of Charlie Chan get off to a fresh start, with Sidney Toler handling the title role in most capable fashion. His Chan has more poise and lightness, and is less theatric than previously. Followers of the series should quickly accept him as Chan, and if comparisons with the late Warner Oland's conception are made they will gener-

---

1. Victor Sen Yung interview *St Louis Post Dispatch* November 4, 1971
2. Victor Sen Yung interview *The Lincoln Star* August 24, 1977
3. "Charlie Chan in Honolulu" *Variety* December 21, 1938

ally be made in his favor. In addition to Toler, sees the temporary - and likely permanent - departure of Keye Luke, who handled the part of Lee Chan, oldest son of the detective. Second son, Jimmy, is introduced to carry prominent spot in future pictures. Sen Yung has been tied by the studio for the role, but possible return of Keye Luke is carried in dialog, which describes his departure for art school in the east. Story is typical of previous Chan murder mysteries, providing several suspects for Chan to gradually eliminate. It's all quite interesting, with direction okay for this type of picture.

At about the time this movie was being filmed, Alfred Andioloa began a Charlie Chan comic series that was syndicated in Sunday newspapers. The comics, which ran until 1942, were based on the films featuring Warner Oland, and Lee Chan was prominently featured in many strips. Oland's impact was still resonating years after his death. However, as far as the movies were concerned, the transition was effectively made. The Chan series with Sidney Toler would continue to enjoy the same level of quality, and success. For his next film, Charlie Chan would travel from his Honolulu home to Reno, where divorces lead to murders.

Charlie Chan In Reno

Director: Norman Foster
Assistant Director: Jasper Blystone
Screenplay: Frances Hyland, Albert Ray, and Robert E. Kent
Based on the character "Charlie Chan" created by Earl Derr Biggers
Based on the original story *Death Makes a Decree* by Philip Wylie
Producer: John Stone (associate producer)
Cinematography: Virgil Miller
Film Editor: Fred Allen

Cast:
Sidney Toler: Charlie Chan
Ricardo Cortez: Dr. Ainsley
Phyllis Brooks: Vivian Wells
Slim Summerville: Sheriff Fletcher
Kane Richmond: Curtis Whitman
Sen Yung: James [Jimmy] Chan
Pauline Moore: Mary Whitman
Eddie Collins: Cab Driver
Kay Linaker: Mrs. Russell
Louise Henry: Jeanne Bentley
Robert Lowery: Wally Burke
Charles D. Brown: Chief of Police King
Iris Wong: Choy Wong
Morgan Conway: George Bentley
Hamilton MacFadden: Night Clerk
Arthur Rankin: Bellboy
Virginia Sale: Maid
Fred Kelsey: Desk Sergeant

Al Kikume: Honolulu Police Officer
Ed Stanley: Police Chemist
Stanley Blystone: Police Officer at Lineup
Jimmy Aubrey: Wisecracker in Lineup
Hank Mann: "Injured" Con Man
Harry Hayden: Chemistry Professor
Dick Hogan: Jack
Jack Perry: Jones
Barbara MacLain: College Girl
Brooks Benedict, Blue Washington: Men in Line-up
Heinie Conklin, Chuck Hamilton: Police Officers

Shooting days: January 23 to February 24, 1939
Released June 16, 1939 by Twentieth Century-Fox Film Corporation
Running Time: 70 minutes. Black and white

CHARLIE CHAN IN RENO BEGAN shooting after its predecessor *Charlie Chan in Honolulu* enjoyed a successful premiere and was in release for about ten days. Critics and moviegoers accepted Sidney Toler as Chan, and Fox executives were pleased that their lucrative franchise would continue. *Charlie Chan in Reno* is one of the best entries in the entire series.

The film opens at the Hotel Sierra in Reno, Nevada which was established as the divorce capital. People would go there for a six week residency in order to file for a divorce. That is the intention of Mary Whitman, who arrives and immediately connects with social director Vivien Wells. However, Mary is soon confronted by Jeanne Bentley, the woman who plans to wed Mary's husband once the divorce is final. Due to her disruptive actions, Jeanne is asked by hotel owner Mrs. Russell, to leave in the morning. Later that night, Jeanne is found dead with Mary standing over the body. Charlie Chan, a family friend is called to the case, traveling with Mary's husband Curtis Whitman. Jimmy Chan reads about the case and heads there by auto from his California University.

Once Charlie arrives, he meets up with an assortment of characters connected to the suspect and the victim, including Dr. Ainsley who is staying at the hotel and is connected to the other, working especially closely with Vivian; and Wally Burke, who has been dumped by Louise in favor of Curtis Whitman. He is also introduced to the Sheriff, Tombstone Fletcher, who is on the case but finds it complicated and confusing.

Sidney Toler becomes serious as Charlie Chan

Clues are tampered with, including pages ripped from a scrapbook, the murder weapon is missing, and it is discovered that big money was being given by the murdered woman to doctor Ainsley. Acid burns on clothing that match those on the floor where the murdered woman is found also add to the clues of the case. Charlie finally assembles the suspects in his room, goes over the case, and not only reveals the murderer, but an attempted murder that had been thwarted, involving another suspect (see Appendix A).

Reno, Nevada had been established as the "divorce capital" back in 1910, and by 1931, the six week residency rule made it an even more popular place for quickie divorces. By 1940 Nevada accounted for 49 out of 1000 divorces in the United States. Using Phillip Wylie's story in *Liberty* magazine, "Death Makes a Decree," as source material, the screenwriters fashioned a Charlie Chan film from the author's vision. A very prolific writer, Wylie is perhaps best known for having written the novel *Gladiator* in 1930, which helped inspire the idea for the Superman comic. *Gladiator* was made into a comedy movie with Joe E. Brown in 1938, the same year Superman first appeared in Action Comics.

Along with its mystery, *Charlie Chan in Reno* features a great deal of comedy and further presents the character of Jimmy Chan in contrast to Lee Chan in the earlier films. Jimmy is trembling in comic fear over staying in the hotel room of the murdered woman. Lee would more likely be intrigued. And while he is entrusted with helping his father, Jimmy is never given as much authority as Lee was. Although he plays most of his scenes for comedy, actor Victor Sen Yung is a delightful counterpart to the sturdiness of Sidney Toler's interpretation of the Charlie Chan character. When he is allowed his own scenes, Jimmy Chan comically stumbles into unfortunate situations, from causing an explosion in his chemistry lab at school, to being robbed of a borrowed car and all of his clothes in a hitchhiking scam on his way to Reno.

Slim Summerville plays Sheriff Tombstone. A lanky, imposing presence, Summerville also adds a veteran comic sensibility to the film. Summerville started out in movies as a Keystone Cop for Mack Sennett in 1912, acting and directing in dozens of short comedies during that early era of the moving picture. He transitioned easily to talkies, appearing in dramas like the Oscar-winning *All Quiet on the Western Front* (1930), and *Captain January* (1936) with Shirley Temple, but specialized in comic roles, including a series of movies teamed with ZaSu Pitts. Here he assumes the role of the befuddled lawman who is at once crowded by Charlie Chan's joining the case, and frequently exhibits confused frustration at his methods and the trajectory of the investigation. Director Norman Foster will often cut away to a reaction shot from Summerville, further enhancing the comic aspect of the film.

The comedy is never a distraction, and the mystery portion is dotted with appearances by what was, at the time, considered the finest supporting cast of all the Charlie Chan features up to this point. Interestingly enough, many of the actors in this movie had played, or would soon play,

Victor Sen Yung and Iris Wong

crime fighters. Ricardo Cortez had portrayed Sam Spade in the 1931 version of *The Maltese Falcon*, Kane Richmond would play the title role in the *Spy Smasher* serial, Morgan Conway would portray Dick Tracy in a couple of features, and Robert Lowery would appear as Batman in a popular serial some ten years later.

The budget for *Charlie Chan in Reno* exceeded $100,000 which was a very large sum for a B movie in 1939. Promotional materials emphasized that the film would have more appeal to women than the usual Chan feature, but would also continue to attract men and children. *Motion Picture Daily* wrote, "There is more mystery than has been the case in any of the Chans. At the same time, the production has all the comedy that any of the series ever had." *Showmen's Trade Review* emphasized "the best supporting cast to be seen so far in this series" and said, "Sidney Toler now stands on his own feet as Chan, and will probably make the Oland fans clamor for more of him." They also said that it was director Norman Foster's "best stint to date."

Norman Foster had directed most of the Mr. Moto series for Twentieth Century Fox when he was assigned this Charlie Chan film. Very superstitious, Foster insisted on having a black cat appear in at least one scene in every one of his films. However, Slim Summerville was equally superstitious and insisted black cats were bad luck. Refusing to do a scene with the animal, he actually managed to shut down production until he finally backed down and agreed to do the scene. Foster would go on to direct the next two Charlie Chan features.

The studio realized with the release of *Charlie Chan in Reno* that there was no need for them to have worried about the recasting of the title character. Sidney Toler's first two Chan films were the most lucrative at the box office to date. The studio executives realized that the financial success of the first Toler film could be due to curiosity. But the even greater success of *Charlie Chan in Reno* helped them realize their franchise remained strong. Fox followed up the success of *Charlie Chan in Reno* with what many consider to be the very best film in the entire series.

Charlie Chan At Treasure Island

Director: Norman Foster
Assistant Director: Charles Hall
Original Story and Screenplay: John Larkin
Based on the character "Charlie Chan" created by Earl Derr Biggers
Executive Producer: Sol M. Wurtzel
Associate Producer: Edward Kaufman
Cinematography: Virgil Miller
Film Editor: Norman Colbert

Cast:
Sidney Toler: Charlie Chan
Cesar Romero: Fred Rhadini
Pauline Moore: Eve Cairo
Sen Yung: Jimmy Chan
Douglas Fowley: Pete Lewis
June Gale: Myra Rhadini
Douglas Dumbrille: Thomas Gregory
Sally Blane: Stella Essex
Billie Seward: Bessie Sibley
Wally Vernon: Elmer Kelner
Donald MacBride: Deputy Chief J.J. Kilvaine
Charles Halton: Redley
Trevor Bardette: Abdul ("The Turk")
Louis Jean Heydt: Paul Essex
Fred Kelsey: Detective
John Elliott: Backstage Doctor
Kay Linaker: Séance Apparition
Gerald Mohr: Dr. Zodiac

Edith Hallor: Toots
Al Kikume: Waiter
Harry Strang: Taxicab Dispatcher
Heinie Conklin, Hank Mann: Taxicab Drivers
Harold Goodwin: Airline Steward
Tom Quinn: Person at Arrival Gate
Arthur Rankin: Airline Official
Bruce Mitchell: Police Desk Sergeant
Bud Geary: Police Officer
Frank Meredith: Second Detective
Margaret Mann, Imboden Parrish, Gloria Roy, Charles Tannen: Airline Passengers
Jack Chefe, Sayre Dearing, Harold Miller, Bert Moorhouse, David Newell: Audience Members

Note: John Carradine and Joyce Compton were set to be in this film, but they do not appear. Photos of each of them are visible in one scene.

Shooting days: April 17 to May 13, 1939
Released September 8, 1939 by Twentieth Century-Fox Film Corporation
Running Time: 74 minutes. Black and White
Working title: *Charlie Chan at the World's Fair*

IN ONE OF THE STRONGEST FILMS in the entire series, *Charlie Chan at Treasure Island* explores fake mystics and superstitious believers in the occult. As with all of the better efforts in the series, *Charlie Chan at Treasure Island* peppers the serious mystery with just enough light comedy. The story is compelling, the performances by a strong cast are effective, and Norman Foster's direction allows for the usual brisk pace.

Charlie Chan and his number two son Jimmy are traveling to San Francisco by plane when their friend, writer Paul Essex, who has just finished a novel about phony occultists, dies mysteriously. A radiogram he just received issued a warning about the dangers when "ignoring the zodiac." Also, Paul's briefcase is suddenly missing, and Jimmy suspects a mysterious passenger who goes by the name Thomas Gregory. Charlie arrives in San Francisco and must break the sad news to Paul's wife, who is waiting for him as the plane lands. He meets up with his friends,

Victor Sen Yung, Cesar Romero, Sidney Toler

deputy Kilvaine and reporter Pete Lewis, along with Fred Rhadini, a magician, who is helping to expose phony psychics. Their immediate target is a Dr. Zodiac, who is performing at the Treasure Island section in the city's World's Fair.

Charlie, the reporter, and the magician go to see Zodiac, whom Rhadini and Lewis proclaim to be a fake. Charlie remains silent and appears to have Zodiac's respect, despite his disdain for the men accompanying him. At a party later that night, Rhadini performs a mind reading bit with Eve Cairo, who is his assistant and Lewis's girlfriend. Charlie is impressed, and is told that it is actual mind reading, and there is no trick to it. He tests her by giving her a card with Chinese characters, and is surprised she is able to read them due to Charlie's concentration on the translation. Soon Eve becomes very upset, indicating a murder is about to be committed. A knife is then thrown at Charlie, narrowly missing him.

After the party, Charlie, Lewis, and Rhadini return to Zodiac's home and are surprised to find Jimmy there attempting to help the investigation. They discover a variety of illusions including masks and other props that

Victor Sen Yung, Sidney Toler

alter appearances. They are confronted by Zodiac's servant, The Turk, whom they attempt to capture, but the lights go out and he escapes. In a back office, through a secret panel, Charlie, Jimmy, Rhadini, and Lewis discover papers of information on Zodiac's victims, including blackmailing Paul Essex for money. Charlie removes all of the files from a large filing cabinet and burns them. "We are destroying web of spider," Charlie states. "Now let's find spider."

Mr Gregory, the mysterious man from the train, turns out to be Stewart Salzbury, an insurance investigator who works with Charlie Chan when Rhadini issues a challenge to Dr. Zodiac's psychic powers. During the performance, Zodiac is murdered and the removal of his mask reveals The Turk. The trick is performed again to discover who killed The Turk. During the performance, an attempt appears to be made on Rhadini's life, and he is wounded. Psychic Eve Cairo uses her mind reading powers to discover that Zodiac is alive and in the audience. Charlie finds and arrests the actual killer (see Appendix A).

Creepy and absorbing, *Charlie Chan at Treasure Island* remains an enduring favorite among fans of the series for being perhaps the most effective example of the series' formula of featuring a strong mystery benefited by dollops of humor. The humorous touches often involve Jimmy Chan. He first establishes his comic sensibilities in the opening scene, where he shows fear on a turbulent flight. When Mr. Gregory states that airplanes are now as safe as one's bath tub, Jimmy responds, quite earnestly, "I'd rather be taking a bath!"

During the scene where Jimmy is assisting in searching the Zodiac mansion and the lights go out upon confronting The Turk, the Chan son tries to turn the lights back on by trying every button and switch his hands can find in the dark. This causes all of Zodiac's various exhibits to start flying about the scene. Director Foster cuts to a medium shot, where a faint light reveals the actor in the darkness, while several glowing objects, including a full skeleton, come floating by. It is a neat visual, and offers a short, amusing break from the seriousness of the narrative. In another scene, Jimmy goes out to address the audience, quickly grabbing a magician's coat to look "presentable." As he gets on stage, several tricks start to spring on him from the coat, creating an uproar from the audience. Jimmy also offers comic timidity in being part of the levitation trick that Rhadini performs so Charlie can discover the killer, and is part of the film's closing gag, falling through a trap door as his father smiles with amusement.

There are a couple of warm moments regarding the relationship of Charlie and Jimmy Chan. At one point, father comforts his frightened son on their turbulent flight, and later, when Jimmy disappears into the basement during an illusion, a concerned Charlie searches the area calling for him. The bond, the affection, is discernible in these scenes, offering an added dimension that had been much more predominant in the Warner Oland-Keye Luke films, but was utilized less frequently by this time.

The supporting cast is bolstered nicely by an actor at the level of handsome Cesar Romero, a leading man who enjoyed success at the studio, but is best remembered for his later appearances as The Joker on TV's *Batman* series. Donald MacBride, one of the sturdiest and most enjoyable character actors of the 30s, 40s, and 50s, is great as the Deputy Sheriff, while Douglas Fowley, no stranger to the Chan films, plays Pete Lewis as the sort of fast-talking reporter that was a staple in B movies of the era.

Pauline Moore, in her third and final Chan film, turns in an effectively jittery performance as the mind-reader Eve Cairo. Ms. Moore would soon leave Fox and join Republic studios as leading lady to cowboy star Roy Rogers for several successful films. Finally, a touch of extra comedy is offered by comedian Wally Vernon, who is amusing without being overbearing. Vernon would also appear as comic relief in many westerns and later team up with Eddie Quillan for a series of two reel comedies at Columbia pictures.

During the scene where Charlie Chan burns the files, there were several fire prevention methods to which Sidney Toler had to adhere. There were two firemen present who were equipped with extinguishers, a fully manned fire engine at the soundstage door, and two other sets were removed from the soundstage. One newspaper article stated, "Sidney Toler could have burned dollar bills in his own home for less money than it cost 20th Century Fox to have him burn an equal amount of paper."

Toler had now settled quite comfortably in the Charlie Chan role. He had been active for decades with little recognition until taking over the Chan role. Now he was a famous and popular actor. In a syndicated newspaper article, Toler stated:[1]

> Isn't it strange how some of us actors lose ourselves in the characters we portray unless we play only on character? I had been proud of my versatility. I've played everything from romantic leads to whiskey-soaked bums. But now I see that when an actor passes the leading man stage, he ought to pick out one characterization and stick to it if he wants fame.

Director Norman Foster's shooting script was filled with notes to himself, including "take it easy, it's only a movie" and "Relax, don't work so hard!" Foster told a reporter,[2] "As I work over the script, my nerves tighten up like watch springs. Suddenly I realize I am getting too tense – then I write myself these notes – and when I see them I remember to relax." Foster, best known for helming most of the Mr. Moto series, would direct just one more Chan movie but would remain with Fox's B movie unit. This was John Larkin's first Chan screenplay, but he would pen four more due

---

1. "35 Years' Obscure Success Finally over for Actor Toler" *Detroit Free Press* June 27, 1939

2. "Script Notes Help Director to Relax" *Panama City Pilot* September 15, 1939

to the success of this one. *Charlie Chan at Treasure Island* was made for a budget of only $120,000 and grossed a nice profit for the studio.

Charlie Chan at Treasure Island has a great, creepy atmosphere. The cinematography makes good use of shadows and highlights to enhance the suspense as well as the supernatural undertones to the story. Even though it isn't integral to the story, the San Francisco World's Fair setting enhances the narrative (there are some aerial shots providing actual footage). The story leads the viewer in different directions, and the final reveal is a surprise.

Moviegoers continued to embrace the Chan series with this film, and critics were also duly impressed. *The Motion Picture Herald* stated:[3]

> Excitement plus mystery, comedy, and romance are the ingredients being blended in this newest Charlie Chan feature. With Treasure Island, the site of San Francisco's Fair as the setting, thrills that provide smiles and chills are promised to pile upon one another from the moment a China Clipper flies through the Golden Gate with a mysteriously dead man aboard until the final moment when the great detective traps the least suspected character as the perpetrator of the crime.

This review was designed to attract theater owners, coming out in this trade magazine a month before the film's September, 1939 release date. *Variety* stated:[4]

> In this one, Charlie Chan bumps into a murder mystery involved with the psychic and astrological and proceeds to unravel the affair at a performance in a Treasure Island (San Francisco Fair) theatre. With Chan's gumshoeing abilities now well known to film audiences, solution is secondary to the story unwinding through a maze of weird and spooky episodes. Picture holds up generally to pace set by previous Chan adventures to satisfy the whodunit fans in the subsequent runs as supporting feature. Only reason for the Treasure Island tab in title is to tie into topical situation. Aside from a few stock shots of the

---

3. "Charlie Chan at Treasure Island" *Motion Picture Herald* August 5, 1939
4. "Charlie Chan at Treasure Island" *Variety* February 21, 1940

western fair, theatre supposedly on the grounds could be anywhere. Chan is assisted by Cesar Romero, operating illusionist theatre at the Fair, and Douglas Fowley, reporter exposing rackets of the mystics and astrologists. After usual confusing trails presented to the audience, with Douglas Dumbrille pointed as most likely suspect, Chan discloses the identity of Zodiac during performance on the theatre stage. Romero, Dumbrille, Donald McBride and Fowley are most prominent in support. Chan's No. 2 son, Victor Sen Yung, does much to confuse things with amateurish display of detecting abilities. Production background is up to standard set by previous releases in the series.

Just as 20th Century Fox had produced the Mr. Moto series with Peter Lorre due to the popularity of the Charlie Chan series, the low budget Monogram studios followed suit. Boris Karloff was hired by that studio to play the similar Chinese detective Mr. Wong. Karloff left the series after five features and was replaced for one last effort by none other than Keye Luke, who added far greater authenticity to the role.

With the continued success of the series, several more Chan features were announced. His next was set to be *Charlie Chan in the City in Darkness* which, for marquee reasons, was shortened to exclude the Chan name from the title. Other films, such as *Charlie Chan on the 20th Century* and *Charlie Chan at the Mardi Gras* were either ideas that never materialized, or were subsequently retitled.

There is an unsettling footnote to *Charlie Chan at Treasure Island*. An actual serial murderer who called himself The Zodiac Killer terrorized the San Francisco area during the 1960s and 1970s. There are many theories that allude to the possibility that the Zodiac Killer was at least partially inspired by Zodiac in this Charlie Chan movie. According to criminologists who have studied the case and watched the movie, there are so many parallels, it is difficult to believe they are all merely coincidental. Another theory, perhaps even more far-fetched, is that the serial killer named himself after the Zodiac Watch, popular during the 60s. The Zodiac Killer was never found. This actual murderer was said to have inspired the villain in *Dirty Harry* (1971) and was the subject of the film *Zodiac* (2007).

City In Darkness

Director: Herbert I. Leeds
Assistant Director: Charles Hall
Screenplay: Robert Ellis and Helen Logan
Based on a play by Gina Kaus and Ladislaus Foder
Based on the character "Charlie Chan" created by Earl Derr Biggers
Executive Producer: Sol M. Wurtzel
Associate Producer: John Stone
Cinematography: Virgil Miller
Film Editor: Harry Reynolds

Cast:
Sidney Toler: Charlie Chan
Lynn Bari: Marie Dubon
Richard Clark: Tony Madero
Harold Huber: Marcel
Pedro de Cordoba: Antoine
Dorothy Tree: Charlotte Ronnell
C. Henry Gordon: Prefect of Police
Douglas Drumbrille: Petroff
Noel Madison: Belescu
Leo Carroll: Louis Santelle
Lon Chaney, Jr.: Pierre
Louis Mercier: Max
George Davis: Alex
Barbara Leonard: Lola
Adrienne d'Ambricourt: Landlady
Frederik Vogeding: Captain
Gino Corrado: Cafe Owner

Ann Codee: Complainant at Police Headquarters
John George: Victor the Gyp
Rlofe Sedan: Hotel Manager
Larry Steers: Man Leaving Paris
Arno Frey: Pilot
Ann Codee: Complainant at Police Headquarters
Jean De Briac: Puppeteer
Harry Fleishmann: Baptiste
Constant Franke: Officer
Paul Irving: Doctor
Michael Mark: Mechanic
Alberto Morin: Clerk
Nita Pike: Telephone Operator
Frank Puglia: Gendarme at Steamship Office
Rolfe Sedan: Hotel Clerk
Tom Seidel: Philip
Lester Sharpe: Market Man
George Sorel: Plainclothes Officer
Larry Steers: Man Leaving Paris
Jean Del Val, Albert Pollet, Marek Windheim: Cab Drivers
Jaques Vanaire, Joseph Romantini, Eugene Borden, Alphonse Martell: Gendarmes
Jeanne Lafayette, Veola Vonn: French Girls

Released December 1, 1939 by Twentieth Century-Fox Film Corporation
Shooting days: July 6, 1939- September 9, 1939
Running Time: 69 minutes. Black and white

CITY IN DARKNESS IS A VERY UNUSUAL Charlie Chan film. The character's name is not in the title. The movie is not a standard murder mystery, it more directly responds to news of the times, the opening establishing scenes referring to Europe being on the precipice of war with stock footage. There is an element of propaganda, with Charlie being directly connected to America's allies. Once this film was released, the war in Europe had begun, so its propaganda is significant to the context of its era.

In Paris to attend the twentieth anniversary of the Intelligence Service, Charlie Chan, becomes involved in the murder of a wealthy arms dealer,

C. Henry Gordon, Sidney Toler

Petroff. He is assisted by the bumbling Inspector Spivak, and the two of them eventually narrow their investigation down to a handful of suspects, including a man Petroff once framed for forgery, some random burglars who had broken into the exporter's house, a locksmith, and the man's butler. The investigation, however, is fraught with foreign agents and spies, Charlie's discoveries extending beyond the immediate parameters of a murder case and venturing into territories like espionage and impending international conflict. Petroff himself turns out to be a foreign agent who was dealing arms to the country's potential enemies. A woman connected to him, Charlotte Ronnell, is a spy helping to ship arms to the enemy. When the killer is revealed (see Appendix A), Charlie Chan states, "In humble opinion, murder is harsh word for act committed in defense of country."

The screenplay was written by Robert Ellis and Helen Logan, who had penned many movies in the Charlie Chan series, but based on a play co-written by Gina Kaus and Ladislaus Foder, who fled Nazi Germany for Paris. Their play was originally purchased by MGM with the intention to film it, but the rights were later sold to 20th Century Fox. Thus, the source material was quite unusual to be adapted to a Charlie Chan movie, but the message very effectively reaches the American mainstream this way. That is why this very unusual Charlie Chan entry stands out from the others in the series. Ms. Kaus would do rather well in Hollywood, working on the screenplays of everything from *Julia Misbehaves* (1948) to *The Robe* (1953), but her work did not blend well when adapted to a Charlie Chan feature. *City in Darkness* is historically interesting, but not a particularly good Chan film.

The propaganda in *City in Darkness* has a sociocultural interest as per the context of its era, but it doesn't age well, especially in its attempt to settle into the Charlie Chan world. This altered that world a bit too drastically. For instance, the presence of Victor Sen Yung as Jimmy Chan is sorely missing, the studio believing his particular brand of comic relief would clash with the seriousness of the movie's message (oddly, early announcements in the trades indicated Sen Yung would be appearing in the movie). The bumbling of the police inspector is hardly an acceptable substitute for comic relief. Huber, a good character actor in many films, plays his role in an over-the-top manner that upsets the proceedings so greatly, it appears that Charlie Chan is a supporting character rather than the central one. If anything, Jimmy Chan would be a more subdued character than the Inspector turns out to be. For the most part, Jimmy and Lee in the previous films provided comic relief without interfering too much with the mystery. Here, it's a mess. Rather than complimenting Chan's calm demeanor, the inspector often overwhelms him.

Even a review by Herbert Cohn noticed this, stating:[1]

> Reel by reel, the charming Charlie Chan is slipping to oblivion. Charlie, in the person of Sidney Toler, is kept in the dark background while Harold Huber, a mamby-pamby godson of a French police prefect, takes charge of law and order. It is a sad day for the memory of Earl Derr Biggers when his family-loving Mr. Chan isn't the whole works, but merely a minor cog in the wheel of the constabulary.

But perhaps the biggest problem with *City in Darkness* is that the murder victim isn't that interesting, nor are a good amount of the suspects.

Still, it is admittedly impressive that a film shot before the war in Europe offers support for France over a possible invasion by Nazi Germany, right up to Charlie Chan's closing line "Wise man once said, 'Beware of spider who invites fly into parlor.'" The fact that Charlie Chan was wise to Germany's intentions before any other mainstream American movie character is a fascinating element of the character. The choice for the studio to use this popular franchise to make that statement shows a prescience on the part of those involved. Early in the film, Charlie Chan states, "Most ironic that reunion to celebrate end of one war finds us waiting zero hour which may start a new one."

Even though it didn't work as a Chan film, or even really just as a good film in general, the backdrop of this movie is an interesting historical curiosity. It gives viewers today a peek into the mood and attitudes of people from different countries leading up to World War II. *Variety* was not impressed with this Charlie Chan entry, stating in its review:[2]

> Charlie Chan gets tangled in a murder mystery in Paris during the Munich crisis, unravels a spy ring, blocks shipment of contraband, rounds up numerous suspects, and finally solves the crime with intuitive deductions. *City in Darkness'* is decidedly weak in story factors, and slow in proceeding through to the eventual finish. It's one

---

1. "City in Darkness" *Brooklyn Daily Eagle* December 18, 1939

2. "City in Darkness" *Variety* November 18, 1939

> of the weakest in the 'Chan' series. A moderate supporting programmer. Story is threadbare of essential drama generally concocted for the Chan pictures, and struggles through without sufficient interest for a murder mystery. Chan, in trying to book passage out of France, is catapulted into the middle of a murder mystery. Proceeding to untangle the mess, hampered by wild deductor Harold Huber, roundup finds smashing of a spy ring in addition to other elements of the government. Direction is inadequate, further hampered by poor story material. Attempts to provide Huber with comedy as a jittery police novice are ineffectual. The audience is never presented with sufficient interest in the murder or culprit, and the mystery just unwinds without much attention.

The film does feature another solid supporting cast, and one publicity article from the studio pointed out that the film is filled with actors who were noted for committing murders on screen:[3]

> Deadliest is Harold Huber, who has killed over 125 gangsters, policemen, foreign legionnaires and others who had the misfortune or bad taste to oppose him in films. C. Henry Gordon estimated he has shot, stabbed, poisoned, or otherwise killed about 100 of his screen enemies. Pedro de Cordoba is the sissy. He has put to death but seven people. Other members of the cast – Douglas Dumbrille, Dorothy Tree and Noel Madison – between them have had over 100 victims.

Perhaps the most interesting aspect of *City in Darkness* was an impressively elaborate publicity idea that was dreamed up by R.M. Thomason, who was manager of the Princess Theater in Bowling Green, Kentucky. He created a device with peep holes one would look into, press a button, and see a silhouette of Charlie Chan. There were buildings in the background, and lights illuminating the images. This idea is far more entertaining and elaborate than the movie it serves to promote.

In the context of the Charlie Chan movie series, *City in Darkness* comes off as a rare entry that has limited entertainment value and re-

---

3. *The Press Democrat* Santa Rosa, California July 19, 1939

Lynn Bari, Sidney Toler, Noel Madison

mains perhaps the weakest film in the entire series. However, it managed to continue the success of the series to the point where the studio decided to abandon the Mr. Moto films that were being produced and concentrate solely on the Charlie Chan mysteries. Although the Moto films were popular, the studio did not even find it necessary to make an official announcement to the press as to the ending of the series. They just simply ceased production. This movie's director, Herbert Leeds, directed *Mr. Moto in Danger Island*, the last of the Moto series to be shot (but not the last to be released), before starting work on this Charlie Chan film. It would be the only effort in the Chan series that he would direct.

Victor Sen Yung, Sidney Toler

Charlie Chan In Panama

Director: Norman Foster
Assistant Director: Saul Wurtzel
Original Screenplay: John Larkin and Lester Ziffren
Source: Based on the character "Charlie Chan" created by Earl Derr Biggers
Executive Producer: Sol M. Wurtzel
Director of Photography: Virgil Miller
Film Editor: Fred Allen

Cast:
Sidney Toler: Charlie Chan
Jean Rogers: Kathi Lenesch
Lionel Atwill: Clivedon Compton
Mary Nash: Miss Finch
Sen Yung: Jimmy Chan
Kane Richmond: Richard Cabot
Chris-Pin Martin: Montero
Lionel Royce: Dr. Rudolph Grosser
Helen Ericson: Stewardess
Jack La Rue: Manolo
Edwin Stanley: Webster
Don Douglas: Captain Lewis
Frank Puglia: Achmed Halide
Addison Richards: Godley
Edward Keane: Dr. Fredericks
Charles Stevens: Spy on Dock
Harold Goodwin: Military Police Officer
Gloria Roy: Hostess

Lane Chandler: Officer at Powerhouse
Edward Gargan: Plant Workman
Philip Morris: Plainclothesman
Albert Morin: Hotel Desk Clerk
Jimmy Aubrey: Drunk at Club
Brooks Benedict: Nightclub Dancer
Chuck Hamilton: Dancer
Franklin Farnum: Marine Officer
Max Wagner, Alan Davis, Charles Sherlock: Soldiers
Eddie Acuff: Sailor

Released March 1, 1940 by Twentieth Century-Fox Film Corporation
Shooting days: October 18-December 29th, 1939
Running Time: 67 minutes. Black and white

ONCE AGAIN, SPIES AND SABOTEURS invade Charlie Chan's world, but *Charlie Chan in Panama* is a big improvement over *City in Darkness*. A strong cast, a good script, and tight direction help make it among the best of the series.

A sea plane containing a group of suspicious characters arrives in Balboa. A government agent goes to a hat store where Charlie Chan is working undercover as the proprietor. He takes one drag from a cigarette and falls over dead. Charlie is taken to jail and when behind bars, discovers Jimmy shooting craps with a group of other prisoners. After receiving his son's explanation as to how he ended up there, a quick investigation gets them both released. Charlie is now on the case with Jimmy's assistance.

The agent's reason for visiting Chan was part of his effort to capture a spy named Reiner. Once the agent dies, it is up to Charlie to capture Reiner before his plans to trap US Ships via the Panama Canal are carried out. Along the way, a cabaret owner evading police, and a government engineer are also murdered.

A school marm who was on board the plane with the others is enlisted to assist Charlie and Jimmy, along with an intelligence officer named Lewis. Entrapped in a tomb while searching through a cemetery, Charlie, Jimmy, the school marm, and the officer discover several cans that had once contained explosives. The group escapes the tomb, and head to the place where Charlie believes the sabotage will take place. He rounds up the suspects and holds a gun on them, as they wait impatiently for the sabotage to occur. The murderer is revealed by pulling a gun on Charlie (see Appendix A). The explosive device is disarmed.

After the disappointing *City in Darkness*, this film is comparatively much better. Director Norman Foster works from the original screenplay and offers some clever ideas. For instance, Charlie Chan's first appearance, after several of the suspects are revealed, is while acting undercover as a hat salesman. The agent enters the shop, and Charlie, turns around to reveal who he is to the audience. Foster shoots this in close-up, then cuts back to a two-shot. It is a nice establishing shot and one of the best moments in the film. As with most of the best Chan movies, the direction fluctuates from detective drama to film noir, with deep focus shots and dark imagery abounding, but never clashing.

The cast is filled with such top B actors as Jack LaRue, Kane Richmond, Jean Rogers, and Mary Nash. Lionel Atwill is at his creepy best. Chris Pin-Martin is a bombastic delight, taking a break from playing Poncho in the studio's Cisco Kid series featuring Cesar Romero, who had appeared a couple of Chan films earlier, in the title role. LaRue, in fact, took the role upon returning to Hollywood after a successful personal appearance tour of the Midwest. LaRue complained to reporters that while driving back to the west coast, he was frequently recognized by gas station attendants and other townspeople along the way. The problem is, they couldn't place just why they found his face familiar, and frequently concluded he was an actual gangster. LaRue had to explain who he was to police nearly twenty times along the way, after which he was cheerfully asked for an autograph.

It is reassuring that Victor Sen Yung is back for *Charlie Chan in Panama*. He is at his comical best, and purely in support of his father, who returns to the central portion of the narrative. Just prior to starting work on this film, Sen Yung was signed by the studio to a long term contract. As usual, Jimmy's presence and sense of humor in the film enhances the story. During the filming of this movie, Sen Yung spent time teaching Sidney Toler the Chinese language and some of its customs, something Toler's predecessor Warner Oland made a point of doing during his tenure in the role. Toler reciprocated by teaching Sen Yung a bit about writing plays. Toler told reporters:[1]

---

1. "Portrayer of Chan Learns Chinese" *Democrat and Chronicle* December 18, 1939

> So many people ask me about Chinese customs, books, and people that I find it almost compulsory to learn something of the language. Sen is a fine teacher. He wants to be a playwright and I am helping him along. When we get through, Sen won't have to listen to me murder the Chinese language and I won't have to read his plays.

The emotional connection in Charlie and Jimmy's relationship is again portrayed in this film. Charlie still admonishes Jimmy a lot, but during a scene where Charlie rescues him, he asks Jimmy if he is ok with the most genuine look of concern on his face. It's brief, but extremely effective.

Production on this film was not without its hazards. Veteran stuntman Harvey Parry, whose career dated back to silent movies, did a dive off a pier where he was supposed to the swim away while under fire from soldiers. A bullet fragment grazed Peary's neck, causing only a minor injury. A half-inch difference could have killed him. Parry's talents were used often at Fox, the 5 foot, 2 inch, 120 pound actor even doubling Shir-

Victor Sen Yung, Jack LaRue, Sidney Toler

ley Temple for some stunts. Parry was still doing stunt work at the time of his death at age 85, "doing the easy stuff like getting hit by cars and falling down stairs"

Charlie Chan in Panama was screened for the U.S. Navy prior to its commercial released, and the studio was quite pleased with their reaction. Not one change was recommended by a board of officials which viewed the film, offering a enthusiastic vote of approval.

Charlie Chan in Panama was paired up with another Fox film, *The Blue Bird* featuring Shirley Temple, in many markets. In Milwaukee, this double feature was the second highest grossing show of the season, after Warner's *It All Came True* with Humphrey Bogart alongside United Artists' *House Across the Bay* with George Raft and Joan Bennett. And while the Shirley Temple movie was an expensive production shot in color, it received mostly negative reviews, making this Charlie Chan second-feature the more attractive movie of the pair. Another pairing was with the Laurel and Hardy feature *The Flying Deuces*, an RKO release produced by Boris Morros, and not the duo's usual producer Hal Roach, who was now releasing through United Artists after decades with MGM.

Critics were pleased with this latest Charlie Chan entry, and several offered positive reactions to the proceedings. *Motion Picture Herald* said the film had "a maximum of entertainment with a minimum of extraneous matter." *Film Daily* stated that *Charlie Chan in Panama*, "is first rate entertainment raking with the best in the Chan series to date." *Variety* said it was "equipped with a far more exciting screenplay than its predecessors and carrying a stronger supporting cast.." *The Hollywood Reporter* called it "solid entertainment in its class." However, there were also reports in the press that since Warner Oland died, the box office receipts had dropped off. Contrarily, other articles referred to the Charlie Chan films as Twentieth Century Fox's "record breaking series."

The next Charlie Chan film announced by the studio was *Charlie Chan on the Orient Express*. By the time it hit theaters, the following Chan film was titled *Charlie Chan's Murder Cruise* and was a remake of *Charlie Chan Carries On*, the now-lost first Warner Oland appearance as Chan.

Victor Sen Yung, Sidney Toler, Lionel Atwill, Leo G. Carroll

Charlie Chan's Murder Cruise

Director: Eugene Forde
Assistant Director: Saul Wurtzel
Screenplay: Robertson White and Lester Ziffren
Based on the story Charlie Chan Carries On
by Earl Derr Biggers (Indianapolis, 1930)
Executive Producer: Sol M. Wurtzel
Associate Producer: John Stone
Cinematography: Virgil Miller
Film Editor: Harry Reynolds

Cast:
Sidney Toler: Charlie Chan
Marjorie Weaver: Paula Drake
Lionel Atwill: Dr. Suderman
Sen Yung: Jimmy Chan
Robert Lowery: Dick Kenyon
Don Beddoe: Ross
Leo Carroll: Professor Gordon
Cora Witherspoon: Suzie Watson
Kay Linaker: Mrs. Pendleton
Harlan Briggs: Coroner
Charles Middleton: Mr. Walters
Claire Du Brey: Mrs. Walters
Leonard Mudie: Gerald Pendleton
James Burke: Wilkie
Richard Keene: Buttons
Layne Tom, Jr.: Willie Chan
Montague Shaw: Inspector Duff

Walter Miller: Office boy
Harry Strang: Hotel Guard
Wade Boteler: Honolulu Police Chief Inspector
Cliff Clark: Lt. Wilson
John Dilson: Police Doctor
Emmett Vogan: Hotel Manager
Sherry Hall: Radio Operator
J. Anthony Hughes: Detective
Paul McVey: Mrs. Pendleton's Doctor

Released June 21, 1940 by Twentieth Century-Fox Film Corporation
Running time: 75 minutes. Black and White

CHARLIE CHAN'S MURDER CRUISE is another of the better efforts from the Sidney Toler period, made more interesting by being a remake of the lost film *Charlie Chan Carries On* (1931). Since *Charlie Chan Carries On* is the first to star Warner Oland, its significance to the series is substantial and its being unavailable for screening is a frustration. Our attempts to compare and contrast the two movies is limited to what our research can reveal about the original.

The plot of this film has Charlie Chan boarding a cruise ship after his friend, Inspector Duff of Scotland Yard, asks him to help capture a strangler who is among the members of this cruise. The cruise party is led by Dr. Suderman, whose piercing eyes and sinister demeanor arouse suspicion. The other members of the cruise range from a fluttery spinster and her attractive secretary, a handsome young man and his uncle, a wisecracking playboy named Ross, and a sober archeologist, to a creepy couple of soothsayers and a jittery man who claims to be under a doctor's care for a nervous condition. These people are in Honolulu during a stopover, and are staying at a nearby hotel. When Chan briefly leaves his office, he returns to find Duff strangled, but not dead, and must continue with the case without further information until the Inspector recovers. When Charlie arrives at the hotel, he finds another murder. The victim, the playboy's uncle, is found to have 30 dimes in a small bag; a symbolic gesture which dates back to the Bible story of Judas being paid 30 pieces of silver to betray Jesus Christ.

When Pendelton, the nervous man, is found murdered, Charlie examines a radiogram he had just sent to his wife. It conflicts with what

Pendelton had revealed his intentions were. Charlie decides to rely on some photos taken at a shipboard party during the time Pendelton was killed, believing the murderer would be conspicuous by his absence from the party. As the pictures are being developed, the murderer enters the darkroom and steals them. He flees and his pursued. He is eludes his pursuants but is discovered dead. When his disguise is removed, it turns out to be Ross. Charlie is skeptical that Ross is the murderer and believes him to be another victim.

The ship docks and the suspects are gathered at the coroner's office, when Pendelton's widow enters with bandages around her eyes. She reveals that the killer is her ex-husband Eberhardt and he had forced Ross to be an accomplice. When she is about to remove the bandages and point out the killer, Dr. Suderman begins shouting his innocence and Charlie orders him to be captured. But this is a ruse, the lights go out, and the actual murderer is revealed in a surprise twist (see Appendix A).

While we cannot screen *Charlie Chan Carries On* to compare it with this remake, information provided by the American Film Institute offers a synopsis that has only a sketchy similarity. In the previous film, the Charlie Chan series was not in full swing, so Chan's appearance isn't the focal point as in this version. There is a great deal of establishing footage featuring Inspector Duff, who is shot in the back when he finally summons Charlie Chan. In this film, the strangled Duff is not dead until later in the film. In the original, he is shot dead. It is this circumstance that causes Charlie Chan to take over the case. One of the more significant elements of this later version is how detective Chan is treated. In this film, his name is quite well known. When he is introduced, the people around are impressed that so famous a sleuth is involved with their case. In the earlier movie, Chan is unknown. Finally, the previous film has Charlie Chan writing identical letters to the various suspects in an effort to reveal the culprit. That isn't done here.

Charlie Chan's Murder Cruise is a tight mystery with interesting suspects and a surprise ending. With such noted movie villains as Lionel Atwill and Charles Middleton, in the cast, it is not easy to guess the outcome. The cast is further filled out by such capable supporting players as Marjorie Weaver, Robert Lowery, Don Beddoe, Leo G. Carroll, and Cora Witherspoon. Ms. Witherspoon's comic performance as an amusingly edgy type exhibits her versatility as a fun character actress who specialized in comedy. This same year, she did a creative turn as W.C. Fields' sarcastically detached wife in *The Bank Dick*. Witherspoon's performance is a good example of comic

Sidney Toler, Lionel Atwill, Leo G. Carroll

relief that serves the narrative as opposed to overwhelming or distracting from it. Much was made in the press about Lowery winning the girl in the end, as he often came up short in his other films. Marjorie Weaver is, according to one article, "the prize worth waiting for. Smaller parts played by the reliably amusing James Burke as a hotel detective, Harlan Briggs as a harried coroner, and the majestic presence of Montague Shaw as the ill-fated Inspector Duff. Leonard Mudie and Wade Boteler are among the other welcome veterans expanding the cast.

Victor Sen Yung once again enlivens the proceedings as Jimmy Chan, whose earnest assistance is alternately a help and a hindrance to his father, and Charlie responds accordingly. His heartfelt determination is irresistible and his comic reactions are delightful. Perhaps his most amusing comic bit is when he stumbles quite accidentally upon Ross's body while they are in pursuit. Before realizing just what he has found, Victor Sen Yung offers a full gamut of comic expressions, doing an artful double-take and never sloppily expanding to a more blatant triple or quadruple take. It has been argued that Keye Luke was the better actor, but it is Sen Yung's performance that most effectively identified the Charlie's son character for all time. Even in a 1950s *Honeymooners* episode, Ralph and Ed are up late watching a Charlie Chan movie (they were among the first major studio films to be released to the small screen during TV's infancy) and remark how "the number one son is really in trouble." This more aptly identifies the situations involving Jimmy, the number two son. Since Sen Yung played the character for the most films, it is his interpretation that is more specifically recalled.

Layne Tom, jr. makes his final appearance as one of the younger Chan children (this time he is Willie, the number 7 son). There is an amusing establishing scene where brother Jimmy helps give young Willie advice on how to remove an unfortunate report card from their father's mail (of course Charlie is already in possession of the mailing). Layne Tom would recall in later interviews that Victor Sen Yung really was like a brother to him when they made the films, and they remained in contact until Sen Yung's death.

Sidney Toler was now quite settled in the Charlie Chan role, and a newspaper article discussing *Charlie Chan's Murder Cruise* remarked that "Sidney Toler won unexpected acclaim....picked up where Oland left off when every Hollywood sage declared it couldn't be done." Another newspaper article promoting this film joked how Charlie Chan was not easily fooled, but actor Toler apparently was. For years he had been wearing what he believed was an expensive jade ring, once owned by his grandfather. While attending an exhibition, Toler showed his ring to an expert, who proclaimed it "a beautiful piece of agate."

One of the more interesting promotional events tied to *Charlie Chan's Murder Cruise* was a special "food matinee' held by three Boy Scout troops at a Dallas theater. A can of non-perishable food was allowed as admission to the movie during this matinee, the scouts distributing these articles to the needy people of the community.

Critics and moviegoers were once again pleased with this latest Charlie Chan production, especially since it did not deal with foreign intrigue and was once again a more typical murder mystery where the detective could flourish. *Variety* stated:[1]

> Everybody takes cruises these days, so why not Charlie Chan? It's sort of a busman's holiday, however, as the "Murder Cruise" title naturally indicates, and again the Chinese detective comes through with not only the cul-

---

1. "Charlie Chan's Murder Cruise" *Variety* February 21, 1940

prit, but also a fair enough mystery meller that'll nicely take care of the action half in dual situations. The Chan series follows a general pattern, plus the philosophic platitudes, and this one's no exception. Even with three murders by strangulation in the story, the Honolulu detective hardly becomes perturbed and never seems to want for a 'Confucius Say.' He plays with the criminal like a cat with a mouse, then uncovers the least-suspected suspect within the cheerful confines of the San Francisco morgue. Sidney Toler, who replaced the late Warner Oland in the title role, does a good job with the detective part. He had a pretty good supporting cast in this edition, Lionel Atwill, Cora Witherspoon, Leo Carroll and Don Beddoe carrying through the mystery motif in nice fashion. The romantic angle is injected by pert Marjorie Weaver and stumbling Robert Lowery, but it's not very important to the general works. Sen Yung, as Chan's meddling son, is okay. Both the direction and camera work are up to the Chan series average.

The writer must take umbrage with the *Variety* critics tacit dismissal of Victor Sen Yung's contribution to *Charlie Chan's Murder Cruise,* as it remains one of the true highlights of the movie.

Despite the popularity of the series, there were conflicting stories regarding the next film, *Charlie Chan at the Wax Museum.* Some articles claimed the series was going strong and that Sidney Toler had written a story that was going to be filmed. Others claimed that *Charlie Chan at the Wax Museum* would be the last film in the series.

Charlie Chan At the Wax Museum

Director: Lynn Shores
Assistant Director: Jasper Blystone
Original Screenplay: John Larkin
Based on the character Charlie Chan created by Earl Derr Biggers
Associate Producers: Walter Morosco and Ralph Dietrich
Cinematography: Virgil Miller
Film Editor: James B. Clark

Cast:
Sidney Toler: Charlie Chan
Sen Yung: Jimmy Chan
C. Henry Gordon: Dr. Cream
Marc Lawrence: Steve McBirney
Joan Valerie: Lily Latimer
Marguerite Chapman: Mary Bolton
Ted Osborn: Tom Agnew
Michael Visaroff: Dr. Otto von Brom
Hilda Vaughn: Mrs. Rocke
Charles Wagenheim: Willie Fern
Archie Twitchell: Carter Lane
Edward Marr: Grenock
Joe King: Inspector O'Matthews
Harold Goodwin: Edwards
Stanley Blystone: Bailiff
Jimmy Conlin: Tour Guide
Charles Trowbridge: Judge
Emmett Vogan: Prosecuting Attorney

Shooting days: Began May 17 – July 5, 1940
Released September 6, 1940 by Twentieth Century-Fox Film Corporation
Running Time: 63 minutes. Black and white

Charlie Chan at the Wax Museum was rumored in the trades to be the last movie appearance of the beloved Chinese detective. 20th Century Fox was considering deemphasizing its B unit, and concentrating on more prestigious movies. Of course this would not occur that quickly. Production head Darryl Zanuck would join the military for eighteen months in 1941, while his duties were performed by William Goetz who preferred lighter, more entertaining films. The Chan series continued to flourish, Betty Grable became the studio's most popular star, and the studio acquired Laurel and Hardy for a series of comedy features. It was not until Spyros Skouras became President of the studio in 1942 when the Chan series would be discontinued, only to find a home a couple of years later at the low budget Monogram studios. So the death knell being sounded by rumors in the trades at the time of *Charlie Chan in the Wax Museum* were unfounded. In fact, at least one newspaper article that came out when this movie was released indicated that Sidney Toler signed a contract to continue with the series.

In this one, convicted murderer Steve McBirney escapes from custody and seeks revenge on Charlie Chan whose testimony was instrumental in his being arrested. He goes to a wax museum where Dr. Cream, a mob associate, alters his face. Charlie Chan is invited to the wax museum to participate in a radio broadcast discussing an old murder case where the convicted Joe Rocke is believed by Charlie to have been innocent, believing he had been framed by his business partner Dagan. Another member of the panel, Dr. Von Brom, had offered the testimony that was instrumental in Rocke's subsequent execution. However, this broadcast has been set up by Dr. Cream so McBirney can get revenge on Charlie Chan. The detective's chair is wired up, but at the last minute he changes sheets with Von Brom, who is killed, but not by electrocution. On inspection, a blow dart is the murder weapon. One of those involved in the broadcast murders McBirney and attempts to kill Charlie but fails. It is then revealed that this person is actually Dagan, with his face altered by Dr. Cream (see Appendix A).

More compact and much more of a programmer, *Charlie Chan at the Wax Museum* is an entertaining effort but decidedly below average.

Victor Sen Yung, Sidney Toler, C. Henry Gordon

The performances are first rate, with supporting players like Marc Lawrence, C. Henry Gordon, and Stanley Blystone having appeared in previous Charlie Chan movies. And once again, Victor Sen Yung offers his usual dollop of humor and action to lighten the proceedings, but never disrupt them. Newspapers promoting this film indicated that Sen Yung was interested in obtaining his Masters degree in political science from Washington University with an interest in becoming an international diplomat, "If I'm not too busy in pictures."

Lynn Shores was a curious choice to direct *Charlie Chan at the Wax Museum*. Shores was at the end of a rather unremarkable career that included around 20 directorial assignments, this one being among his last. There is no real style to his approach to the material, allowing the screenplay and actors to carry the proceedings. This is ok, as the talent involved in this production is solid, but other directors were able to infuse a bit of style to elevate the proceedings beyond the merely standard. However, Shore did host a wrap party after the movie, with the entire cast and crew invited, all sitting in the dark and hearing actor Ted Osborne recite Edgar Allen Poe's *The Fall of the House of Usher*. Osborne's recitation was punctuated by sound effects provided by Sidney Toler.

Variety was not only unimpressed, but alluded to the rumor that this might be the final Charlie Chan picture:[1].

> As a horrible example of what can happen to series pictures if they're continued indefinitely, *Charlie Chan at the Wax Museum* has a certain interest. But it has little other value. If, as reported, this is the last of the series, it's neither surprising nor regrettable. For the picture is a feeble effort which should get playing time only on the strength of its probable series audience. Nothing much is to be said of the story, except that it follows the obvious slant indicated at the title. There's a hodge-podge of action in the wax museum as the pigeon-English hero strolls comfortably among villainous facial surgeons and their molls, escaped murderers, imbecile janitors, avenging widows, suspicious lawyers, radio announcers and engineers and a pulp mag version of a girl reporter. There are wax figures all over the place and before long even the scripters seem to have been unable to distinguish between them and the real characters, or between their scenario and the remnants of a plot lying around a cutting room floor. It's all flimsy, muddled, absurd and never for an instant believable. But frequently it's just preposterous enough to be amusing. Direction and production are routine, befitting the inglorious end of a once-popular series

While it was not as much a misfire as this review would lead one to believe, and it was not the final movie in the series, *Charlie Chan at the Wax Museum* was a standard entry in the series that would continue for another four features. Newspapers stated that subsequent films would no longer use the Charlie Chan name in the title. Thus, the next feature in the Chan series was *Murder Over New York*.

---

1. "Charlie Chan at the Wax Museum" *Variety* October 2, 1940

Murder Over New York

Director: Harry Lachman
Assistant Director: William Eckhardt
Original Screenplay: Lester Ziffren
Based on the character "Charlie Chan" created by Earl Derr Biggers
Executive Producer: Sol M. Wurzel
Cinematography: Virgil Miller
Film Editor: Louis Loeffler

Cast:
Sidney Toler: Charlie Chan
Marjorie Weaver: Patricia
Sen Yung: Jimmy Chan
Robert Lowrey: David Elliott
Ricardo Cortez: George Kirby
Donald MacBride: Inspector Vance
Shemp Howard: "Shorty" McCoy
Melville Cooper: Herbert Fenton
Joan Valerie: June Preston
Kane Richmond: Ralph Percy
John Sutton: Keith Jeffrey
Leyland Hodgson: Boggs
Clarence Muse: Butler
Frederick Worlock: Hugh Drake
Lal Chand Mehra: Ramullah
Dorothy Dearing: Mrs. Percy
Frank Coghlan, Jr.: Frankie
Shirley Warde: Mrs. Felton
Catherine Craig: Stewardess

Lee Phelps: First Policeman
Stanley Blystone: Fingerprint Expert
Ralph Dunn: Second Policeman
George Walcott: First Mechanic
Paul Kruger: Guard
Alan Davis: Pilot
Carl Faulkner, Jimmie Dundee, Eddy Chandler,
   Frank Fanning: Policemen
Trevor Burdette: Hindu Businessman
Bud Geary: Second Mechanic
Jack "Tiny" Lipson: Hindu in Police Lineup

Released December 13, 1940 by Twentieth Century-Fox Film
   Corporation
Running Time: 65 minutes. Black and White.
Working title: *Charlie Chan in New York*

THE ORIGINAL TITLE for this entry was *Charlie Chan in New York*, but the producers felt that it was too generic and could be confused with other, older, movies in the series. Thus, for the first time since *City in Darkness* (which itself was billed as *Charlie Chan in the City in Darkness* in some markets), we have a Charlie Chan film that does not include the character name in the title.

A shorter, more streamlined, and nicely paced mystery, *Murder Over New York* once again has Charlie Chan responding to spies involved in the war effort overseas. The film opens with Charlie traveling by plane to a police convention in New York, bumping into Hugh Drake, an old friend who had once worked for Scotland Yard but is now involved with British intelligence. Drake reveals he is on the trail of a spy named Paul Narvo, who has been sabotaging US-made bombers being used by England for the war effort. The plane lands and Charlie is invited to a party for Drake being held by George Kirby, an airplane tycoon who is assisting with the case. Charlie is met by his friend Vance, a police inspector, and is surprised to also be met by son Jimmy, in town for the fair.

After the police banquet, Charlie and Jimmy arrive at the party and are shown to Kirby's office wear Drake is found dead. Initially believed to have had a heart attack, the discovery that a pet canary in a cage is also dead allows Charlie to conclude that a poison gas was the culprit.

Soon, remnants of the pellet are found, and Jimmy recognizes the smell of tetrogene gas. Several guests are interrogated by Charlie, Jimmy, and Inspector Vance, including Drake's school friend Herbert Fenton, an actress named June Preston, stockbroker Keith Jeffrey, aircraft designer Ralph Percy, and Boggs, Kirby's butler. Chan eventually tracks down the ex-wife of Narvo, the spy that Drake had been seeking, and she reveals she left her husband upon realizing he was a spy. She also explains he had an accom-

Sidney Toler, Donald MacBride

Victor Sen Yung, Sidney Toler, Marjorie Weaver, Robert Lowery

plice, Ramullah, who acted as his servant. Ramullah is shot dead from a window while he is being questioned by Charlie and the police.

Charlie assembles the suspects aboard a T-4 bomber which has been set up to cause a gas pellet to explode at a certain elevation. Charlie examines the reactions of the passengers as the plane flies. The pellet drops but is caught by Fenton who uses it to threaten the others. When the plane lands, Fenton throws it to the ground and escapes, only to be captured by police waiting outside. The passengers exit unharmed, the pellet's gas having been replaced ahead of time. The suspects are gathered at police headquarters where an attempt to poison Fenton reveals who Narvo really is (see Appendix A).

The tightness of this film's structure, its breezy nature, the less elaborate sets, and the dollops of humor make *Murder Over New York* to appear as something of a harbinger to what the films would look like once they left the prestigious 20th Century Fox studios for Monogram Pictures in a couple of years. The cast is once again filled with welcome veterans, many of whom had appeared in other Charlie Chan movies: Donald MacBride as a blustery inspector, Ricardo Cortez as the mysterious Kirby, as well as Robert Lowery, Marjorie Weaver, and Kane Richmond.

This film has generated a latter day interest in some quarters due to a funny cameo by Shemp Howard who would later be known as one of The Three Stooges. Shemp was freelancing at this point in his career, his short comedy series at Vitaphone having ended, and his solo series at Columbia not having yet begun. Shemp had started doing the Glove Slingers series at Columbia, and appeared in a couple of Andy Clyde comedies, but he also free-lanced in feature films, playing small parts at Universal studios for W.C. Fields, Abbott and Costello, and The Dead End Kids, among others. Shemp appeared in ten movies in 1940 alone, mostly for Columbia or Universal, but also did this film for Fox and *Millionaires in Prison* for RKO. Having achieved iconic status for his Three Stooges work, it is fun for modern day audiences to see Shemp in this Charlie Chan mystery.

Jimmy Chan once again enlivens the proceedings with enthusiasm and humor. *Murder Over New York* might feature the character's best initial appearance. Charlie has landed for the convention and suddenly is surprised to hear his son's voice calling in the distance. He turns to find a happy Jimmy Chan approaching him. Taking the viewer off guard and disrupting the action, Jimmy's sudden appearance was reportedly met with applause in some theaters at the time of the film's initial release.

Murder Over New York has special interest in the Charlie Chan series as it is a reworking of *Charlie Chan's Chance*, one of the lost films featuring Warner Oland. In the earlier movie, the first murder victim is found in a room where a pet cat, not a canary, is also dead, leading to the conclusion that he was gassed. The earlier movie's trajectory is different, but there are enough similarities to state that *Murder Over New York* was at least inspired by *Charlie Chan's Chance*. It is unfortunate we do not have the earlier movie to screen for a true comparison. None of the articles or ads about this production made reference to the older movie.

There is some historical interest in the aircraft used in the movie's conclusion, which is a Lockheed Model 10, similar to the one Amelia Earhart had flown on her final voyage. It is revealed where the guns are mounted once all test flights have been done.

Harry Lachman was an interesting director to take over the series. He had directed Warner Oland in *Charlie Chan at the Circus* (1936), and that same year Sidney Toler in the Laurel and Hardy feature *Our Relations* in which Toler played a wonderfully bombastic comic role as the captain of the duo's navy ship. Lachman would finish out the Chan series at Fox as their director, making the last few films for the studio among the more enjoyable efforts in the entire series.

164 • *The Charlie Chan Films*

Sidney Toler, Victor Sen Yung

Dead Men Tell

Director: Harry Lachman
Assistant Director: Saul Wurzel
Original Screenplay: John Larkin
Based on the character "Charlie Chan" created by Earl Derr Biggers
Associate Producers: Walter Morosco and Ralph Dietrich
Cinematography: Charles Clarke
Film Editor: Harry Reynolds

Cast:
Sidney Toler: Charlie Chan
Shiela Ryan: Kate Ransome
Robert Weldon: Steve Daniels
Sen Yung: Jimmy Chan
Don Douglas: Jed Thomasson
Katharine Aldridge: Laura Thursday
Paul McGrath: Charles Thursday
George Reeves: Bill Lydig
Truman Bradley: Captain Kane
Ethel Griffies: Miss Nodbury
Lenita Lane: Dr. Anne Bonney
Milton Parsons: Gene LaFarge
Lee Tung Foo: Wu Mei
Ralph Dunn: Homicide Desk Sergeant
Lee Phelps: Detective
Stanley Andrews: Inspector Vesey
Pat Flaherty: Policeman
Tim Ryan: Red Eye
Jimmy Aubrey: English Sailor

John Wallace: Peg Leg
Charles Tannen: Sailor
O.G. "Dutch" Hendrian: Saloon Dancer

Shooting days: December 14, 1940 - January 21, 1941
Released May 28, 1941 by Twentieth Century-Fox Film Corporation
Running Time: 61 minutes. Black and White

ONE OF THE INITIAL THINGS that makes *Dead Men Tell* especially interesting is that it opens with a curious, adventurous Jimmy Chan trying to stow away on a ship, getting captured in his attempt. Jimmy has heretofore been presented as satisfying his curiosity via shadowing his father and helping to solve the murder cases in which Charlie is involved. But here he is rebellious enough to try running away to sea.

Charlie Chan arrives on board ship, almost immediately running into Miss Nodbury who states the ship will not sail in the morning as someone tried to steal her portion of a treasure map. Charlie inquires, and she explains that her grandfather was a pirate who was murdered at sea. She has torn a treasure map of his in four pieces and distributed three of them to other passengers. She states that the restless spirit of her grandfather, known as The Black Hook, appears every time a Nodbury is about to die. This proves true when he later does appear to her and she dies.

Among the suspects on board ship are Steve Daniels who arranged the trip, journalist Bill Lydig, coin collector Jed Thomasson, secretary Kate Ransome, and a newly married couple, Charles and Laura Thursday. It is Kate who discovers Miss Nodbury's body while Charlie finds the costume and hook that the assailant wore. Charlie collects the other portions of the treasure map from the passengers who have them and after Jimmy finds clues in the cabin of Steve Daniels, who insists he has been framed. Charlie goes ashore and finds Captain Kane, who claims to not have met any of the passengers. But he admits he his involved with this impending voyage because he was once stranded by a partner on the island to which they are going and where the treasure is said to exist. He believes the partner might try to join the voyage and he can seek revenge. Daniels is arrested due to the evidence in hand, but Charlie Chan is confronted by the Black Hook and manages to unmask him (see Appendix A). He is then captured with the help of Captain Kane, who reveals him to be the man who once left him to die.

Now that the Charlie Chan films are compact B movies that run around an hour and adhere to a specific formula, one would think that little could be said other than to acknowledge how effective each movie was within those parameters. However, director Harry Lachman often liked to add artistic visuals to his films, even when they were at the B level such as this one. For the scene in which Miss Nodbury dies, Lachman shoots the Black Hook in shadow form as it approaches her. When she sees him, Lachman shoots from the Hook's perspective. The pace is steady, even when Lachman cuts away to closeups of Miss Nodbury's fearful expressions. It is one of the more impressive murder scenes in the entire Charlie Chan series, even though the woman actually dies from being frightened to death by the image. Fox publicity played up the fact that Lachman had to direct similarly spooky scenes in *Dante's Inferno* many years earlier.

Cinematographer Charles Clarke experimented with using a coated lens when shooting this movie, adding to the darkness of its atmosphere. Most of the production is filmed in low key effect lighting. So, rather than bringing the contrast and definition to the values of an average production, Clarke tried to take advantage of what coated lenses could do with the studio's new cameras. These cameras were noted for well-defined cinematography because of the shutter placement and silent operation, so there was no need to use a glass window before the lens. So, for *Dead Men Tell*, no diffusion was used on any scene, close-up, or otherwise. This added to the murky nature of the setting on board ship.

The supporting cast is decidedly less interesting in this effort, with the notable exception of George Reeves, who achieved iconic status as television's Superman in the 1950s. Sheila Ryan is perhaps best known for appearing at Fox in Laurel and Hardy's first two features for Fox: *Great Guns* (1941) and *A-Haunting We Will Go* (1942). She met her future husband, Pat Buttram, on the set of a Gene Autry feature in which both appeared. Jean Rogers was announced as playing the character of Laura Thursday, but was replaced by Katherine Aldrich when she became ill with the flu once shooting began. Milton Parsons offers perhaps the most interesting performance.

Critics were not terribly impressed with this Charlie Chan entry, failing to appreciate its success at the B movie level. *Variety* stated:[1]

> *Dead Men Tell* is a standard entry in the Charlie Chan series, carrying familiar ingredients of a couple of mur-

---

1. "Dead Men Tell" *Variety* March 26, 1941

ders and a mystery over four portions of a map of buried treasure. It's a programmer that will get by as supporting fare in the houses where the Oriental detective built up a following with his crime deductions. The picture is a *Grand Hotel* aboard the docked ship, and played close to the shore - with the four-piece map another familiar piece of story construction.

This review clearly indicates that understanding that a set formula was now being followed for the Charlie Chan series. However, this formula works effectively, and *Dead Men Tell* is one of the better films among the later Fox productions.

Audiences enjoyed *Dead Men Tell* as part of a weekend program that often included a western, a comedy, and a cartoon. Such B movie matinees became even more popular after America entered the war effort. Wartime audiences hungered for escapist fare. Unfortunately, 20th Century Fox was becoming less and less interested in continuing this series.

Charlie Chan In Rio

Director: Harry Lachman
Assistant Director: William Eckhardt
Screenplay: Samuel G. Engel and Lester Ziffren
Based on the character "Charlie Chan" created by Earl Derr Biggers
Executive Producer: Sol M. Wurtzel
Cinematography: Joseph P. MacDonald
Film Editor: Alexander Troffey

Cast:
Sidney Toler: Charlie Chan
Mary Beth Hughes: Joan Reynolds
Cobina Wright, Jr.: Grace Ellis
Victor Sen Yung: Jimmy Chan
Ted North: Clark B. Denton
Victor Jory: Alfredo Marana
Harold Huber: Delegado
Richard Derr: Ken Reynolds
Jacqueline Dalya: Lola Dean
Kay Linaker: Helen Ashby
Truman Bradley: Paul Wagner
Hamilton MacFadden: Bill Kellogg
Leslie Denison: Rice
Iris Wong: Lili
Eugene Borden: Armando
Anne Codee: Margo

Shooting days: May 8 to May 29, 1941

Released September 5, 1941 by Twentieth Century-Fox Film Corporation
Running Time: 60 minutes. Black and White

THIS REMAKE OF THE 1931 film *The Black Camel* does not hold up in comparison to the earlier film and for a number of reasons. The first movie was a well mounted detective mystery with film noir elements, directly inspired by an original Charlie Chan novel. *Charlie Chan in Rio* uses the same complications from the original story, but offers none of the location settings, nor does it have as strong of a cast (Bela Lugosi, Dwight Frye, Marjorie White, C. Henry Gordon, and Murray Kinnell are somewhat more impressive than the likes of Cobina Wright Jr., Ted North, and Jacqueline Dalya).

Charlie Chan is in Rio de Janiero to arrest nightclub singer Lola Dean who was recently engaged to Clark Denton. Lola is accused of murdering a man named Manuel Cardosa. Lola visits a psychic, Alfredo Marana, on the advice of Helen, her secretary, and, after taking a drug he gives her, confesses to the murder . A party is planned for her engagement to Clark, but she is found stabbed to death in her apartment. Complications continue with the introduction of Lola's ex husband Paul Wagner. Meanwhile, Marana demonstrates his hypnotic powers on Jimmy, while also telling Charlie about Lola's confession. Some of Lola's jewelry is missing, including a pin from a broken brooch, which Charlie believes will be imbedded in the sole of the murderer's shoe. The murderer is revealed through some brief confusion when an innocent person confesses to spare the life of the actual culprit, but Charlie sees through the ruse. (see Appendix A).

The film ends with Jimmy asking his Pop if he can bring his pretty new lady acquaintance, Lili, back to Honolulu. Charlie refuses, revealing that Jimmy's mother has sent a cable indicating he has been drafted. Jimmy valiantly states that with him in the military, winning the war will be a cinch. It should be noted that *Charlie Chan in Rio* was the last film in the series to be released before the Pearl Harbor attack and America's becoming involved in the war.

A big comedown from the original film, *Charlie Chan in Rio* is still a compact, amusing B mystery, with Victor Sen Yung appearing in most of the movie's best scenes. Jimmy Chan finally gets to exhibit his skills as a fighter (something brother Lee did in earlier movies rather frequently) when he tussles with a servant who is found with the murdered woman's jewels. His interest in pretty Iris Wong, who plays Lili, includes some amusing romantic comedy, and his hypnosis scene is a delightfully funny exhibition where he not only reveals he "goes for" her, he also admits to skipping Math class and getting in an accident with his father's car.

There is a scene where Sen Yung and Sidney Toler have a conversation in Chinese. Toler learned the scene phonetically, but since Sen Yung could speak the language, he was expected to have no problem. In fact,

Victor Sen Yung, Harold Huber, Sidney Toler

the actor kept blowing his lines. The director stated that it was ok, most moviegoers won't know he's making errors. Sen Yung stated, "my father and relatives sure will!" He insisted on doing the scene until he got it right.

The Charlie Chan series had challenged racial stereotypes in the past, but in the scene with Charlie and Jimmy conversing in Chinese; one of the characters turns to Lili and asks her what they are saying, automatically assuming that because she is Chinese she knows the language. She replies to the other person's surprise that she was raised in San Francisco and doesn't know the language. Iris Wong had appeared in two earlier Charlie Chan films. In *Charlie Chan in Honolulu* she was one of the Chan daughters, and in *Charlie Chan in Reno* she had another role that distracted Jimmy. This is probably her strongest part in a Charlie Chan movie. Many years later, when Victor Sen Yung traveled to Hawaii to appear in a *Hawaii Five-O* episode, the PanAm reservations supervisor was Iris Wong (then Iris Ching). According to a newspaper account, they

Victor Sen Yung, Iris Wong

were delighted to see each other and spent some time talking over their Charlie Chan experience.

Curiously, Sheila Ryan, who had appeared in the previous Chan movie, *Murder Over New York*, was apparently slated to appear in this movie as well. A newspaper blurb stated that she was "making her bid for an important place on the cinematic road of fame in *Charlie Chan in Rio*." However, Ryan remained busy on the Laurel and Hardy feature *Great Guns* and could not appear in the Chan mystery.

One amusing bit of trivia is the fact that Hamilton MacFadden, director of *The Black Camel*, made a cameo appearance in this movie, just as he had in the original. As indicated earlier in this text, MacFadden started work on *Charlie Chan in Paris* but was replaced when Darryl Zanuck took over as head of production at the studio. MacFadden had last directed in 1937, and was functioning as an actor in small roles by the time this Charlie Chan picture was in production.

An amusing B movie trifle that does not measure up to the original screen version of the story, *Charlie Chan in Rio* was the penultimate Charlie Chan film at 20th Century Fox. The final film for the studio would begin shooting the following September.

Sidney Toler

Castle In the Desert

Director: Harry Lachman
Assistant Directors: Hal Herman and Saul Wurzell (neither credited)
Screenplay: John Larkin
Based on the character "Charlie Chan" created by Earl Derr Biggers
Producer: Ralph Dietrich
Cinematography: Virgil Miller
Film Editor: John Brady

Cast:
Sidney Toler: Charlie Chan
Arleen Whelan: Brenda Hartford
Victor Sen Yung: Jimmy Chan
Richard Derr: Carl Detheridge
Douglas Dumbrille: Paul Manderley
Henry Daniell: Watson King
Edmund MacDonald: Walter Hartford
Lenita Lane: Lucy Manderley
Ethel Griffies: Madame Saturnia
Milton Parsons: Arthur Fletcher
Steve Geray: Dr. Retling
Lucien Littlefield: Professor Gleason
George Chandler: Bus Driver
Oliver Prickett: Hank
Eric Wilton: Wilson
Paul Kruger: Servant

Shooting days: September 23 to October 12, 1941

Released: February 27, 1942 by Twentieth Century-Fox Film Corporation
Running Time: 63 minutes. Black and White

CASTLE IN THE DESERT FINISHED filming in October of 1941 and by early November the trades were announcing that this was the final Charlie Chan movie that the studio would produce. The films were still popular, but the war caused the European market to become more limited, and this loss of revenue made continuing the series to become less feasible. Also, Sol Wurtzel's B movie unit at Fox was giving most of its attention to Laurel and Hardy, whose first film for the company, *Great Guns*, was a huge hit.

The general consensus regarding the aesthetic quality of *Castle in the Desert* was that it was not the best, nor the worst, Charlie Chan effort. Thus, as with Warner Oland's last Chan film, *Charlie Chan at Monte Carlo*, this swan song for Sidney Toler at Fox studio was a rather run-of-the-mill entry.

The initial focus is on Mr. and Mrs. Manderly, two millionaires who are hosting several guests at their castle. When one of them is murdered with poison, Manderly asks other guests to bring the body elsewhere and make it appear natural. Mrs. Manderly is a descendent of the Borgias, and her husband is concerned that she will become a prime suspect. Charlie Chan arrives on the case, indicating he has been summoned by Mrs. Manderly. But she insists she never sent him the note. He stays anyway, suspicious of the activities and the people. At about the same time, sculptor Watson King arrives as he has been hired to do a bust of Mrs. Manderly. Jimmy Chan shows up at the castle soon afterward, with concerns for his Pop's safety. Jimmy received his draft notice at the end of the previous film, *Charlie Chan in Rio*, so in order for him to appear in *Castle on the Desert*, the story has him on a one week furlough during which he offers his assistance to Charlie's latest murder case.

The list of suspects becomes rather complicated, including a lawyer, his wife, a fortune teller, a doctor, and a private detective. Attempts are made to convince others that Mrs. Manderly is insane and dangerous. Charlie, however, comes to a different conclusion after more murders are committed, and reveals the actual killer, who turns out to be Cesare Borgia with a disguise and altered features (see Appendix A).

By this time, *Variety* had pretty much given up on the Charlie Chan series, especially once it was announced that this would be the last film:

> The last of the Charlie Chan whodunits, *Castle in the Desert* is a very mild murder mystery, without clear-cut reasons for action. Original script by John Larkin is unimaginative and seems to have been tossed together hurriedly in order to get the final Chan to the barrier. After Chan walks through sufficient footage, and segregates the various suspicious characters around the place, he makes the inevitable solution which to the onlooker seems like a 'whydunit.' Direction by Harry Lachman is slow in development, and efforts to inject slapstick laughs via antics of Jimmy Chan fail to catch on. Cast is standard for picture of this type.

Motion Picture Herald was more impressed, stating: "For its final item in the long series of Charlie Chan melodramas, the studio which gave the Earl Derr Biggers character its screen career offers one of the most fascinating films in the series." However, this review also admits that, "Chan's solution of the mystery leaves a number of story threads hanging loose...."

The supporting cast is good, with returning actors like Douglas Dumbrille, Richard Derr, Ethel Griffies, and Milton Parsons, along with welcome veterans like Lucien Littlefield and George Chandler in smaller roles. Actress Arleen Whelan was not pleased to be cast in this B movie, believing she should be used in more prestigious films. She had initially been cast in such A pictures as *Kidnapped* (1938) and *Young Mr. Lincoln* (1939), but by 1942 she was in B movies like this Chan film and *Sundown Jim*. When she turned down the femme lead in the Laurel and Hardy feature *Jitterbugs* (1943), the studio suspended her and she found herself blackballed from the studios. Her next film was not until 1947, and she finished out the few remaining years of her career mostly in independent movies, including decent roles in *Never Wave at a Wac* (1953) and John Ford's *The Sun Shines Bright* (1953). Whalen told the press,[1] "I was ordered to play leading lady for Laurel and Hardy. I just wouldn't do it. I think they pushed me too fast. And I saw the whole United States at the

---

1. "Big Buildup Failed, Question is Why." *The Morning News* Wilmington, Delaware July 11, 1942

expense of 20th Century Fox. Whenever anybody wanted a movie actress to make a personal appearance, the studio always sent me. It was tough, all that traveling and all that smiling when I didn't feel like smiling, but it was a good experience."

The ending of the series was a difficult situation for Sidney Toler, who, like Warner Oland before him, had become so identified with the Charlie Chan role, there was little else this talented actor could do. Moviegoers would send him scores of letters seeking his professional assistance in solving their personal mysteries. Often it would be help in finding clues that could lead to the whereabouts of missing persons. Losing the role for which he had become identified was a real blow to his career. To add insult to injury, once America became involved in what evolved into World War Two, Toler was forced to close an expensive, elaborate golf driving range and restaurant he had just opened due to dim-out regulations.

There was one intriguing idea put forth by Bryan Foy at 20th Century Fox. He wanted to put together a movie featuring all of the famous movie detectives including Toler and Chan, George Sanders as The Falcon, even Peter Lorre as Mr. Moto, playing his scenes from behind the bars of an interment camp! But, unfortunately, this fascinating idea never came to fruition.

Sidney Toler was undaunted. He began looking into the possibility of bringing the Charlie Chan series to another studio.

Charlie Chan In Transition

From Fox to Monogram

THE CHARLIE CHAN SERIES offered no movies in 1943. It was the first time since 1931 that a year went by without a Charlie Chan film in release. During this time, Sidney Toler was in negotiation to secure the rights to the series and bring it to another studio. Toler told the press: "I can tell you, I was seriously worried when William Goetz, the Fox executive, called me in to say it was not my fault, but Chan was dead." The studio wanted to concentrate more on A pictures, and scale back on its lower budget B unit, maintaining only the profitable Laurel and Hardy features they'd just begun to produce (ironically, the duo was unhappy at the studio and left movies altogether in 1945).

Toler secured the rights from the widow of Earl Derr Biggers with an advance from Fox, who were supportive of the actor bringing the series to another studio. He shopped around, discussing the possibility with several different studios before settling on Monogram Pictures. Monogram was a poverty row studio, specializing in B movies for neighborhood theaters or as part of a double feature. Their most profitable series was The East Side Kids, which would soon morph into The Bowery Boys and enjoy even greater popularity.

Monogram was eager to obtain the Chan series at their studio, and offered the production talents of Phil Krasne and James S. Burkett to spearhead the series. The producers originally considered Lynn Shores to direct. Shores had directed only 16 features since the 1920s, including *Charlie Chan in the Wax Museum* at Fox. His latest film, also at Fox, was a second-rate family film, *Golden Hoofs* starring Jane Withers, released two years earlier. Shores was chosen because he was available, and because he had helmed a Charlie Chan movie already. But the studio preferred to use a director who was already active at the studio, so Shores was replaced by Phil Rosen before filming began. Shores remained active as a second unit director until his death in 1949, but never directed another film.

Phil Rosen seemed like a much more logical choice, not only because he was already active at Monogram, but he was also known for being able to work in a variety of genres. One of the films he directed is the Mr. Wong mystery *Phantom of Chinatown* (1940) in which Keye Luke takes over the leading role from Boris Karloff. Rosen would not only direct the first Chan mystery at Monogram, but also the next six. Because his background was in cinematography, and because he was adept at working successfully within a small budget, the films Rosen directed belie their poverty row limitations and come off as perfectly strong efforts in the series. Along with the rights to the series, Sidney Toler insisted on having some level of creative input. Monogram was open to this sort of freedom and Rosen encouraged it.

Monogram's approach was different, and Toler approved their intent on offering more comedy in the films, including adding a new character, chauffeur Birgmingham Brown, played by African American actor Mantan Moreland. Moreland recalled in a 1971 phone conversation with the author: "I was doing parts in a dozen pictures a year in those days. I would ride a bicycle from one set to another and do small parts in three movies in one day. I worked with everybody. When they called and gave me a steady job in the Charlie Chan series, I snapped it right up. It is one of the best experiences of my career."

One snag that came along was the casting of Chan's offspring, which had become a real mainstay of the series. Victor Sen Yung had enlisted in the military in real life just as his character was drafted in the movies. He was on active duty overseas when the series resumed production. Toler suggested that they try to hire Keye Luke to return as Lee Chan. Luke remained active since leaving the role, and had a good reputation at Monogram having played the title role in the last Mr. Wong movie. Unfortunately, Keye was currently under contract at MGM, appearing fairly regularly in their Dr. Kildare series, so he could not take the role. A nationwide search was conducted before the studio hired Benson Fong, owner of a grocery store who took small film roles from time to time, usually playing wily Japanese villains, even though he was American-born and of Chinese descent. Fong had a bit in *Charlie Chan at the Opera*, but very little experience when cast in the role of Tommy Chan, Toler's number three son. After a rough start, Fong connected competently and continued in the role for the next several years, until Victor Sen Yung was discharged from the service and resumed the role in 1946.

When the series resumed production toward the end of 1943, the entertainment sections of newspapers printed cheerful stories welcoming Charlie Chan back to the movie screens. Columnist Fredrick Othman stated:[1] "This afternoon, *Charlie Chan in the Secret Service* was in production with good old Charlie and his number three son Benny Fong. We're glad the magnificent Chan has returned to the job." So were moviegoers, who embraced the return of Charlie Chan to their movie screens with box office success.

---

1. "Magnificent Charlie Chan is Making Great Comeback" *The Cincinnati Enquirer* September 17, 1943

Trade ad announcing the first film for Monogram Pictures

Charlie Chan In the Secret Service

Director: Phil Rosen
Assistant Director: George Moskov
Original Screenplay: George Callihan
Suggested by the original character created by Earl Derr Biggers
Cinematography: Ira Morgan
Film Editor: Martin G. Cohn

Cast:
Sidney Toler: Charlie Chan
Mantan Moreland: Birmingham Brown
Arthur Loft: Jones
Gwen Kenyon: Inez Aranto
Sarah Edwards: Mrs. Hargue
George Lewis: Paul Aranto
Marianne Quon: Iris Chan
Benson Fong: Tommy Chan
Muni Seroff: Peter Laska
Barry Bernard: David Blake
Gene Stutenroth: Louis Philipe Vega
Eddie Chandler: Lewis
Lelah Tyler: Mrs. Winters
George Lessey: Slade
Stan Jolley: Coroner's Assistant

Released: February 14, 1944 by Monogram Pictures Corporation
Shooting days: September 4-19, 1943
Running Time: 65 minutes. Black and White

FOR THE FIRST CHARLIE CHAN FILM at Monogram, the studio made sure all elements were in place for an entertaining feature. Not only was Benson Fong on hand as Number Three Son Tommy, but also Marianne Quon appears, for the first and only time, as daughter Iris. It was determined that the film needed two Chan children to take the place of Victor Sen Yung or Keye Luke, neither of whom could return to the series. For further insurance, the comedy of Mantan Moreland is also included. And, finally, Charlie Chan is no longer a Honolulu detective. He is now working with the Secret Service for the war effort.

An inventor who is developing an explosive for the American war effort dies mysteriously and plans for his torpedo disappear. Charlie Chan, now stationed in Washington with the secret service, is called in to investigate. He is currently being visited by two of his children, Tommy and Iris, who want to see the sites in the nation's capital and end up going along to help out. The suspects are gathered at the inventor's house, having been invited to a cocktail party before the murder.

The film then concentrates on the various characters maneuvering about with murder attempts and shootouts occurring at regular intervals. Charlie uses some various methods of technology to realize how the murder of the inventor occurred, and demonstrates to the assembled suspects. During the subsequent questioning, one of the suspects, Mr. Vega, is shot in the back. A rigged gun in a nearby safe nearly shoots Charlie Chan. A similar gun hanging on the wall turns out to be the weapon that killed Vega. It is discovered to have been activated by a switch under the piano.

Several of the suspects seem likely. They include the flighty Mrs. Winters, war refugee Louis Vega, the wheelchair bound Paul Aranto and his sister Inez, politician David Blake, housekeeper Mrs. Hargue; and valet Peter Laska. Peter Laska is originally named the murderer by Charlie Chan. Charlie indicates that Laska feared Vega would implicate him in the death of the inventor. However, this was a ruse and as Laska is taken away, the actual murderer tries to hurry away, but is blocked by a returning Laska. The identity of the correct culprit is then revealed (See Appendix).

While the studio was desperate to give Charlie Chan a son to play off of, Benson Fong seems a bit tentative in his performance as Tommy Chan. Marianne Quon appears more confident in her role as Iris Chan. Fong would improve as he went along, but in his first Chan movie he is decidedly less charismatic than either Victor Sen Yung or Keye Luke had been. Quon would appear in only four other films in her entire acting career, but she is quite engaging in her only Charlie Chan appearance. She and Fong play off each other nicely, with him as a more bumbling sort, while she has a smug cuteness. This first appearance of Mantan Moreland as Birmingham Brown seemed to give him attention mostly in isolated scenes to break up the serious moments with comedy. He'd become more integral to the plots as the series continued.

There are some amusing moments with the newcomers to the series. When both Tommy and Iris try to explain themselves to their Pop in their native tongue, Birmingham asks what they're saying and Charlie replies, "It's all Chinese to me." Charlie responds to the snappy forties slang of the kids with a disdainful, "speak English please," which is especially funny in that both the younger Chans are American born and do not have Charlie's accent. Mantan's appearances are always a lot of fun, especially since he is so frequently left alone to command the scene. The stereotypical black comic fear of dangerous situations is only part of his characterization. He mostly plays the outsider, the observer who is less a part of the action as on the periphery. Even Charlie is rather amusing here, lightening up the seriousness of his quest to find a murderer. When he is detained by a flighty woman, he excuses himself with a rather sarcastic, "excuse please, must catch murderer." Charlie Chan is more sarcastic at Monogram, including with his children-helpers. He has more of an edge.

Because the series has gone from the prestigious 20th Century Fox to the lower budget Monogram studios, the sets are cheaper and the music more perfunctory. The confined setting is not as interesting as, say, a wax museum or a pirate ship. However, director Phil Rosen exhibits his background in cinematography by offering some rather artistic shots throughout. One scene is established with a nice medium shot of Charlie getting into a cab, the expanse of the frame including a great deal of the cityscape behind him. A dark conversation features two people in silhouette. There are a number of tracking shots that transition from one scene to another. For a low budget B movie, these are impressive choices on the part of the director.

Technology became more relevant to the war effort, and now with Charlie Chan in the secret service, his solving of the murder involves a lot of technological gadgetry. Some of it appears complicated, but Charlie explains it carefully and effectively.

Charlie Chan in the Secret Service is decidedly better than the last few Fox features had been. The added humor to lighten the proceedings never distracts from the story, even when the comedy is tangential rather than organic to the plot. While the film does follow the formula established at Fox, and the murder mystery remains heavily dramatic, the comedy punctuates the overall production and adds to the film's entertainment value. Perhaps it is the cheap, aggressive nature of the Monogram studio methods that offer a greater urgency to this Charlie Chan production, but as a portent to the new direction of the series.

The review in *Motion Picture Daily* pointed out that the comedy, especially by Mantan Moreland, "provoked plenty of laughter from a weeknight audience at the Orpheum Theater in downtown Los Angeles." *Film Daily* called it a "first rate mystery" that kept the "Charlie Chan series up to date." *Variety*, however, commented instead on the "stodginess" of the series now being produced by a low budget poverty row studio, pointing out that the action mostly confines itself to the inventor's home, with no real expansion beyond that. However, it is these elements that add a certain B-level movie charm to this effort. *Charlie Chan in the Secret Service* is the best film in the series since *Charlie Chan's Murder Cruise*.

Monogram studio president W. Ray Johnston, a former independent producer whose career dated back to the old Thanhouser company during the silent era, issued a three-colored brochure to movie theater owners as a guide to what exhibitors could expect from the "New Monogram" this season. The kickoff of their Charlie Chan series was one of the headline pieces. The studio released *Charlie Chan in the Secret Service* on Valentine's Day in 1944, and by that time they already had another Chan feature already completed.

The Chinese Cat

Director: Phil Rosen
Assistant Director: Bobby Ray
Original Screenplay: George Callahan
Based on the character created by Earl Derr Biggers
Producers: Phillip N. Krasne and James S. Burkett
Cinematography: Ira Morgan
Film Editors: Fred Allen and Martin Cohn

Cast:
Sidney Toler: Charlie Chan
Joan Woodbury: Leah Manning
Mantan Moreland: Birmingham Brown
Benson Fong: Tommy Chan
Ian Keith: Dr. Paul Reknik
Cy Kendall: Webster Deacon
Weldon Heyburn: Harvey Dennis
Anthony Ward: Catlen
John Davidson: Karl Karzos/Kurt Karzos
Dewey Robinson: Salos
Stan Jolley: Gannett
Betty Blythe: Mrs. Manning
Daisy Bufford: Carolina
Jack Norton: Hotel Desk Manager
Luke Chan: Wu Song
Sam Flint: Thomas P. Manning
George Chandler: Taxicab Dispatcher
Danny Desmond: Bellboy
Terry Frost: Policeman Writing Ticket

Released May 20, 1944 by Krasne-Burkett Productions
Distributed by Monogram Pictures Corporation
Shooting days: January 11-19, 1944
Running Time: 65 minutes. Black and White

Working title: *Murder in the Funhouse*

ONCE AGAIN SCREENWRITER GEORGE CALLAHAN and director Phil Rosen combine to offer a darker, edgier Charlie Chan movie, that responds well to its low budget and uses all of the actors to the best of their respective abilities.

Thomas Manning is shot dead while alone in his locked study, the police are baffled and the case is eventually dropped by the district attorney. Charlie is spending some time in San Francisco, getting away from his Secret Service work in Washington, and discovers that his number three son Tommy has promised that he would take the Manning case. This is to Charlie's chagrin, because he is no longer interested in taking private cases, but he refuses to break his son's promise. Charlie must leave in two days, and that is all he has to solve a murder that the police could not solve in six months.

Charlie is delighted to reconnect with Birmingham Brown, who is now driving a cab in San Francisco. Charlie Chan's initial appearance in the film is to take a cab and discover Birmingham Brown is the driver. Charlie is glad to see him, but Birmingham refers to the previous film, stating the last time he saw detective Chan was in Washington and "I ain't in the mood for no more murders!" He speeds away after dropping Charlie off, and forgets to collect his fare. That gives him an excuse to go back and, of course, end up involved in the proceedings.

The crooks are shown at their hideout on the pier near a fun house. A man named Catlin reports that Charlie Chan is investigating the Manning case. One of the criminals has a twin brother who phones Chan and sets up a meeting. Birmingham is enlisted to drive Charlie and Tommy to a destination after the detective receives the phone call, but the man who awaits him is instead confronted by a mysterious figure that the director only shows the visitor's feet walking in and a close-up of the man being murdered. It is a brutal, impressively filmed murder scene that sets the tone for the remainder of the movie.

Charlie Chan examines a book about the Manning case, *Murder By Madame*, which implicates Mrs. Manning. Chan interviews the author

Sidney Toler, Benson Fong, Betty Blythe

and exhibits his skepticism, while the author insists he is right, even to the point of betting the detective 10-1. Not a gambling man, Charlie Chan takes the bet, planning to donate his winnings to the war effort.

While examining the Manning home, Charlie Chan is confronted by Manning's business partner Webster Deacon, who does not want the case reopened as it is bad for his business. Chan looks over Manning's desk and notices a large area that is less dusty than the rest, indicating a large item was removed from it recently. As they leave in Birmingham's cab, Birmingham mentions he hears two meters clicking, stating, "it must be inflation!" Turns out there is a bomb in the cab. The three escape the explosion, but Birmingham's car is destroyed.

The Chans go visit artisan Wu Song, who is found to have created the statues found at both murder scenes. Compartments in each reveal large diamonds. A cat statue turns out to be the central clue in the mystery. Deacon is confronted in his office about these findings, but he escapes out the back way. He is pursued to a fun house near the pier where there is a hideout, but find him strangled to death. When they return to their hotel room, Tommy faints and Charlie discovers someone trying to shoot poison gas through the keyhole.

Later at the fun house, Charlie is kidnapped and Tommy attempts to rescue him, but is beaten. Birmingham offers a distraction and is chased, allowing both Chans to escape. Charlie and Birmingham get the crooks involved in a chase through the fun house and, with the help of Tommy, all are captured. It is revealed that while Deacon killed Manning, another man killed Deacon (see Appendix A).

With his second series appearance, Benson Fong is beginning to settle into his role as Tommy Chan. Still, his bumbling, tentative manner is without the heroics of older brother Lee or the wisecracking nature of other brother Jimmy, and he lacks the charisma of either actor who played the roles. Thus, it is good that Mantan Moreland is on hand as Birmingham, as he provides the comedy that Mr. Fong is less capable of offering.

Mantan is delightful, first refusing to follow the Chans into the murder scene, and soon disliking having to wait outside alone. In either case he is frightened and plays it beautifully. There is a lot of fun with the twin brother aspect where Mantan sees one man lying dead, and his identical brother outside walking around. He also has a funny bit trying to light his cigar, but each time he brings a match near the keyhole, the gas being let in blows the match out. He blames Tommy, thinking a prank is being pulled. When Tommy faints from the gas, Mantan believes "he must have lost his strength blowing out my matches!"

The small role of African American actress Daisy Bufford allows for a bit of a romantic interest for Mantan, who responds flirtatiously to her. She smiles with delight when he asks, "what are you doing later tonight? I am going to be busy till midnight chasing murderers. Crazy isn't it?"

The mystery is not complicated as in the previous film, and follows the usual formula. As with most Monogram features, the sets are limited, the outdoor photography is minor, and the back projection during the driving scenes is especially chintzy. Charlie Chan continues to be edgier and more sarcastic, even seeming less patient with Tommy, but since this number three son is far more bumbling than one or two, it stands to reason that Pop would be less tolerant. When the crooks start beating up on Tommy in order to make Charlie reveal information, he remains stoic where in earlier films he would have some concern over the safety of his offspring.

Along with the aforementioned murder scene, director Phil Rosen offers some good noirish imagery, especially as Charlie and Tommy are sneaking through the dark fun house surrounded by creepy images. Rosen also has fun with Moreland in this setting, from a fun house mirror to a closet containing a skeleton. "This is just like walking around in a nightmare," he exclaims.

From its noir set pieces, to its comic relief, to its edgier presentation of the central character, *The Chinese Cat* is a good example of how Monogram would continue to present the Charlie Chan series. Along with good direction and top performances by Sidney Toler and Mantan Moreland, the supporting cast boasts solid B actors like Joan Woodbury, Cy Kendall, Dewey Robinson, even former silent movie star Betty Blythe. Benson Fong continues to be the weak link in his second Charlie Chan appearance, but he saves the day at the end with a well aimed fire extinguisher.

Made for a budget, the Charlie Chan series at Monogram continued to be successful, albeit predominantly for matinees and second features. In any case, the studio was pleased with the success of the first two films and preparations were already underway for the third Monogram entry in the series.

Poster for *Black Magic*, which is also known by the title *Meeting at Midnight*

Black Magic

Director: Phil Rosen
Assistant Director: Bobby Ray
Original Screenplay: George Callahan
Suggested by Earl Derr Biggers' character
Producers: Phillip N. Krasne and James S. Burkett
Cinematography: Arthur Martinelli
Film Editor: John Link

Cast:
Sidney Toler: Charlie Chan
Mantan Moreland: Birmingham Brown
Frances Chan: Frances Chan
Joseph Crehan: Sergeant Matthews
Helen Beverly: Norma Duncan
Jacqueline deWit: Justine Bonner
Geraldine Wall: Harriett Green
Ralph Peters: Rafferty
Frank Jaquet: Paul Hamlin
Edward Earle: Dawson
Harry Depp: Charles Edwards
Claudia Dell: Vera Starkey
Charles Jordan: Tom Starkey
Richard Gordon: William Bonner
Darby Jones: Mr. Johnson

Shooting days: May 3 to May 18, 1944
Released September 9, 1944 by Monogram Pictures Corporation
Running Time: 65 minutes. Black and White

Working title: *Murder Chamber*
Reissue title: *Meeting at Midnight*

THE CHARLIE CHAN SERIES very quickly regained its stride after moving from 20th Century Fox to Monogram, and picked up where it left off rather comfortably. The only real drawback in the first two movies is the fact that actor Benson Fong, playing Number Three Son Tommy Chong, did not have the same charisma as Keye Luke or Victor Sen Yung before him. So, it is interesting that in the third Charlie Chan feature for Monogram, Fong is replaced by Frances Chan who plays Charlie's daughter, also named Frances. Perhaps the convenience of her name actually being Chan caused producers to allow her to use her real name for her character.

Benson Fong had worked better when teamed with an actress playing his sister in *Charlie Chan in the Secret Service*, but needed to rely on the comedy of Mantan Moreland, as Birmingham Brown, when working alone in *The Chinese Cat*. Frances, however, holds her own quite well in this movie, and the antics of Mantan are an enhancement rather than a replacement.

As with the previous movie, Charlie Chan is attempting to enjoy a bit of vacation from his responsibilities in Washington, but is once again drawn into a murder investigation. This time a man conducting a séance by the name of William Bonner dies mysteriously. The séance participants include his wife Justine Bonner, Harriet Green, Paul Hamlin, Charles Edwards, and Nancy Woods. Another one of the séance participants is Frances Chan, so this implication necessitates Charlie Chan's involvement in solving the crime. Birmingham Brown gets involved because he had just been hired as the houseboy for the home where the séances are conducted. He did not realize this was the case, as his friend Mr. Johnson, who got him the job, conveniently left that information out. When the murder is committed, Birmingham notices Frances and says, "What's your father going to say?" It is established here that Birmingham is acquainted with Charlie Chan's large family.

Frances provides the same dynamic as the sons – she wants to get involved in the case but Charlie recommends she stay out of it. There doesn't appear to be any inherent sexism in his decision, as would happen often in older movies, he responds to her the same way as he does the boys. He even acknowledges she is as smart as she is pretty. Of course, Frances is determined, and cannot be easily deterred. She eventually becomes a helpful aid, just as her brothers often were.

As Charlie investigates, he realizes the phoniness of the séances and finds that one of the participants has been attending in order to expose them. Charlie's investigation reveals the various gadgetry that allows the effects of the séance to be performed. The detective also finds that the dead man's wife was planning to kill him for his infidelities. When she jumps to her death off of a tall building, it is determined by police that she committed suicide out of remorse for killing her husband and close the case. Charlie, however is unconvinced and continues to investigate.

In one of the most stirring scenes in the Charlie Chan series, Chan is captured, drugged, and hypnotized into climbing a tall building and jumping to his death. Having taken an antidote ahead of time, he comes out of his trance prior to jumping, just as daughter Francis and a detective are about to grab him.

The séance is reconvened at Charlie Chan's insistence, and when the lights are darkened, a shot rings out. When the lights come back on, the bullet is shown to have gone through the chair at which Charlie had been seated. He reveals the murderer as Chardo, a magician, who has altered his face and joined the séance to kill the murder victim and his wife, the woman who walked off the building. She had been Chardo's wife and ran away with the murder victim. Chardo came to the séance under an assumed name to get even (see Appendix A).

During Charlie Chan's investigation, there are several cutaways to Birmingham in the same house, being startled by every noise and shadow. When Charlie starts to test the various gadgetry in the basement, Birmingham, who is upstairs, responds to hearing the sound of his voice. While these sorts of comic reactions can be dismissed as perfunctory and mechanical, Mantan Moreland is talented enough to make them seem fresh and clever. Decades later, after the Civil Rights movement, actors like Moreland were admonished for playing stereotyped characters. In a 1971 interview with the author, Moreland stated, "I was a comedian. If I wasn't afraid of ghosts, I wouldn't have been funny." He is indeed quite funny and offers many of this movie's highlights.

There are a few running gags. Charlie Chan, who has purchased several novelty items for his children and grandchildren, amuses himself by using them to baffle detectives while conducting his investigation. Birmingham keeps trying to make himself disappear by using the instructions in a book.

Frances Chan and Mantan Moreland play nicely off of each other, proving again that Mantan can work effectively with anyone. When Frances wants to follow the culprits, Birmingham refuses to go along with her. She says, "Fine, stay here with the spooks." Birmingham quickly responds, "wait till I get my hat." Frances also plays well with Charlie Chan. "I'm going to get a backless dress and toeless shoes," she tells her Pop. "Don't the stores have any complete clothing?" he asks.

Black Magic was retitled *Meeting at Midnight* for television and video release, but its original title has since been restored. The retitling is likely to avoid confusion with the 1949 Orson Welles feature *Black Magic*. In any case, it is one of the better Charlie Chan movies from the Monogram period, maintaining the formula but offering a lot of good humor, and tense situations. Critics and moviegoers both enjoyed the film, and many pointed out how much Frances Chan added to the proceedings. Some even acknowledged that she had appeared as a small child in *Charlie Chan's Greatest Case,* an early Warner Oland appearance as Charlie Chan (and a film that is now lost). She was one of the Chan brood then also. Unfortunately, Frances Chan never appeared in another Charlie Chan film. She only appeared in six movies total, but lived until 2004.

Benson Fong does not return for the next Charlie Chan feature, *The Jade Mask*. Instead, Edwin Luke, brother of Keye Luke, makes his only appearance in a Charlie Chan movie.

The Jade Mask

Director: Phil Rosen
Screenplay by George Callahan
Based on the character created by Earl Derr Biggers
Producer: James S. Burkett
Cinematographer: Harry Neumann
Film Editors: John C. Fuller

Cast:
Sidney Toler: Charlie Chan
Mantan Moreland: Birmingham Brown
Edwin Luke: Eddie Chan
Hardie Albright: Walter Meeker
Frank Reicher: Harper
Janet Warren: Jean Kent
Cyril DeLevanti: Roth
Alan Bridge: Sheriff Mack
Ralph Lewis: Jim Kimball
Dorothy Granger: Stella Graham
Edith Evanson: Louise Harper
Joe Whitehead: Dr. Samuel R. Peabody
Henry Hall: Inspector Godfrey
Jack Ingram: Lloyd Archer
Danny Desmond: Bellboy
Lester Dorr: Michael Strong

Shooting days: September 2-20, 1944
Released: January 26, 1945 by Monogram Pictures Corporation
Running Time: 69 minutes. Black and White

Working title: *Mystery Mansion*

WHILE THE CHARLIE CHAN FILMS had long settled into an effective formula, and their adaption from the Fox studios to the lower budgets at Monogram maintained their effectiveness, the series continued to struggle in finding an actor who could pick up the slack left by Keye Luke and Victor Sen Yung. This time, Keye Luke's actor brother Edwin is cast as Number Four son Eddie Chan. But, as with Frances Chan in the previous film *Black Magic*, this would be the only time Edwin Luke would appear in a Charlie Chan movie. With the next film, Benson Fong returned, and eventually hit his stride in the role of Number Three son Tommy Chan.

This would not be worth as much discussion if it wasn't for the fact that the son character is a quintessential ingredient in the series' successful formula. Mantan Moreland was hired for the Monogram films to offer the comic relief that was missing, and he fit the bill quite well. But the familiar connection, the engaging support, and maddening bumbling, were all factors that added to each Charlie Chan movie. That was the one thing missing in the Monogram films. Otherwise, *The Jade Mask* is yet another good Charlie Chan effort.

Detective Chan is back in Washington working with the Secret Service, when a scientist working for the war effort disappears. In an opening scene, we are shown that he was murdered by a man posing as a police officer, and his body was removed from the premises The scientist was currently working on an experiment that made wood as sturdy as metal. Charlie, Inspector Godfrey, and Sheriff Mack gather all those who live with the scientist and question them. They include the scientist's sister Louise, his niece Jean Kent, his butler Roth, his mute chauffeur Michael and his assistants Walter and Stella. Later, the murdered man's nephew, Lloyd Archer, shows up claiming that Harper stole a secret formula from his father. This questioning quickly reveals that the scientist was hated by his live-in relatives as they were forced to be his servants. Charlie finds the scientist's body and reveals it to the suspects in order to gauge their individual reactions. He realizes he must find the murderer in order to find the scientist's formula, which is important for the war effort. Roth, the scientist's butler, indicates he knows the killer, but is himself murdered before he can tell Charlie. It is revealed that these murders were performed with a poison dart, the same weapon that nearly kills Char-

Poster for *The Jade Mask*

lie in one instance. Charlie Chan gathers the suspects and reveals the method used to murder and that there is a culprit and an accomplice (see Appendix A).

Director Phil Rosen continues to draw from his past as a cinematographer, and add nice noir touches to the proceedings, especially his establishing shots. The opening shot of *The Jade Mask* pans the scientist's grounds where a murky fog surrounds the premises. The mysterious figure shown at the gate, who buzzes to come in, adds to the macabre aspect of the opening, especially when the quietness is disrupted by a gunshot. While all of this is going on, the scientist is working carefully with his assistant Walter, oblivious of all that is going on. When the scientist is alerted by the butler as to the mysterious figure and the gunshot, his response is "what happened this time?" This is not a random occurrence. The government work the scientist is doing is important to the enemy. His demeanor, being hated by his own live-in relatives, is another factor. He smiles rather fiendishly when describing how a locked room filled with gasses will kill anyone who goes in – and only the voice of the scientist indicating a secret code will free the victim. The film cleverly has the mysterious figure overpower the policeman and dress in his uniform so he can enter the mansion and have access to the scientist. This opening sets up the plot, the atmosphere, and some of the central characters within the first ten minutes, before Charlie Chan is introduced to the narrative.

When Charlie Chan is introduced, he is trying to sit on a heavily packed trunk in order to close the lid, as Birmingham tries to assist him. This is our first look at Eddie Chan, who insists on being called Edward. He is far more bookish and pedantic than his older brothers, and it is this dynamic that the film attempts to use as a conflict for humorous purposes, while his academic approach occasionally helps with the case. This works better as a straight man to Birmingham's comical bits. Luke has none of the personality or presence of his brother, and his line readings are quite stiff. But this was his film debut, and he remained active in movies and on television through the 1950s. Mantan Moreland carries every scene in which the two appear. The edgier aspects of the Charlie Chan character are amusing, as he introduces Eddie Chan as "number four son who is number one problem."

Along with the scientific aspect, connecting it to the war effort, there is another creative idea in *The Jade Mask* in making one of the suspects a puppeteer who is strong enough to manipulate the dead bodies so, from a distance, it appears they are walking about. It is an offbeat element that is significant to the narrative. But perhaps the most interesting bit of creativity is the idea that the scientist's own gas chamber cannot be opened unless the code is said in his voice. When his pretty young niece is trapped in the room, Charlie Chan must play the scientist's voice on a dictaphone saying the code in order to free the woman.

The supporting cast is good, with veterans like Dorothy Granger and Al Bridge adding experience to a cast where Hardie Albright's sinister performance as the scientist's assistant Walter truly stands out. All of this is put together nicely by director Rosen's vision, bathing each scene in darkness and pacing the proceedings. *Film Daily* made notice of the many layers to this Chan effort:[1]

> An easy-to-explain, hard-to-understand Charlie Chan detective mystery tale with only four murders to solve. Sliding doors, gas chambers, face masks, secret formulas, dictaphones, warning bells, puppet strings, poison darts,

---
1. "The Jade Mask" *Film Daily* February 1, 1945

air guns, stage dummies, and the war effort are all combined to add intrigue to dispense. An imaginative plot tailor-made to suit the followers of this series.

Other reviews also offered kudos to *The Jade Mask* as an effective Charlie Chan mystery, but not without errors. *Motion Picture Daily* goofed and indicated it was Keye Luke in the film, rather than brother Edwin. And the review in *Variety* identified Edwin correctly, but stated that his character name was Tommy Chan.

One of the cast, Janet Warren, who plays the niece, was performing under this name for the first time. She had heretofore been known as Elaine Morey. In 1944, newspaper accounts reported her missing for several days. A widespread police search was launched. Her husband, Robert W. Major, a dramatic coach, said the actress disappeared last week after leaving a note which read: "Good-bye forever. I am going away." Apparently the actress was upset over not getting a coveted role in a major film. She was eventually found safe and cast in this Charlie Chan feature. It would not be her last Chan movie.

The Jade Mask was more mystery than comedy, with Mantan Moreland's humor being a bit more separate and less organic to the immediate narrative structure. The actor, however, continued to enjoy a lot of freedom when playing the Birmingham Brown role. In a 1971 interview with the author, Moreland stated: "Sidney Toler was the boss. He could tell the producer what to do. So he left it open for me to ad-lib a lot of lines so there'd be more jokes. Sometimes I'd think of one during rehearsal and use it, other times I'd give one when the cameras were rolling. Mr. Toler liked the humor I added and always gave me his support."

Edwin Luke's lack of charisma, his inability to connect on screen with the Charlie Chan character (even his affectionately calling him Pop didn't ring true), and his stuff line readings resulted in less screen time for him and, therefore, Mantan Moreland. After a few experiments, it was decided to bring Benson Fong back, not only for the next movie, but for the next four.

Sidney Toler, Mantan Moreland, Benson Fong

The Scarlet Clue

Director: Phil Rosen
Assistant Director: Eddie Davis
Original Screenplay: George Callahan
Based on the Charlie Chan character created by Earl Derr Biggers
Producer: James S. Burkett
Cinematography: William Sickner
Film Editor: Richard Currier

Cast:
Sidney Toler: Charlie Chan
Mantan Moreland: Birmingham Brown
Ben Carter: Ben Carter
Benson Fong: Tommy Chan
Virginia Brissac: Mrs. Marsh
Robert E. Homans: Captain Flynn
Jack Norton: Willie Rand
Janet Shaw: Gloria Bayne
Helen Devereaux: Diane Hall
Victoria Faust: Hulda Swenson
Milt Kibbee: Herbert Sinclair
I. Stanford Jolley: Ralph Brett
Reid Kilpatrick: Wilbur Chester
Charles Sherlock: Sergeant McGraw
Leonard Mudie: Horace Karlos
Frank Mayo: Hodge
Emmett Vogan: Hamilton
Crane Whitley: Cooper
Charles Jordan: Nelson

Charles Wagenheim: Rausch
Tom Quinn: Chemist
Kernan Cripps: Detective

Shooting days: January 3-18, 1945
Released May 11, 1945 by Monogram Pictures Corporation
Running Time: 65 minutes. Black and White.

Working title: *Robot Murder*

WITH EACH NEW RELEASE, it appears that the Monogram screenwriters got a better idea as to how one wrote for the Charlie Chan series. While the formula was set and the series regained its stride immediately, each film seemed to better understand the quirks of the character and made him more interesting. Chan had already gone from peaceful and benevolent to a bit edgier and more sarcastic. These were the war years, and there were serious issues at stake.

This time, Charlie Chan is working as a federal agent who is trying to crack a spy ring that is stealing radar plans. When one of the spies is killed by his boss, due to being followed by suspicious police, the case now involves murder. Charlie realizes he must find out who that boss is. Chan is informed that many attempts to break into a laboratory and steal plans have occurred, so he places phony plans in the lab's safe, hoping this will lure criminals. The lab is in the same building as a radio studio, where a program sponsored by a Mrs. Marsh is broadcast. Actresses Gloria Bayen and Diane Hall, as well as studio manager Ralph Brett, are suspects. Brett is an especially suspicious character, and is mysteriously killed when it is assumed the police are onto him. Another actor, Willie Rand, informs Chan he may have some information that will be helpful, but he is soon murdered as well, and so is one of the show's pretty actresses. Charlie, along with number three son Tommy and Birmingham Brown, does a search of the studio and discovers the head of the spy ring, whose attempt to escape results in death (see Appendix A).

Director Rosen once again utilizes his penchant for dark noir imagery with his opening shot of two detectives walking in a blurred, foggy area, following the suspicious character who is ultimately killed by his boss as a result. There is no dialog, just a series of shots within the murky visuals, and Edward Kay's music score. When Charlie first meets up with one of the detectives, established as being an old friend, he admonishes their methods in the same manner as he would Tommy Chan. This is justified when the man in question is found dead. It is a good idea to then cut to a scene introducing Tommy Chan and Birmingham Brown to the proceeding. The light comical aspect of their presence immediately diffuses the seriousness of the opening scene

The fact that radio actors are part of the mystery makes this Charlie Chan film something of a cultural artifact. Made during the pre-television era when radio was the significant home entertainment, the methods of presenting a radio program, the creative process that goes into a show, generates a cultural and historical interest. The performance is actually an experimental television production, as that medium was in its infancy when the movie was made. While radio is not the focal point, it maintains its tangential connection to the proceedings. And because these are actors, there are a myriad of pretentions that make the characters more colorful and amusing. Leonard Mudie appears to enjoy himself while chewing up the scenery as an affected Shakespearean actor who has relegated to the mainstream media. His character name – Horace Karlos – is an obvious takeoff of Boris Karloff During bits where a radio performance is being shown, the actors contorting their voices is part of the fun. One cheeky line: "You can't believe any of these actors are murderers, they're too busy murdering the English language!" It is admittedly absurd that a laboratory housing important plans would be in the same building as a radio station, but the premise allows for some entertaining scenes. The radio actors contorting their faces to fit the voices of the characters they are playing was a neat touch.

Another interesting cultural aspect of this film are the scenes where various technology is presented, and explained, on screen to Charlie Chan and to the period moviegoer fascinated by such things. They would also diffuse these serious scenes with humor. Tommy Chan fumbles an attempt at explaining radar, and Birmingham turns on the wrong switch and is suddenly surrounded by buzzing machines and flying sparks.

The murders here are cleverly designed, with the puff of a cigarette causing one young lady's demise. A snooping maid picks up the discarded cigarette, but Tommy picks her pocket and keeps it as a clue. And unlike other movies, Charlie seems to have his eye on the killer early in the mystery. He makes mention of his assuredness that it is one of a specific group, and that he has his eye on whom he believes is guilty. His choice to patiently step back and observe as the culprit further reveals himself is a long standing Charlie Chan character trait. Still, Charlie Chan in these Monogram productions continues to be edgier and more sarcastic. Perhaps due to the extra seriousness of the war effort, Charlie is a no-nonsense sort.

Benson Fong returns as Tommy Chan after a two film absence, and exhibits a level of enthusiasm and charisma that almost matches predecessor Victor Sen Yung. He displays a curiosity, even a courageousness, that proves he is adapting to the character and settling into the series formula more effectively. The dialog is dry and funny between him and Pop. When Tommy insists "when it comes to detective work, I know my p's and q's," Charlie Chan counters with, "but do you know the rest of the alphabet?"

One of the real highlights of *The Scarlet Clue* was when Birmingham meets up with Ben Carter, who was Mantan Moreland's straight man on stage for years. Their precise timing during their signature "unfinished sentence" routines are delightfully funny at the same level as Abbott and Costello's wordplay sketches, such as the classic "Who's on First." The review in *Motion Picture Daily* pointed out that "Mantan Moreland and Ben Carter contribute importantly to the humorous content." *Motion Picture Herald* stated, "Mantan Moreland and Ben Carter take over for stretches of unfinished conversation of the kind which they've been making people laugh both on the stage and over the air." Mantan Moreland recalled for the author in a 1971 interview, "I asked Mr. Toler if Ben and I could do a routine in the picture, and he liked the idea. But the producer insisted Benson Fong be in the scene, and just stand there, so they had one the Chans doing a reaction. It worked out and we did it again in another picture."

Mantan has plenty of his own scenes to add even more comedy. One of his funniest is when an elevator on which Birmingham is riding loses its floor. By the time the Chans find Birmingham, the floor has returned. This was a significant clue to the mystery, but also one of the best comedy bits in the feature.

Jack Norton provides another kind of comedy with his eccentric performance as one of the radio actors, and the act he performs for the experimental TV show is a pantomime in which he does his famous drunk act. However, when he frantically gets ready to reveal some info to Chan, he suddenly drops dead, another victim in this mystery.

A topical story that now provides interesting cultural history, a good supporting cast, a tight mystery story, and some funny moments make

The Scarlet Clue one of the better Charlie Chan mysteries for Monogram. Made for a set amount of $70,000 per production, The Charlie Chan features always turned a profit, and *The Scarlet Clue* was no exception. The series continued to respond well to the lower budgets, and explore wartime areas that added a greater significance to the stories.

Poster for *The Shanghai Cobra*

The Shanghai Cobra

Director: Phil Karlson
Assistant Director: Eddie Davis
Screenplay: George Callahan and George Wallace Sayre
Original Story: George Callahan
Based on the Charlie Chan character created by Earl Derr Biggers
Producer: James S. Burkett
Cinematography: Vincent Farrar
Film Editor: Ace Herman

Cast:
Sidney Toler: Charlie Chan
Mantan Moreland: Birmingham Brown
Benson Fong: Tommy Chan
James Caldwell: Ned Stewart
Joan Barclay: Paula Webb
Addison Richards: John Adams
Arthur Loft: Bradford Harris
Janet Warren: Lorraine, record machine operator
Gene Stutenroth: Morgan
Joe Devlin: Taylor
James Flavin: H.R. Jarvis
Roy Gordon: Walter Fletcher
Walter Fenner: Inspector Harry Davis
George Chandler: Joe Nelson
Cyril Delevanti: Larkin
Stephan Gregory: Samuel Black
Mary Moore: Rita
Bob Blair: Corning

Bill Ruhl: Gregory
John Goldsworthy: Manwaring
Tiny Newlin: Guard
Andy Andrews: Policeman
Karen Knight: Telephone Switchboard Supervisor
Dianne Quillan: Telephone Operator
Jack Richardson: Mailman

Released September 29, 1945 by Monogram Pictures Corporation
Production: May 29 to June 14, 1945
Running Time: 64 minutes. Black and White

THE SHANGHAI COBRA HAS THE DISTINCTION of being the first Charlie Chan movie to play Grauman's Chinese Theater. There is a certain irony that a film series celebrating a Chinese detective would take this long to play Grauman's.

Charlie Chan continues to work for the US Government, but is summoned to New York by his friend, homicide detective Harry Davis, when a series of deaths due to cobra bites parallel a similar case Chan worked on in Shanghai years earlier. The victims were all working for a bank that kept a vault filled with radium owned by the US Government. The case is complicated by a private detective hired to watch the bank president's secretary, the disappearance of an undercover agent working at the bank, and a couple of noted gangsters whom Tommy Chan and Birmingham Brown follow, where the discover the undercover man's dead body. A coffee shop owner receives a video juke box that is being operated elsewhere Charlie Chan finds that the juke box emits the cobra venom when the coin return is activated. After nearly being killed in the debris of an explosion, along with Tommy and Birmingham, Charlie Chan and the others are rescued by police who catch the gangsters. Charlie later reveals that one of the suspects is actually Jan Van Horn, who was disfigured during the Shanghai case and remained at large since (see Appendix A).

The director changes from Phil Rosen to Phil Karlson with this film. Karlson would soon build a reputation for realism in crime films like *Kansas City Confidential* (1952) and *The Phenix City Story* (1955), and his opening scenes in *The Shanghai Cobra* exhibit his style immediately; short, energetic scenes, bathed in darkness, with bursts of action and augmented by comedy. George Chandler diffuses the drama as an amusingly wisecracking soda jerk, while murder takes place just outside of his establishment. When Charlie Chan is introduced, the narrative is given its backstory with a flashback and the detective tells about the exploits of Jan Van Horn, who had eluded him in Shanghai. This offers the ominous foreshadowing for when the mystery starts to move. Karlson keeps the opening scenes dark, the characters casting deep shadows that enhance the sense of foreboding. This style belies film's low budget.

The first scene with Tommy Chan and Birmingham Brown is worth noting. As usual, they amusingly get into trouble, by talking in a bank about how easy it would be to rob. A guard overhears them so they hastily leave. They meet Charlie outside the bank, who clears them, then scolds them and insists they go wait in the car. When they do so, there is a shot of Charlie smiling after them. Since beginning the Monogram series, the Chan character had been so edgy and sarcastic whereas he had been presented more warmly in the Fox features. This smile, only seconds long, returns the warmth to the character that had been missing from these more recent efforts.

The comical aspects coming from Tommy and Birmingham increases with each film, and here it appears that Benson Fong has settled comfortably in the role of the Number Three son. He is quick with his dialog and it never seems stilted or tentative as with earlier performances. And Mantan Moreland continues to be delightful as Birmingham. The two play off each other nicely, helping to lighten the heavier aspects of the murder mystery. They even get to do a bit of a wordplay routine, where Birmingham must explain a traffic ticket to Charlie. Tommy insists he told the driver "no U turn," and Birmingham heard it as, "no, you turn!" Their attempt to explain this to Charlie causes him to exclaim, "I need to find a dog house that will fit both of you!" In another scene they sneak into the back of a laundry and search in the dark, giving Mantan the opportunity to do his scare comedy. The chemistry that Fong and Moreland have created continues to improve with each movie. Fong is definitely more appealing in his role by now, and he is able to play off of Moreland's more over-the-top antics without distracting from the mystery.

Sidney Toler's performance as Chan, though exhibiting warmth toward his assistants, maintains his edgy command in a stirring scene where he is confronted in the dark by a man with a gun who wants information. As with all of these films, the man reacts respectfully when he realizes who Charlie Chan is. The detective's celebrity status is used effectively this way. And Charlie wavers from amused coyness (when the girl operating the video juke box calls Charlie "cute") to the hardened edge that is necessary to convey in certain serious aspects.

One of the most interesting scenes is when Charlie, Tommy, and Birmingham are trapped by debris after an explosion. Charlie communicates with a live phone wire by tapping out a morse code, which is understood by one of the operators (something that might not have been so far-fetched during wartime).

Under Karlson's direction, *The Shanghai Cobra* is very taut, and moves along quite methodically. Karlson was new to directing, but not to film, and it is interesting to see him explore what would become identifying aspects of his style. Since Karlson defined his career with noir and action (his biggest moneymaker was 1973's *Walking Tall*), it is interesting to see his early development. Despite the lightness and humor that permeate every Chan movie, Karlson makes *The Shanghai Cobra* an otherwise very dark film with each suspect having his or her own eeriness (including the voice of the video juke box girl).

Karlson chooses to end the film on a gag, with Charlie Chan getting in trouble for making an illegal U turn, and being confused by the No U Turn comment the same way Birmingham had been. Tommy and Birmingham laugh with Charlie, but stop when he looks at them sternly. But he smiles when he walks away. Edgy Charlie Chan is crowded out by a kinder gentler version in more than one scene. Phil Karlson would direct one more Charlie Chan film, but not the next one. Phil Rosen returns for one last time to direct *The Red Dragon*.

The Red Dragon

Director: Phil Rosen
Assistant Director: Eddie Davis
Original Screenplay: George Callahan
Based on the character created by Earl Derr Biggers
Producer: James S. Burkett
Cinematography: Vincent Farrar
Film Editor: Ace Herman

Cast:
Sidney Toler: Charlie Chan
Fortunio Bonanova: Inspector Luis Carvero
Benson Fong: Tommy Chan
Robert E. Keane: Alfred Wyans
Willie Best: Chattanooga Brown
Carol Hughes: Marguerite Fontan
Marjorie Hoshelle: Countess Irena
Barton Yarborough: Joseph Bradish
George Meeker: Edmund Slade
Don Costello: Charles Massack
Charles Trowbridge: Prentiss
Mildred Boyd: Josephine
Jean Wong: Iris Ling
Donald Dexter Taylor: Walter Dorn
Lucio Villegas: Chemist
Toni Raimondo: Woman in Powder Room
Richard Lopez: Bellboy
Augie Gomez: Cab Driver

Shooting days: September 1-29, 1945
Released February 2, 1946 by Monogram Pictures Corporation
Running Time: 64 minutes. Black and White

Working title: *Charlie Chan in Mexico*

DIRECTOR PHIL ROSEN returned to the Chan series for one last movie, once again bringing his noirish vision to the proceedings. While Phil Karlson would emerge as a more noted noir director, one cannot dismiss Rosen's contribution to the Chan films at Monogram. The only factor that is a bit jarring and disruptive to the continued flow of the series is the absence of Mantan Moreland as Birmingham Brown. He is replaced by Willie Best in the role of Chattanooga Brown.

Charlie Chan continues to work for the government, and is called to Mexico City when Dorn, an undercover government agent, is killed while acting as secretary for Alfred Wyans. An attempt was made to steal important papers from Wyans that contain information about an element to be used to create a powerful explosive that surpasses even the atomic bomb. The agent summoned Chan before being killed. Chan arrives with Tommy and Chattanooga, meeting up with his old friend Inspector Carvero. His suspects include Marguerite Fontan, with whom the inspector is smitten; gunrunner Edmund Slade; smuggler Joseph Bradish; a singer known as the Countess Irena; and nazi propagandist Charles Massack. Wyans' typewriter is stolen, and then he is later murdered. Irena, the singer, is also murdered, and an attempt is made on Charlie's life as well. Charlie Chan is intrigued by some Chinese ink known as "red dragon," which he finds among Wyans' things, and traces to artist Iris Ling. Chan later finds that messages written in the ink are on the ribbon from Wyans' stolen typewriter, which had been recovered by him and the Inspector. A clue that Dorn had attempted to write turns out to be "thermostat," and it is that method the killer has used as a remote control to cause bullets planted in victims to explode. Charlie Chan uses this information to reveal the killer (see Appendix A).

Red Dragon isn't nearly as dark and noirish as other Charlie Chan movies from this period, and plays out like a more standard detective mystery. And while other Chan films like to investigate newer technology, this one instead uses older materials like a typewriter and ink that goes back to ancient times. Director Rosen does do a nice job stationing his actors during the first murder. As the Inspector enters upon hearing a shot, the suspects have already run in and are standing in the room. And Charlie Chan's entrance includes the delightful revelation that Tommy Chan is fluent in Spanish, and that Chattanooga is Birmingham's cousin (explaining the appearance of Willie Best and the absence of Mantan Moreland).

The absence of Birmingham is basically the fault of the Chan series' popularity. Mantan Moreland had just done three Charlie Chan movies in a row and had become so popular that he was sought after for comic relief at other studios. So, 20th Century Fox loaned him to Columbia for a small bit in *She Wouldn't Say Yes*, and to Republic for a larger role in *Captain Tugboat Annie*. When he returned to Fox, it was to play a supporting role in *The Spider*. That film was still in production when shooting began on *The Red Dragon*, so Willie Best was cast.

Best had already perfected his own style of scare comedy, and had been quite popular in his own right. When given a larger role in movies like *Down the Stretch* (1937) with Mickey Rooney, or *Nothing But The Truth* (1941) with Bob Hope, he was able to exhibit his talents more fully.

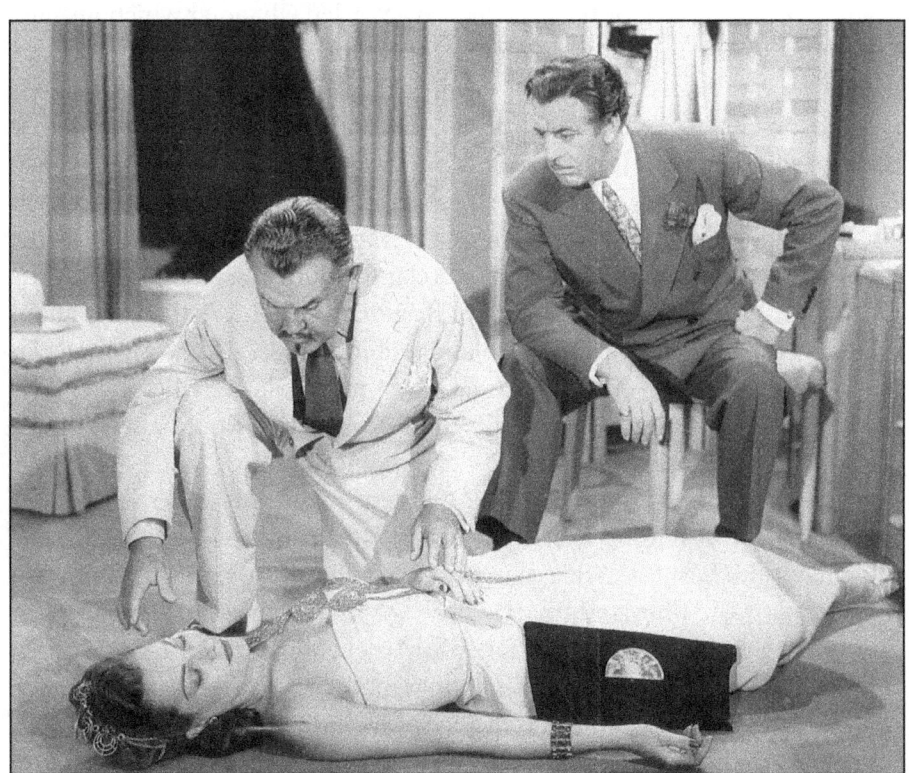

Marjorie Hoshelle, Sidney Toler, Fortunio Bonanova

He does not seem to rise to that opportunity in this Charlie Chan movie. Best trades off of stereotyped humor moreso than Mantan, and it is decidedly less effective. Benson Fong has comfortably established himself as Tommy Chan, bringing his own ideas to the character, while exhibiting the courage of Lee Chan and the comic sensibilities of Jimmy Chan. He has a nice bit when he attempts a dance with pretty Jean Wong, but is interrupted by his father, who cuts in.

Charlie Chan's interaction with Tommy and Chattanooga is a bit more limited here than in other films. Chan concentrates on the mystery at hand more completely, and any assistance he gets from the others is uncalled for. He will occasionally react with some indignation to their hijinks, but overall he tolerates them without the sarcastic edge found in other Chan movies. And he dances a great rhumba upon cutting in a Tommy.

The supporting cast includes familiar faces like Carol Hughes, Robert Emmett Keane, Barton Yarbrough, Don Costello, and Fortunio Bonanova. It is also notable that Marjorie Hoshelle stars as the singer, and gets her own song number, a rarity in the Chan films, especially at Monogram. Ms. Hoshelle is perhaps better known for her marriage to actor Jeff Chandler which resulted in two daughters. Sadly, both daughters succumbed to cancer before the age of 60, the same disease that ended the life of Ms. Hoshelle at 71.

Unfortunately, the formula that had been working so effectively since the Charlie Chan series restarted at Monogram seems a bit tired in *The Red Dragon*. The sudden murders, the close calls, and the comic relief all seem a bit lacking. And while there are a smattering of amusing moments, Willie Best is no Mantan Moreland. Mr. Moreland would engage more with the Chans and the surrounding mystery. Best does little more than fret about the dangers with a quivering voice and widened eyes. He hasn't the layer of character that Moreland added. His best moments are when he is flirting with a pretty maid (played by Mildred Boyd). This would not be Willie Best's final appearance in a Charlie Chan movie, however.

Charlie Chan fans seem to be divided in their opinion of this entry. Some call it among the worst of the later films, while others argue it is one of the best. As with many such conflicts, the truth is somewhat in-between. The film is not particularly good, nor particularly bad. Just average. And sometimes that makes for an even less interesting subject.

Phil Karlson's noir sensibilities returned for the next Charlie Chan feature, *Dark Alibi*, as did Mantan Moreland, and another appearance by his comic partner Ben Carter. It would also be the final Charlie Chan film appearance for Benson Fong as Tommy Chan.

Dark Alibi

Director: Phil Karlson
Assistant Director: Theodore Joos
Second Assistant Director: Joel Kronish
Original Screenplay: George Callahan
Based on the character created by Earl Derr Biggers
Producer: James S. Burkett
Cinematography: William Sickner
Supervising Film Editor: Richard Currier
Film Editor: Ace Herman

Cast:
Sidney Toler: Charlie Chan
Mantan Moreland: Birmingham Brown
Benson Fong: Tommy Chan
Teala Loring: June Harley
Edward Earle: Thomas Harley
George Holmes: Hugh Kensey
Joyce Compton: Emily Evans
John Eldredge: Anthony R. Morgan
Ben Carter: Ben Carter
Russell Hicks: Warden Cameron
Janet Shaw: Miss Petrie
Ray Walker: Danvers
Milton Parsons: Johnson
Edna Holland: Mrs. Foss
Anthony Warde: Jimmy Slade
Tim Ryan: Foggy
Meyer Grace: Punchy

William Ruhl: Thompson
Frank Marlowe: Barker
George Eldredge: Brand
Tom Quinn: Criminologist
Chet Brandeburg, Matthew McCue (Convicts)

Shooting days: December 18, 1945 - January 8, 1946
Released May 25, 1946 by Monogram Pictures Corporation
Running Time: 61 minutes. Black and White.

Working titles: *Fatal Fingerprints, Fatal Fingertips, Charlie Chan in Alcatraz*

MANTAN MORELAND RETURNS as Birmingham Brown, and he is just one of the factors that makes *Dark Alibi* one of the better Charlie Chan films from this later period. Phil Karlson's direction, George Callahan's screenplay, and a solid supporting cast all contribute. Perhaps the fact that Charlie Chan is no longer working for the government, now that the war is over, and is instead back to investigating murders is another positive factor. Maybe the setting, set in the gritty world of crime rather than a world of spies and espionage, has an earthier and more lasting appeal. Whatever the reason, *Dark Alibi* works at every level.

Charlie Chan is summoned to a case by a young woman, June Harley, whose father, Thomas, has been sentenced to death for a bank robbery and the killing of a bank guard. She insists he is innocent but a jury did not believe his alibi. Charlie sees that there are a few things that don't add up, so he takes the case. Thomas Harley's alibi is that he received a note from Dave Wyatt, an old cellmate, to meet him at a warehouse, and got locked inside. The police state that Wyatt has been dead for years. Charlie Chan discovers that the note Thomas received was written on a typewriter owned by Mrs. Foss, the landlady of the boarding house where the Harleys live. He also questions several other boarders. Charlie, Tommy, and Birmingham go to San Quentin prison to speak to Harley, and are shot at on their way. Charlie realizes only the inhabitants at the boarding house were aware of his destination. The case then delves into forged fingerprints, another attempt on Charlie's life when a truck attempts to run him over, another murder when that same truck strikes one of the suspects, and a gun that backfires, killing another suspect as he attempts

John Eldredge, Teala Loring, Sidney Toler

to escape from prison. Charlie Chan discovers how the fingerprints were forged, realizes how Harley was framed and who the culprit is (see Appendix A).

Once again director Phil Karlson opens with a dark establishing scene, this time with the safecracking taking place. This leads seamlessly into establishing the police accusing Harley and his subsequent trial, which is shown as a montage. Charlie Chan getting involved in the case is done in an amusing manner. Handing the woman a note containing the name of a detective who may help with the case, she opens the note after Charlie leaves and sees his name written. The comic touch continues as Charlie walks out front to where Tommy Chan and Birmingham Brown have carefully packed and have the auto ready to return home. But Charlie instructs them to unpack, stating, "I will wait in car while you have nervous breakdown."

It is interesting and revealing how Charlie Chan immediately begins unraveling the case as he speaks to the landlady and other tenants of the boarding house. Alibis, excuses, and dodges are easily seen through by the clever detective. And since Sidney Toler does this scene without his assistants, it allows him to command center frame. Director Karlson concentrates mostly on medium shots, but will cut to close-ups to enhance certain pieces of dialog. But what is most effective are the tracking shots as Charlie walks about the room, addressing the seated suspects. Despite any budgetary limitations, Karlson's directorial eye belies these limitations.

Toler plays Chan with the edginess that became more evident in the Monogram efforts, but the warmth from the Fox period that was sometimes missing. Even after the questioning scene, when the landlady indicates she owns the building and can do what she wants, Chan smiles like a Cheshire cat, exhibiting the sort of secure emotional control of the situation that would result in so relaxed a manner.

The rhythm of the film allows comic scenes to effectively act as relief from the more serious ones. When the group goes to San Quentin, the scene cuts from Charlie's serious conversation with the warden to Birmingham and Tommy running into Ben Carter, allowing him and Mantan to do a very funny unfinished sentence routine. Tommy and Birmingham get into more trouble by following a couple of contacts and getting themselves locked up. This allows Tim Ryan and Meyer Grace to appear as a couple of bumbling prisoners who look upon Charlie as a visiting celebrity. It is all a lot of comical fun and adds a great deal to the proceedings. Tommy and Birmingham also connect to the murder mystery, doing their best to assist Charlie Chan as he continues his investigation. Tommy is less helpful than Lee or Jimmy had been in earlier films. In fact, Charlie pretty much avoids Tommy's attempts to contribute beyond the menial tasks he and Birmingham are assigned.

Karlson offers a particularly nice shot through a stairwell from an upper floor while Charlie Chan questions some suspects on the lower floor. That shot is maintained when a woman goes up the staircase, ostensibly into danger. When the scene cuts back to Charlie Chan on the first floor, a scream is heard. This nicely filmed sequence is another example of Karlson's vision as a director surpassing the material at hand. In another scene where a woman is run down by a truck, Karlson's use of quick editing and the right camera angles makes the scene jarring and realistic.

While most of the Charlie Chan films benefit from comic scenes where Tommy and Birmingham walk through a dark, creepy area surrounded by spooky artifacts, in this film such a scene distracts from the flow of the narrative. However, in spite of this, Mantan Moreland is left alone to completely take over a comic scene where he walks among stuffed animals, dinosaur replicas, even a faux skeleton. Moreland is completely in his element here, performing his scare comedy specialty at its most effective. The scene is so funny, the fact that it disrupts the narrative is forgiven.

At one point, the film lifts a gag from *Charlie Chan's Murder Cruise* where a man claims to be hard of hearing, and the drop of a coin causes him to turn his head and reveal his ruse. It is Tommy's idea and he says so proudly as he pockets the coin. Charlie says, "your idea, but my dollar!" Benson Fong plays this nicely, his facial expression as he reaches in his pocket and hands Charlie the coin exhibits triumph replaced with sorrow. It is a nice comic reaction and shows, in what would be his final Charlie Chan movie, that Benson Fong had completely settled into the role.

Another of the film's highlights is a prison escape sequence when a gun backfires and kills the convict attempting to do so. Karlson often liked to feature sudden bursts of aggressive action in his films, and managed to insert such sequences at just the right moment. The sequence also helps to enhance the narrative and lead closer to the solving of the mystery. Karlson follows it fairly closely with a quieter scene where a fingerprint expert carefully presents how prints can indeed be forged. The climactic action scene with Birmingham and Tommy manning a large truck and chasing down the murderer is expertly filmed, editing from medium shots of the action to shooting from the perspective of the driver. Their further heroics are shown when another of the culprits goes for his gun, and they stick their fingers in his back and saying "we've got you covered!"

Dark Alibi is one of the very best Charlie Chan films from the Monogram period. It contains just enough action and comedy to enhance the narrative, and even when a scene is potentially distracting, it is effectively entertaining. Mantan Moreland's wordplay with Ben Carter appears as a running gag throughout the proceedings, and even involves Charlie Chan as a closing gag. Mantan Moreland recalled, "None of that was in the script. We put all that together ourselves. Ben and I kept working on stage right up until the time he passed away." Ben Carter died in 1946. Mantan said in 1971, "I miss him to this day."

Mantan Moreland is truly given the spotlight in many of this film's scenes, showing how the director, the film's star, were so benevolent to him. "The Charlie Chan pictures gave me every opportunity," Moreland recalled. "Other producers would see me in those and I'd get more work. My stage act would get more bookings. The ads would say 'here is Birmingham from the Chan pictures' and everybody would come to see us. So when they ask me how could I do this or that in those pictures, I tell them that's what put food on my table."

As for the supporting cast, John Eldredge was in *Charlie at the Olympics* with Warner Oland and would later appear in *Sky Dragon* with Roland Winters as Chan. Russell Hicks was in *Charlie Chan in Shanghai* with Oland and will appear in *Shanghai Chest* with Winters. So we've got two performers in *Dark Alibi* who have acted with all three of the actors who played Charlie Chan in this series. It is notable that Eldredge's brother George also appears in *Dark Alibi*.

It had already been decided that when Victor Sen Yung finished his military service, he would be welcomed back into the Charlie Chan series to resume his role as Jimmy Chan. So, while Benson Fong had steadily improved in the role of Tommy Chan, eventually finding his niche and offering a different dynamic to the "son" character, this would be his final Charlie Chan movie. It was also the last for director Phil Karlson, who went on to other projects. The next film, *Shadows Over Chinatown*, featured editor-turned-director Terry Morse at the helm. Morse would direct the next two Charlie Chan movies.

Shadows Over Chinatown

Director: Terry Morse
Assistant Director: William Callahan, Jr.
Original Screenplay: Raymond Schrock
Based on the character created by Earl Derr Biggers
Producer: James S. Burkett
Cinematography: William Sickner
Supervising Film Editor: Richard Currier

Cast:
Sidney Toler: Charlie Chan
Mantan Moreland: Birmingham Brown
Victor Sen Young: Jimmy Chan
Tanis Chandler: Mary
John Hamilton: Pronnet
John Gallaudet: Jeff Hay
Paul Bryar: Mike Rogan
Bruce Kellogg: Jack Tilford
Alan Bridge: Captain Allen
Mary Gordon: Mrs. Conover
Dorothy Granger: Joan Mercer
Jack Norton: Cosgrove
George Eldredge: Lannigan
Tyra Vaughn: Miss Chalmers
Lyle Latell: Police Clerk
Myra McKinney: Kate Johnson
Harry Depp: Dr. Denby
Gladys Blake: Myrtle
Jack Mower: Hobart

Charlie Jordan: Jenkins
Louise Franklin: Maid
Frank Mayo: Police Lieutenant
Kit Carson: Hotel Clerk
Doris Fulton: Angie
Jimmy Dugan: Police driver
James B. Leong: Chinese Curio Shop Owner

Shooting days: March, 1946 (exact dates unknown)
Released July 27, 1946 by Monogram Pictures Corporation
Running Time: 64 minutes. Black and White

Working title: *The Mandarin Secret*

SHADOWS OVER CHINATOWN WAS DIRECTED by Terry Morse, whose career would be defined by *Godzilla: King of the Monsters* (1956). Morse would direct the American scenes featuring Raymond Burr and tacked onto Ishirō Honda's Japanese original. Morse would direct the next two Charlie Chan movies. His editing skill would be so seamless on this movie, many actually believed Burr went to Japan to film his scenes organic to the original movie. Morse was primarily an editor for most of his career, and it is this skill that informed his few films as a director, including this Charlie Chan movie.

Unlike Phil Karlson, Morse does not feature a noirish establishing scene in *Shadows Over Chinatown*. The movie opens with a brief documentary style opening, with establishing shots and a narrator, talking about missing persons and the tragedies that sometimes befall them. Charlie Chan, Number Two Son Jimmy Chan, and Birmingham Brown are all on a bus headed to a murder investigation in San Francisco. This portion of the narrative is interrupted by a scene where the bus breaks down and the riders take shelter from a rainstorm in a bus station. While there, Charlie Chan is shot, but a pocket watch once gifted to him by Jimmy Chan blocks the bullet. Several of the passengers complain they've been robbed, and Charlie realizes the culprit is Cosgrove, another rider. He tells him to return the items, and he will not be arrested. Cosgrove does so and tells Chan he won't forget this favor. The bus ride resumes and includes a new passenger, a Corporal who states he is on a 48 hour furlough. On the trip, Charlie Chan meets an elderly woman who is also

Mantan Moreland, Victor Sen Yung, Sidney Toler

headed to San Francisco to look for her missing granddaughter. Chan agrees to help her.

The case Chan is investigating is particularly gruesome, as it involves a headless, limbless corpse that must be identified. Chan discusses the case with the Bureau of Missing Persons, and clearly identifies that the unidentified torso is not Mary Conover, the woman's missing granddaughter, due to an appendix scar. Charlie believes that the torso is Grace Gorner, a former showgirl who had a rich husband that died after taking out a life insurance policy. Chan sees a photo on a desk at the bureau of an AWOL Marine named Joe Thompson, and recognizes him as the Corporal who joined the bus trip en route. Charlie wants him for questioning.

Charlie Chan spots Mary as a waitress at a diner, and goes to get the grandmother to identify her. Mary is also spotted by a former employer, Mike Rogan, who phones his boss about her. Mary leaves the diner and is followed by Rogan, who is followed by Jimmy and Birmingham. Charlie meets Jimmy and Birmingham at Mary's apartment, along with a detective who introduces himself as Jeff Hay, and discover the grandmother's roommate has been murdered. Charlie deduces that she was mistaken by the killer to be Mary Conover. Mary ends up connected to the AWOL marine, and Gortner is discovered to have once been married to a man named Winfield. Charlie Chan reunites Mary with her grandmother and identifies one of the suspects as Winfield in disguise, who turns out to be the murderer (see Appendix A). This identification occurs with the help of the pickpocket, who owed Charlie a favor and promised to repay him.

The opening scenes establishing the situation are nicely played out. After the documentary styled opening, we are quick brought into the case. The missing granddaughter, the unidentified torso, and Charlie's seriousness working off of the comical manner of Jimmy Chan and Birmingham combine to present this film's story. There is some fun dialog as the trio arrives in San Francisco:

> Charlie: We will go to the Bureau of Missing Persons later
> Mantan: What's the Bureau of Missing Persons
> Jimmy: It's where you go to find things that are missing
> Mantan: I missed my breakfast, let's go find that!

Mantan Moreland

Unfortunately, the comedy is, for the most part, a bit forced in this effort. While Jimmy and Birmingham work well together and have some amusing moments, they do not blend as seamlessly with the story as in previous films. There is a funny bit when they follow Mary to her apartment and don ineffective disguises, and Mantan's asides are always amusing (referring to Confucius as "Confusion"). It appears this director, new to the series, was not quite sure out to incorporate comic relief. Add to that a new screenwriter who had never written a Charlie Chan movie before, and we have one of the weaker efforts in the series.

However, this does not negate the performances. When Charlie is waited on by Mary at the diner, he gives his order and does an artful double take as he realizes who she is. In this same scene, Jimmy's enthusiasm reminds us of how much we had missed Victor Sen Yung's presence in the Monogram features up to now. Sen Yung's last appearance in a Chan film was *Castle in the Desert*, the final movie at Fox. He settles back into the role quite easily, and plays it has he previously had. He is enthusiastic, intelligent, a bit impulsive, and sometimes rather bumbling. But the character's complexities never clashed before and they don't in this film either. Jimmy is allowed to be more a part of the action than Tommy ever was, Victor Sen Yung being the better actor for such situations. When Jimmy and Birmingham are part of the central narrative, and are working on the case, their work blends into the proceedings more effectively and it does not appear forced like the straight up comic relief scenes. Even a sequence where the car won't start and Charlie must take a taxi seems dropped into the plot as a matter of convenience. Even Mantan's obligatory scene walking around a creepy area relies on mechanical gags and doesn't use the comedian's talents as effectively.

Most of the Monogram Chan films had been scripted by George Callahan, who understood how to effectively balance the comedy with the mystery. He became increasingly more comfortable with each project, and reached his peak with what would be his final screenplay, *Dark Alibi*, the previous Charlie Chan movie. Having that script directed by someone with the talent of Phil Karlson made it that much better. The writer of *Shadows Over Chinatown*, Raymond Schrock, was a veteran screenwriter who career lasted from the silent era into early television (he died in 1950). But he wasn't particularly adept at penning a Charlie Chan feature, even with an established formula in place. Although it was good to see Victor Sen Yung back as Jimmy Chan, the script doesn't use him as effectively. And despite good performances with the material at hand, the film just does not measure up to others in the series.

Terry Morse would direct the next Chan film, with a screenplay by Miriam Kissinger who would pen the next two entries in the series. They are the only screenplays for which Ms. Kissinger is credited. And that's a bit of a mystery itself.

Dangerous Money

Director: Terry Morse
Assistant Director: Wesley Barry
Second Assistant Director: Kenny Cossler
Screenplay: Miriam Kissinger[1]
Based on character created by Earl Derr Biggers.
Producer: James S. Burkett
Supervising Film Editor: Richard Currier
Film Editor: William Austin

Cast:
Sidney Toler: Charlie Chan
Gloria Warren: Rona Simmonds
Victor Sen Young: Jimmy Chan
Rick Vallin: Tao Ericson
Joseph Crehan: Captain Black
Willie Best: Chattanooga Brown
John Harmon: Freddie Kirk
Bruce Edwards: Harold Mayfair
Dick Elliot: P.T. Burke
Joe Allen, Jr.: George Brace
Amira Moustafa: Laura Ericson
Tristam Coffin: Scott Pearson
Alan Douglas: Mrs. Whipple
Selmer Jackson: Ship's Doctor
Dudley Dickerson: Big Ben
Rito Punay: Pete

---

1. Screenwriter Jack DeWitt chose to use his wife's name for this screenplay credit, and for *The Trap*

Elaine Lange: Mrs. Cynthia Martin
Emmett Vogan: Professor Henry Martin
Leslie Dennison: Reverend Whipple
Jerry Groves: Polynesian
Kit Carson: Seaman
Mavis Russell: Freddie Kirk's Assistant
Don McCracken: Junior Officer

Shooting days: June 14-30, 1946
Released October 12, 1946 by Monogram Pictures Corporation
Running Time: 66 minutes. Black and White

Working title: *Hot Money*

PERHAPS DIRECTOR TERRY MORSE paid some attention to previous Charlie Chan features before directing his second, and last, entry in the series. *Dangerous Money* returns to a more noirish feel and maintains its status as a compelling murder mystery. Mantan Moreland is once again sorely missing, and again is replaced by the decidedly less amusing Willie Best.

This Charlie Chan mystery responds to the post-war situation, as it deals with valuables stolen during the Japanese invasion. Now that the war is over, such crimes are being investigated. Charlie is sailing to Samoa to take part in this investigation, when his accomplice, undercover agent Scott Pearson, is murdered on board the ship. Chan and the ship's captain also discover that Pearson's room has been searched, but Charlie is relieved to know that the agent's important papers are stored in the ship's safe. The suspects include a knife thrower, a professor who specializes in the study of fish and his wife, a Samoan restaurant owner and his wife, two missionaries, and a female tourist from England. Once the ship docks in Samoa, Charlie has only 24 hours before it resumes its voyage to Australia. Charlie discovers the murderer is actually one of the women disguised as a man, who stabbed his victims with a gun that shoots knives (see Appendix A).

The film opens on shipboard with the actors bathed in fog, adding a noirish tone to the establishing shots. Chan's meeting with Pearson is made more effective by the foggy framework, and Sidney Toler's acting is immediately impressive when he reacts to veteran character actor Tristam Coffin's identifying himself as an undercover agent for the government.

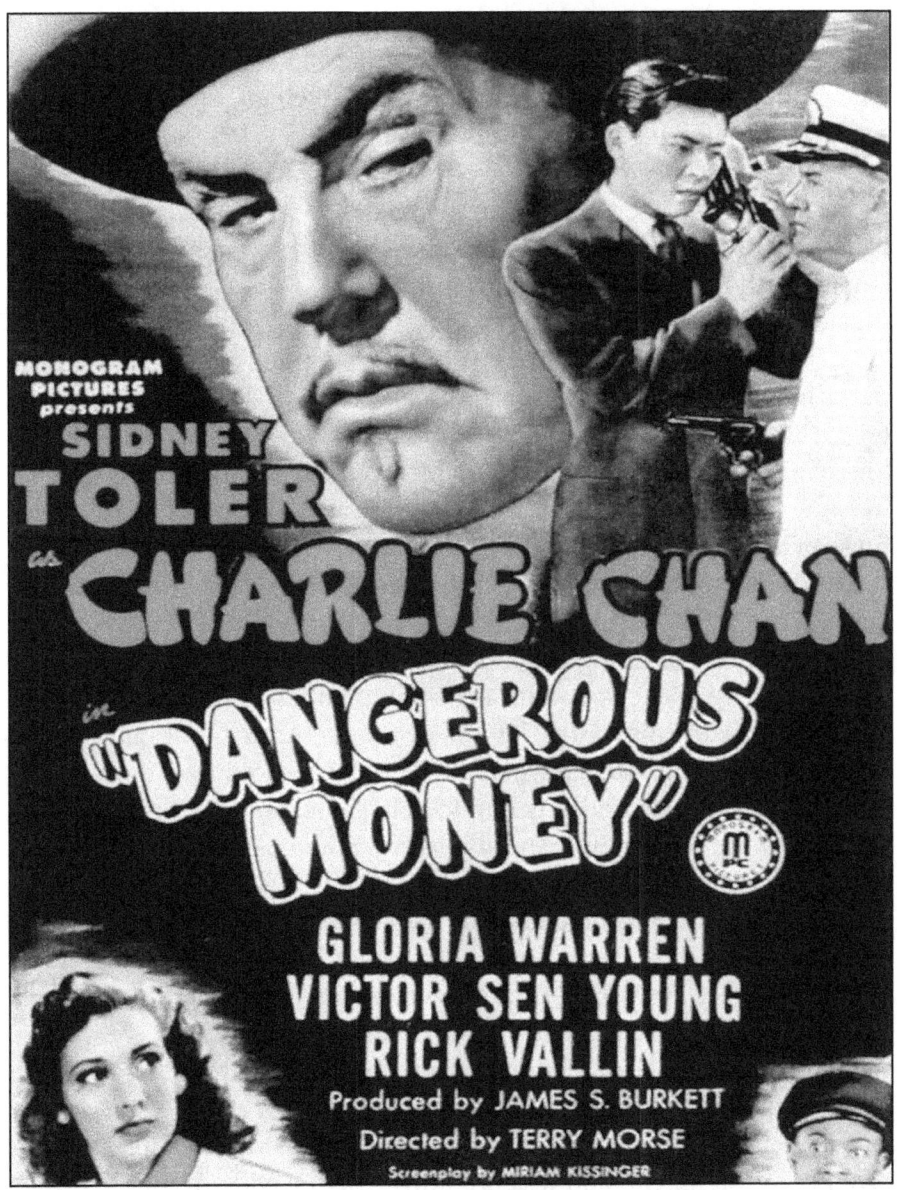

Poster for *Dangerous Money*

His facial reaction exhibits his feelings effectively, showing Toler's continued mastery of the character's nuance. The character's sudden murder, being stabbed in the back in full view of several, including Charlie Chan, adds to the mystery. Thus, within the first seven minutes, the viewer is drawn into the story.

Jimmy Chan gets involved quickly, but Chattanooga is once again timidly trying to avoid the situation. Willie Best again approaches his character differently than Mantan Moreland, relying more on the stereotype, with a quivering voice, wide eyes, and knocking knees. Mantan uses scare bits for comedy also, but Best works within the stereotype while Moreland extends beyond its parameters. One can understand some backstory to the Best character. Birmingham is accustomed to Charlie Chan's methods, but Chattanooga, a substitute, would be less privy, and thus more intimidated.

The comedy bits are once again tangential and not organic to the narrative, a problem with director Morse's previous Chan effort, *Shadows Over Chinatown*. Chattanooga feigning illness, with Jimmy's help, has him lying in bed with white spots on his face. The doctor pulls out a large hypodermic needle and Chattanooga runs off. Their ploy is to obtain fingerprints that might help Charlie Chan's investigation, but that is the extent of this gag's connection to the plot. What's worse, it isn't particularly funny.

Best's most amusing scene is a confrontation with another black comic, Dudley Dickerson, who is best remembered for his appearance in Columbia comedies with The Three Stooges, Andy Clyde, and others. Stumbling upon the kitchen where Big Ben (Dickerson) is working, Chattanooga pays him off and gets him to help gather some information that could help the case. Ben is the ship's porter, and Chattanooga hopes to use whatever he knows to somehow help Charlie Chan.

One of the real problems with the characters of Jimmy and Chattanooga is that they are not immediately connected to the case. Their antics take place away from Charlie, and are not helping out as they have in other films. During the few moments that Sen Yung and Best share screen time with Toler, it seems to only remind us that their characters are connected. It is less effective.

Screenwriter Jack DeWitt had written only two screenplays when given this assignment, and it is unknown why he chose to put his wife's name on the credits (doing so again for the next Charlie Chan movie, *The Trap*). His only other screenplay for 1946 is a Republic release, *Don Ricardo Returns*, which was also directed by Terry Morse. DeWitt is perhaps best known for penning the screenplays for the *Man Called Horse* trilogy of films, the last of which was released two years after he died.

When one recalls the brilliant screenplays offered by Helen Logan and Robert Ellis, or John Larkin, at 20th Century Fox, or even the tighter, equally effective work of George Callahan at Monogram, it is disappointing to see films where the mystery and comedy don't balance effectively. Callahan established an extension of the existing formula with the inclusion of the Birmingham Brown character, but subsequent screenwriters seem unable to present both styles as seamlessly.

Still, *Dangerous Money* is an improvement over its predecessor. *Shadows Over Chinatown* had a far less effective screenplay. At least with this film, the writer knows how to pen a good mystery film. He just doesn't quite know what to do about the comic relief. That makes *Dangerous Money* a better mystery, but with poor use of the Jimmy Chan and Chattanooga characters. It would be Willie Best's last appearance as Chattanooga, but he would have a cameo in another Charlie Chan movie the following year.

Sadly, it is on this film that Sidney Toler felt less energetic and was experiencing some pain. He gets ample screen time as usual, and his performance is good, so it wasn't evident to the viewer or other actors. But Toler himself realized he wasn't feeling as well, so he went to his doctor for a checkup shortly after shooting on this movie ended. It was then that he was told he was suffering from intestinal cancer. Sidney Toler insisted on continuing to work, but his illness is evident in what would be his final film, *The Trap*.

Poster for *The Trap*

The Trap

Director: Howard Bretherton
Assistant Director: Harold Knox
Original Screenplay: Miriam Kissinger
Based on the character created by Earl Derr Biggers
Producer: James S. Burkett
Cinematography: James Brown
Supervising Film Editor: Richard Currier
Film Editor: Ace Herman

Cast:
Sidney Toler: Charlie Chan
Mantan Moreland: Birmingham Brown
Victor Sen Young: Jimmy Chan
Tanis Chandler: Adelaide
Larry Blake: Rick Daniels
Kirk Alyn: Sergeant Reynolds
Rita Quigley: Clementine
Anne Nagel: Marcia
Helen Gerald: Ruby
Howard Negley: Cole King
Lois Austin: Mrs. Irene Thorn
Barbara Jean Wong: San Toy
Minerva Urical: Mrs. Weebles
Margaret Brayton: Madge Mudge
Bettie Best: Winifred
Jan Bryant: Lois
Walden Boyle: George "Doc" Brandt

Production: July 29- August 16, 1946
Released November 30, 1946 by Monogram Pictures Corporation
Running Time: 69 minutes. Black and White

Working title: *Murder in Malibu Beach*

THE *TRAP* IS THE FIRST CHARLIE CHAN film since *The Black Camel* (1931) to be shot mostly on location, this time Malibu Beach. It is also the final film appearance of Sidney Toler, who was suffering from intestinal cancer during filming and died six months after completing his scenes.

This one features a musical variety troupe that is filled with infighting among the performers. When a showgirl, Lois, is found strangled, two of the other troupe members, Adelade and San Toy, are among those accused. San Toy is a friend of Jimmy Chan, so she summons Charlie Chan to the case. As Charlie investigates with the help of Jimmy and Birmingham Brown, another troupe member, Marcia, is found washed up on the beach with a silk belt from a robe wrapped around her neck. Daniels, a press agent, is spotted burying the bathrobe, claiming to Charlie that it was planted on Cole King, the head of the troupe, to frame him. Another member of the troupe attacks San Hoy, and speeds away in a car with Charlie, Jimmy, and Birmingham in pursuit. The car crashes and the attacker confesses to the murders while dying (see Appendix A).

Director Howard Bretherton, whose career dated back to silent movies and would continue into the television era, was something of an action specialist, so he knew how to mount an action mystery shot on location. With the opening scene, Bretherton makes good use of the location filming but presenting an establishing shot that presents a speeding car in the background and a curious traffic cop in the foreground. It is really nicely framed and gives the movie's pacing an immediate shot of adrenaline that continues as the movie progresses. A scene on the beach that soon follows is impressive in that it is shot on the actual Malibu location and not in the studio with back projection.

The first murder is also impressively shot. Lois is bullied by Marcia into searching Adelaide's trunk. As she starts to search, the tempo of the background music increases to maintain the brisk pace of the movie that the director has established. Bretherton then cuts to a shot of the killer holding the silk rope, and then back to the face of Lois begging for her life. The murderer's approach crosses over the lens of the camera. It's really quite effectively shot, and sets the tone for the mystery portion of the movie.

The first comical moment happens when San Toy phones Chan and yells "Jimmy, Jimmy, it's murder." Birmingham, who has answered the phone, misunderstands and thinks Jimmy Chan was murdered. He and Charlie hurry to the scene, and are relieved at the misunderstanding. Jimmy joins them soon afterward, sneaking in a window and almost getting shot by police. It is a typical entrance for the Jimmy Chan character, and this energy helps continue the pace that has been set.

Sadly, though he anchors the narrative, Sidney Toler is much weaker in this film due to his illness. His gait is slower, and his line delivery is a bit sluggish. Fortunately, the dynamic between Victor Sen Yung and Mantan Moreland is enough to carry the scenes in which they appear, allowing the ailing Toler less screen time. Mantan Moreland's obligatory scene where he is walking alone, and scared, in a darkened area, comes much earlier in this movie than in others (he even gets startled by his own reflection in the mirror and then, upon realizing, giggles, waves at the image, and says, "that's me!"). When he walks into a mesh net and starts yelling for help, it is Jimmy who comes to his rescue alone, not Charlie.

While he has less screen time overall, Sidney Toler's scenes are carefully edited throughout the film to give the appearance of his being more predominant. He works hard to command the scenes in which he appears, but his presence is discernibly diminished by his illness. Nearly 25 minutes, close to half the film's running time, has gone by before Charlie Chan makes his first appearance.

One of the real highlights is when Charlie is trying to figure out the method that the strangler used. As he is doing so with Jimmy's help, Birmingham walks in. He sees Jimmy lying on the ground and Charlie standing over him with the silk rope, and states, "Oh Mr. Chan, I figured this would happen some day!"

There are longer scenes in which Charlie Chan is figuring out the logistics of the case, questioning the suspects, and delving further in his investigation, but these scenes are separated by long stretches containing the girls in the troupe, or Jimmy and Birmingham. When one of the girl's drives off, it is a cop with a tangential role who goes after her, not Charlie Chan. It is this cop who searches rooms, without the others. Eventually Jimmy is scene doing the same. Charlie is absent from the entire sequence. Even in the climactic scene when the Chans and Birmingham

Sidney Toler, Victor Sen Yung, Mantan Moreland

have to hurry to catch a speeding car, Charlie slowly walks to his vehicle, with no sense of urgency. The actor was unable to run the few steps to do the scene.

One of the positives of *The Trap* is the fact that Jimmy and Birmingham are very much a part of the investigation. Their antics are not separate from the narrative. Mantan Moreland recalled during a 1971 interview with the author, "Mr. Toler couldn't stand for very long and had to rest a lot. I told him he should be in a hospital. And he said to me, 'Manny, if I quit the picture I'll put all these people out of work.'"

The supporting cast is filled with talented veterans, helping bolster the film nicely. Larry Blake offers a strong role as the press agent, and Minerva Urecal has a delightfully creepy presence as a rather obvious red herring. Kirk Alyn, movie serial Superman does a good job as the cop. Tanis Chandler, Anne Nagel, Helen Gerard, and Jan Bryant are cute and disarming as the girls in the troupe. Barbara Jean Wong, as San Toy, had already appeared in *The Red Dragon* as artist Iris Ling (under the screen name Jean Wong) and would appear in other Charlie Chan films. Years earlier as a child actress, she was once called "the Chinese Shirley Temple" and was a regular on radio's "Amos N Andy" show as Amos's daughter, Arbedella. The only ringer among the women is Rita Quigley, who spends most of the movie screaming and crying over the proceedings.

Larry Blake was not particularly proud of this movie, or the experience of making it. According to his son, author and makeup artist Michael Blake,[1] Larry was not fond of Kirk Alyn, and didn't like that Howard Bretherton didn't give the actors much direction. Michael stated, "even though Sidney was very ill, my dad did enjoy his company." Apparently Toler realized the movie's success rested on him, so despite his illness, he maintained a friendly and jovial presence on the set, even though he was easily fatigued and rested a lot. But Blake stated that his father was so fed up as the production was concluding he just wanted it to be over. In later years he would rarely talk about the movie, dismissing it as "crap."

After filming *The Trap*, Sidney Toler retired to his home and died on February 12, 1947. His funeral was held two days later. Mantan Moreland recalled, "If he lived another 50 years I couldn't repay him for all he did for my career." Moreland's stage bookings had increased so much due to his appearance in these popular movies, it precluded him from taking part in the previous Charlie Chan feature, which is why he had again been replaced by Willie Best. Mantan had to fly in from an engagement in New York to appear in *The Trap*.

As with the death of Warner Oland, the passing of Sidney Toler resulted in another search for an actor to assume the role in the popular series. Eventually, Roland Winters was cast. It was a full year after the completion of *The Trap* before the next Charlie Chan movie, *The Chinese Ring* went into production.

---

1. E-mail to the author on July 3, 2017

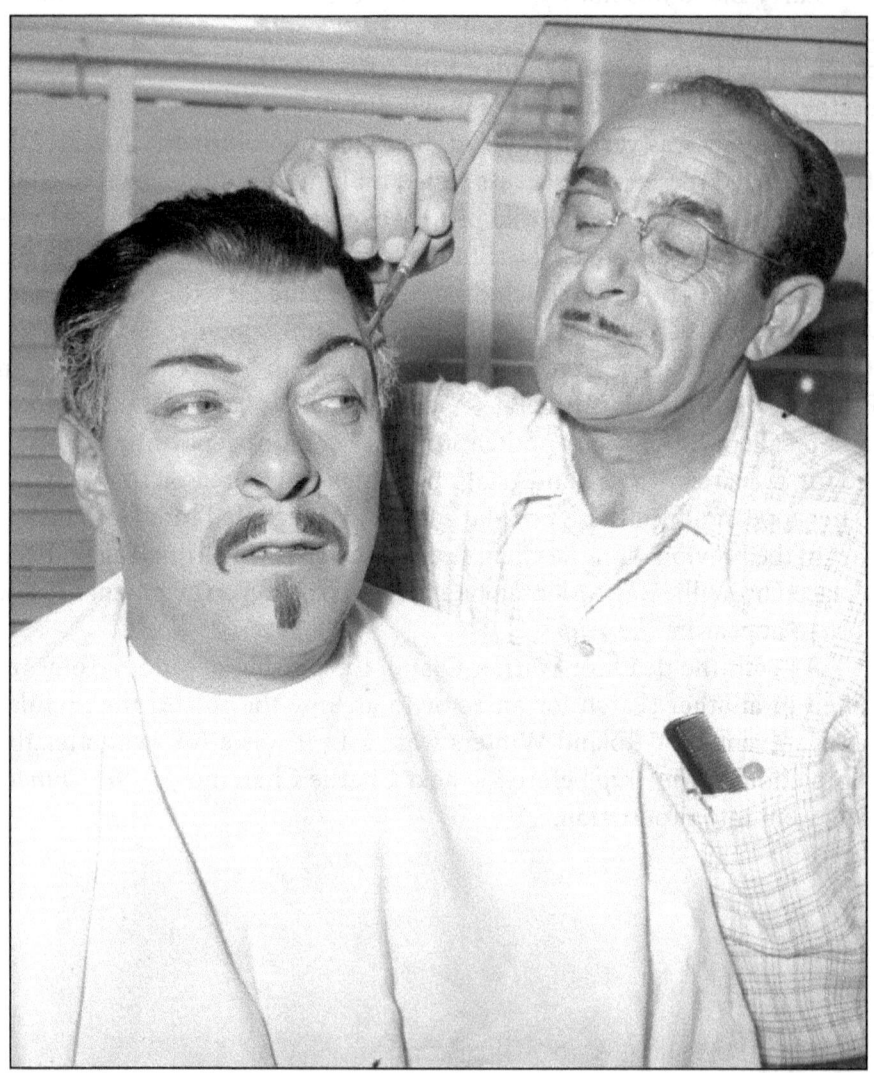
Roland Winters being made up as Charlie Chan by Monogram makeup artist Harry Ross

The Chinese Ring

Director: William Beaudine
Assistant Director: William Calihan, Jr.
Original Screenplay: W. Scott Darling
Based on the character created by Earl Derr Biggers
Producer: James S. Burkett
Cinematography: William Sickner
Film Editor: Richard Heermance

Cast:
Roland Winters: Charlie Chan
Warren Douglas: Sergeant Bill Davidson
Mantan Moreland: Birmingham Brown
Louise Currie: Peggy Cartwright
Victor Sen Young: Tommy Chan
Phillip Ahn: Captain Kong
Byron Foulger: Armstrong
Thayer Roberts: Captain James J. Kelso
Jean Wong: Princess Mei Ling
Chabing: Lilly Mae Wong
George L. Spaulding: Dr. Hickey
Paul Bryar: Sergeant
Thornton Edwards: Hotel Clerk
Lee Tung Foo: Butler
Richard Wang: Hamishin
Spencer Chan: Chinese Officer
Kenneth Chuck: Chinese Boy
Jack Mower: Ballard
Charmienne Harker: Stenographer

Leon Alton: Detective
Jimmy Base: Detective

Shooting days: August 21 to September 3, 1947
Released December 6, 1947 by Monogram Pictures Corporation
Running Time: 68 minutes. Black and White

Working titles: *Mandarin's Secret, The Red Hornet*
A remake of *Mr. Wong in Chinatown*, also scripted by
 W. Scott Darling

DESPITE THE PASSING OF SIDNEY TOLER, Monogram Pictures chose to continue the lucrative Charlie Chan series, just as Fox had when Warner Oland died. Roland Winters was chosen as the new Charlie Chan after 47 actors were tested. His approach to the role is a bit closer to how Warner Oland envisioned it – a relaxed, intuitive approach, rather than the more sardonic Sidney Toler method. He does, however, have several sardonic remarks throughout the film toward his son and the suspects. The thing that is most off-putting is that Winters doesn't pass as Asian as well as the previous two actors, serving as more of a reminder of the whitewashing of the character.

W. Scott Darling, who was a proficient screenwriter in all genres, penning such notable films as Laurel and Hardy's *The Big Noise* and *The Bullfighters*, had scripted one of Warner Oland's best Chan films, *Charlie Chan at the Opera*. He dusted off an old 1939 script, *Mr. Wong in Chinatown* with Boris Karloff, and readapts it for this Charlie Chan movie. William Beaudine was a veteran director who specialized in B movies across every genre, and continues to be respected as one of the most proficient, and efficient, directors of low budget cinema.

Mantan Moreland is back as Birmingham Brown, and Victor Sen Yung is back as well, but rather than being called Jimmy, he is now given the name of Tommy Chan. This was the name of the character when played by Benson Fong. The most likely reason is that writer Darling referenced some of the earlier Monogram scripts, saw that name, used it, and nobody bothered correcting him.

While visiting Charlie Chan in San Francisco, Mei Ling, a Chinese princess is killed by a poison dart. Before she dies, she writes the name Capt. K but perishes before finishing. Chan contacts his friend, police

Victor Sen Yung, Byron Foulger, Mantan Moreland, Roland Winters

sergeant Bill Davidson, and reports the murder. Davidson's girlfriend, reporter Peggy Cartwright, indicates the captain of the ship on which the Princess traveled was named Kong. That apparently identifies Captain K. However Charlie also discovers Mei Ling was in the country to give a Captain Kelso one million dollars for some war planes she planned to give to her brother's army. Charlie and Davidson interview the maid at Mei Ling's apartment, and when Chan returns later he finds he maid has been killed by a poison dart. A mute Chinese boy conveys to Charlie, with gestures, that he saw a masked man enter the apartment. Chan visits the bank where Mei Ling's money was, and is told that little of the million dollars remains. The banker is trapped at his home by both Kong and Kelso, and Charlie is tricked into coming to the home where he and the banker are tied and taken to the ship. Birmingham sees this and follows them. Birmingham summons Tommy Chan, and the two of them get to the ship and free Charlie and the banker. Davidson and Peggy arrive soon afterward and Kelso tries to abduct Peggy, but she alerts the others with her screams. It is then that Charlie reveals who the murderer is in a twist ending (See Appendix A).

Beaudine stages the establishing scenes very effectively. A cheerful Birmingham Brown answers the door and the Chinese princess bursts in, demanding to see Charlie. She does not identify herself, but gives Birmingham a ring to give to Charlie. It is while waiting, that she is shot with a blow dart, and her body is discovered. Darling's script allows Tommy to be effectively involved in the case at the outset. Unfortunately, after that, Tommy is not seen again for a good portion of the movie. Because this adapted script was originally written for one detective, it was perhaps somewhat intrusive to extend the narrative to include Tommy Chan and Birmingham. However, the film does include a scene where Tommy calls from a pay phone to offer information that does help the investigation. But otherwise, Tommy and Birmingham do not return to the film until its climactic scenes.

As it was already a successfully filmed detective mystery plot, *The Chinese Ring* responds effectively to the material and comes off as a good introduction to a new actor playing Charlie Chan. While most of it still works, there are some rather outrageous scenes. When Peggy hides in a closet, a shelf comes down and knocks her out. It's a bit convenient and far-fetched. The ending, where the woman foolishly hurries to report the investigation's results before it has fully concluded, and is playfully admonished for doing so, is performed for a laugh but comes off as sexist in the more enlightened 21st century, especially when Charlie says "Woman not made for heavy thinking, but should always decorate scene like blossom." She doesn't respond to Charlie's remark, and in fact kind of inclines her head in a way that indicates acceptance, which is incongruent with the strong, self-sufficient character she had displayed as up to that point. Whereas throughout the film it appears as if the story is presenting a strong female character, the final scene turns all that around and sends the message that it isn't ok for women to behave the way she does. There is also an awkward scene between the detective and the reporter where he shakes her up a bit, she punches him, and he gets ready to "put up his dukes." It's done in a comic fashion, but awkwardly distracts the flow of the narrative, even though it is attempting to establish more depth to their characters.

The Chinese Ring is, overall, a pretty faithful remake of *Mr. Wong in Chinatown*. It is Captain J instead of Captain K in the original movie, and the mute Chinese boy in *The Chinese Ring* was midget actor Angelo Rossitto in the Wong feature. Also the rough stuff with Peggy and her boyfriend, the Sergeant, was not in the Wong movie (the characters in that were played by Grant Withers and Marjorie Reynolds), nor was Charlie's line about "woman not made for heavy thinking". Lee Tung Foo played Mr Wong's houseboy in the original and in *The Chinese Ring* he plays the bank manager's houseboy.

Roland Winters does a reasonably good job in the Charlie Chan role, something that was quite daunting after not one, but two actors were able to define the character as their own. In a 1947 issue of *Independent Exhibitor's Bulletin*, it was suggested that advertisements play up Winters as the latest, and best, Charlie Chan. *Film Daily*, in its review, referred to Winters as a "worthy successor" to the role. *Motion Picture Herald* called *The Chinese Ring* "as good as any that have gone before and better than most," and called Roland Winters' portrayal "a somewhat more modern and equally convincing personality."

The budget for this film was increased from the usual $75,000 to $100,000. It is well stacked with strong character actors, including Phillip Ahn, who had also appeared in Sidney Toler's first movie as Charlie Chan, Warren Douglas as the detective, and Louise Currie as the reporter. Byron Foulger is another welcome presence as the banker. And while the mystery is good, and Roland Winters settles into the role quite well for his first venture, the fact that Victor Sen Yung and Mantan Moreland have so little to do leaves a real gap in the enjoyment of the movie, despite their showing up to assist Charlie at the end of the movie. Charlie Chan looking directly into the camera as he delivers his closing line is charming and further endears the new actor to the role.

As with any big change, the Charlie Chan series had to adapt to respond to Roland Winters' approach in the central role, as well as a new screenwriter (with at least one Chan film in his credits) and a new director. Since they all remained active on ensuing projects, their understanding grew with each project, and the movies responded favorably.

Poster for *Docks of New Orleans*

Docks of New Orleans

Director: Derwin Abrahams
Assistant Director: Theodore Joos
Original Screenplay: W. Scott Darling
Based on the character created by Earl Derr Biggers
Producer: James S. Burkett
Cinematography: William Sickner
Supervising Film Editor: Otho Lovering
Film Editor: Ace Herman

Cast:
Roland Winters: Charlie Chan
Virginia Dale: Rene Blanchette
Mantan Moreland: Birmingham Brown
John Gallaudet: Captain Pete McNally
Victor Sen Young: Tommy Chan
Carol Forman: Nita Aguirre
Douglas Fowley: Grock
Harry Hayden: Oscar Swendstrom
Howard Negley: Andre Pareaux
Stanley Andrews: Theodore Von Scherbe
Emmett Vogan: Henri Castanaro
Boyd Irwin: Simon Lafontanne
Rory Mallinson: Thompson
George J. Lewis: Sergeant Dansiger
Dian Fauntelle: Mrs. Swendstrom
Ferris Taylor: Dr. Dooble, Coroner
Haywood Jones: Mobile Jones
Eric Wilton: Watkins

Forrest Matthews: Detective
Wally Walker: Chauffeur
Larry Steers: Doctor
Paul Conrad: Man from D.A.'s Office
Frank Stephens: Sergeant
Fred Miller: Armed Guard
Charlie Jordan: Fingerprint Expert

Shooting days: November 17 to November 25, 1947
Released March 21, 1948 by Monogram Pictures Corporation
Running Time: 64 minutes. Black and White

Working title: *Charlie Chan in New Orleans*
A remake of *Mr. Wong, Detective* also scripted by W. Scott Darling

FOR ROLAND WINTERS' SECOND TURN as Charlie Chan, screenwriter W. Scott Darling dusted off another of his old Mr. Wong screenplays, this time *Mr Wong, Detective* (1938). Director Derwin Abrahams was noted for B-level western films, but he handles his only Charlie Chan assignment competently. *The Docks of New Orleans* is not accurately titled (the docks do not figure so prominently in the narrative), but it is one of the better Charlie Chan movies since the move to Monogram, and an improvement on the first Roland Winters effort.

The film opens with Charlie Chan visiting New Orleans along with his son Tommy and chauffeur Birmingham Brown. They are visited by Simon Lafontanne, owner of a chemical company, who believes he is being followed due to a chemical shipment in partnership two foreigners. When Lafontanne goes back to his car, there is a different driver before he gets in, as Birmingham and Jimmy come out with his actual driver. The car drives off, and Lafontanne's actual driver shows signs of having been knocked out. The next day, Lafontanne is visited in his office by the two partners and they draw up an agreement that states if any die, his share of the deal will be divided among the survivors. Another man, Oscar Swendstrom, comes to Lafontanne's office, claiming to have been swindled out of the chemical formula and threatening him with a gun. The police are called, but when they arrive, Lafontanne is dead. Charlie Chan arrives for a scheduled appointment and is told of the death, which is initially attributed to a heart attack. Upon further inspection, Charlie notices the radio is humming when it had been playing music, and finds that a tube is broken. Examining it, Charlie sees that it had been filled with a poison gas that would shatter at a certain sound frequency.

Tommy and Birmingham locate Lafontanne's car which had sped off with the strange driver, and Charlie searches it, discovering more clues. One of the foreign partners dies from similar circumstances as Lafontanne. Other suspects enter the case, including a phony countess, who is accompanied by a man she introduces as her cousin. Later an interrogation leads to the last living partner in the chemical deal, and he is also found dead of the same circumstances as the other two.

Tommy and Birmingham are knocked out by thugs attempting to steal the chemical shipment and locked in a closet. Charlie is held and questioned by these thugs, and explains how the three partners in the deal were killed, including producing a recording containing the right frequency to shatter the tube. The police arrive, arresting the thugs, and Charlie reveals the murderer and his accomplice (see Appendix A).

Director Abrahams opens with an establishing shot of warehouse activity, introducing some of the culprits that would figure more prominently as the narrative progresses. He follows this with the scene where Lafontanne comes to see Charlie Chan. Just prior to his arrival, Tommy Chan tells Birmingham Brown that they should pay close attention so they can help with the case. This allows for an amusing moment when the frightened Lafontanne, as he tells Charlie Chan he is being followed, sees Tommy's shoes under where he is hiding. Charlie is dismissive, but Roland Winters plays it more calmly, without the edge that Sidney Toler offered. While he doesn't exude the natural affection that Warner Oland's portrayal offered, his own take on the character continues to be closer to Oland's more patient manner.

The script is lifted from a Wong movie, but it works in this context immediately. There is a nervous tension among the various characters, including Lafontanne, his two partners, and Swendstrom, who bursts into the room, defying the secretary. Abrahams cuts to a close-up of Swendstrom during the confrontation, the use of this edit enhancing the scene nicely. It is ideas like this that bolster a lower budgeted movie with limited sets to a higher level. This furthers the tension of the scene. When Lafontanne dies with Swendstrom outside of the room, his being alone is the reason for the heart attack conclusion. It is when the coroner states that poison gas was the cause of death, Chan arrives upon the radio tube conclusion.

Tommy and Birmingham show up again with their own scene as they are searching for Lafontanne's car that sped off. They run into Birmingham's friend Mobile Jones, who is played by Haywood Jones, appearing in his only movie. Haywood became Mantan's stage partner after the death of Ben Carter. The two of them go into one of their routines.

> Mantan: I was at home sleeping thinking about that money I owe you and I couldn't sleep. So I came down to tell you I can't pay you.
>
> Haywood: Now you've fixed it so we both can't sleep. Why can't you pay me?
>
> Mantan: Races
>
> Haywood: I play the races. Horse races.
>
> Mantan: What track?
>
> Haywood: Well usually the....
>
> Mantan: That track's crooked...

They then go into one of Mantan Moreland's classic "unfinished sentence" routines. Haywood's timing is impeccable, as Ben Carter's was. Mantan recalled in a 1971 interview with the author.

> I'd do these routines in the picture, and then the people would come see me on stage to hear them again. It was great publicity. We played vaudeville houses, saloons, nightclubs, movie theaters.... Sometimes we'd be hired to play before one of the Chan pictures. So we'd do a routine on stage and then they'd see another one in the picture.

While Sidney Toler had originally been responsible for allowing Moreland the opportunity to use these routines in the movie, producer James Burkett gave the comedian that same freedom after Toler died. Mantan explained that these were never in the script. He'd perform them with his

Boyd Irwin, Roland Winters, Victor Sen Yung

partner and they'd be placed where they best fit. They are always a highlight and never slow up the flow of the narrative.

The use of Tommy and Birmingham more completely in this film, inserting them into the old Wong script, allows for a good scene where they drive out of the garage with the Lafontanne auto, and it is spotted by Charlie and the detectives in another car. This extends to Charlie Chan's being pleased with Tommy and Birmingham's assistance, despite their frequent bumbling. Tommy and Birmingham even get a chance to do a bit of a music jam, playing what they call "the Chop Suey Boogie" with Birmingham on piano and Tommy on violin. It appears like a tangential fun scene, but it figures prominently in the progression of the case. Tommy hits a certain note while jamming with Birmingham, causing the radio tube to pop while Charlie Chan examines it. This allows the detective to conclude how it could have killed Lafontanne.

There is one aspect of Roland Winters' approach to the Chan character that is evident in *The Docks of New Orleans* that separates him from the other actors. Winters' Chan is introduced to the "countess" and immediately indicates he has met her before at a ball in Hawaii. She tries to cover by stating, "oh yes, I remember." Of course Chan's method was simply to reveal an imposter as he never met the woman before. Both

Oland and Toler would likely have Chan be more gradual and methodical in their approach. Winters' version of Charlie Chan forges ahead very quickly. It is an interesting and effective element of the character that helps separate Roland Winters' portrayal from the more noted ones, and shows him as an actor who didn't simply step into an established role and go by the numbers. He has his own approach.

When the thugs enter the Chan home and attack both Birmingham and Tommy, knocking them out, it is a bit convenient, but since this is a remake where only one detective was present, with no help, it was screenwriter Darling's challenge to adapt his old script accordingly. The setup allows for Charlie Chan to exhibit the calm demeanor that Winters used to redefine the character. When he enters and finds the thugs in his home, he maintains his composure. He carefully goes over what he knows about the case up to this point. This allows the moviegoer to catch up with then narrative. It is well done. Following this is the tense scene where a gun is pulled on Chan by the thugs demanding the chemical formula. Charlie Chan pulls out a radio tube indicating it is filled with the poison gas. He stalls, but the thug gives him only three minutes. That is when he plays the record that will activate the breaking glass. When it breaks, he states the gas is now in the room.

This scene shows another aspect of Charlie Chan as played by Roland Winters. Chan is creepily playing on the psychological aspect of the situation. Even though there has been no poison gas emitted by the tube, his mental suggestion has enough power to fool the thugs into believing they are suffocating. This bit of ingenuity is both clever and rather fiendishly courageous; an aspect of the new Charlie Chan that was not evident in the earlier ones. Tommy and Birmingham break out of the closet and Tommy punches out the head thug who had the gun, showing the sort of courage not seen since Lee Chan in the Warner Oland period. Once again, Charlie Chan concludes the film by looking into the camera and addressing the audience.

The supporting cast is good, notably featuring Douglas Fowley, another actor who appeared in a movie with each of the three Charlie Chan actors (*Charlie Chan on Broadway* with Warner Oland, and *Charlie Chan at Treasure Island* with Sidney Toler). Virginia Dale, Harry Hayden, Carol Foreman, and Stanley Andrews are the other welcome veterans who help round out the cast.

For the next Charlie Chan movie, W. Scott Darling created a screenplay that was not a repeat of an earlier script. Its source material was an original story by Sam Newman. William Beaudine was back as director.

The Shanghai Chest

Director: William Beaudine
Assistant Director: Wesley Barry
Screenplay: W. Scott Darling and Sam Newman
Original Story: Sam Newman
Additional Dialogue: Tim Ryan
Based on the character created by Earl Derr Biggers
Producer: James S. Burkett
Photography: William Sickner
Editor: Ace Herman

Cast:
Roland Winters: Charlie Chan
Mantan Moreland: Birmingham Brown
Tim Ryan: Lt. Mike Ruark
Victor Sen Young: Tommy Chan
Deannie Best: Phyllis Powers
Tristam Coffin: Ed Seward
John Alvin: Victor Armstrong
Russell Hicks: District Attorney Frank Bronson
Pierre Watkins: Judge Wesley Armstrong
Willie Best: Himself
Philip Van Zandt: Joseph Pindello
Milton Parsons: Mr. Grail
Olaf Hytten: Bates
Erville Alderson: Walter Somervale
George Eldredge: Pat Finley
Charlie Sullivan: Officer Murphy
Eddie Coke: Thomas Cartwright

William Ruhl: Jailer
Lois Austin: Landlady
Chabing: Insurance Receptionist
John Shay: Stacey
Paul Scardon: Cemetery Custodian
Louis Mason: Custodian

Produced: Early to mid-February 1948
Released July 11, 1948 by Monogram Pictures Corporation
Running Time: 65 minutes

Working title: *Murder by Alphabet*

THE FIRST OF THE CHARLIE CHAN films featuring Roland Winters to be from an original story, *The Shanghai Chest* was penned by Samuel Newman and is his first credited screenplay. He would later do a lot of television writing, including several episodes of TV's *Perry Mason*, on which he also served as a story consultant. The established W. Scott Darling co-wrote the screenplay with Newman, based on Samuel's original story. Another advantage was having William Beaudine was back as director.

A judge, Wesley Armstrong, is murdered while his nephew, Victor Armstrong, is visiting him. The nephew is assaulted. However, when the police are alerted by the judge's secretary, the nephew is found standing over the body and holding the murder weapon. Because of a conflict where the judge was planning to disinherit the nephew, a motive for the murder seems clear. Along with the nephew's fingerprints, the murder weapon contains the prints of Tony Pindello, a criminal who had been executed at San Quentin months earlier after being sentenced by the deceased judge. The judge's lawyer, Ed Seward, had once defended Pindello in court. Charlie Chan is asked to assist with this complicated case, and soon the district attorney, Frank Bronson, is shot and killed. Chan and the police investigate the grave of the executed criminal and find the casket has been removed. Charlie Chan finds a method where fingerprints can be forged. Detective Mike Ruark gathers the suspects and then Joseph Pindello, brother of the executed prisoner, enters and holds all at gunpoint, claiming he took the coffin because wanted to give his brother a proper burial. He is believed to be the murderer of the judge and the others, and is jumped from behind by Tommy, but Charlie Chan reveals otherwise.

William Beaudine's return to the series results in a nice opening scene, sans any dialog, and using a lot of darkness with only the central images in the light. The judge is quietly active at his desk when an intruder comes in and kills him. The nephew then arrives, answers a ringing telephone, and his knocked out by the same assailant. The circumstances reveal him as the most possible culprit, and that usually arouses skepticism in someone as pragmatic as Charlie Chan. However, Beaudine doesn't introduce the detective until this establishing scene, which is followed by some quick character exposition, including the entrance of detective Ruarke.

There is a recurring theme about entering through a window. The assailant does so, then the nephew does, and then the district attorney, having forgotten his key, enters his own home that way. This introduces Tommy Chan and Birmingham Brown, who are walking home from the movies and see the D.A. entering his own home through a window. This mixup gets the two of them locked up in jail. It is then that Charlie enters the film, arriving at the jail to bail the two of them out. The choice to introduce the crime fighting contingent with a comedy scene featuring Victor Sen Yung and Mantan Moreland shows that screenwriter W. Scott Darling had some interest in showcasing their humorous contribution. This was a bit more difficult in earlier movies that were remakes of old Mr. Wong scripts that were designed for one detective. But in this original script for this movie, it works more effectively.

The idea to bring the audience up to date with the backstory of the characters by presenting their exploits in flashback is offbeat but effective. It provides us with an understanding of the conflict between the judge and his nephew, as well as the secretary's connection to each. The judge is shown calling his lawyer, Seward, and stating that he was set to cut off his nephew the next morning. Of course the fact that the judge is murdered that night makes it a convenient conclusion that the nephew is the culprit.

Charlie's arrangement to get Tommy and Birmingham out of jail is to apologize to D.A. Bronson personally, and it is while he's in the D.A.'s office that the revelation that the murder weapon has prints of the nephew and the deceased Tony Pindello. It also offers a very telling scene where someone calls the case a Chinese puzzle, and is amused at having used that expression in the presence of "a Chinese cop." Charlie Chan has a straight faced reaction, quite obviously not amused. This is an interesting post-war reaction as opposed to the earlier films where Charlie essentially laughs off a much more blatantly racist reaction.

There is a charming bit as Birmingham and Tommy are released from jail. Birmingham walks past a cell and recognizes a friend. It is Willie Best, who had appeared in other Chan movies as Birmingham's cousin Chattanooga. Curiously, Best goes by his own name, and not by Chattanooga, which might have been more effective. Best and Mantan Moreland engage in a brief exchange of comic dialog (Best states he got arrested for loitering in a bank – after it was closed). As with any of Mantan's comic tangents, it does not distract from the flow of the narrative and it is a delightfully amusing addition.

As Charlie Chan continues with the investigation, Tommy and Birmingham figure into the proceedings when the script deems it appropriate. When Chan and the detectives investigate Tony Pindello's grave, the detective asks Tommy and Birmingham to stay behind and investigate further. This gives them both a chance to do some scare takes in the graveyard setting. But their scene alone is too brief. Another fun moment is when Tommy sneakily listens on the extension when the detective calls Charlie Chan to report another murder. When Charlie calls for Tommy he foolishly answers through the phone receiver. As a result, Tommy is "grounded," and thus does not appear in the next scene as Charlie continues his investigation. In another cute scene, Charlie is exploring how fingerprints can be faked, with Birmingham's help. As Charlie paints ink on his helper's gloved hands, Birmingham dissolves in ticklish giggles. Scenes like this lighten the triple murder that is central to the story. Mantan once again gets one of his own scenes wandering in a dark room where he has the opportunity to do his scare takes. Finally, as the film moves toward its conclusion, both Tommy and Birmingham figure prominently as the final events unfold. Tommy even gets to exhibit enough heroics to jump and tackle the Pindello brother who is holding the group at gunpoint.

This film was originally titled *The Alphabet Murders* because the three victims' names began with an A, a B, and a C. It would have been a much more accurate title than *The Shanghai Chest*, as there is no Shanghai, nor any chest, in this movie. The alphabet idea is one of many elements layered onto the mystery, which has a lot of details, but never seems heavy or convoluted. The story is solid, and William Beaudine's direction shows his real talent for getting a lot out of a low budget movie. His choice of shots, his use of darkness, and his making the most of the limited settings all combine to make an effective presentation.

The supporting cast features such veterans as Tristam Coffin, Russell Hicks, and Pierre Watkins. Hicks is another actor who worked in films with all three Charlie Chan actors. Tim Ryan makes the first of a few appearances as the detective. Milton Parsons once again offers his unsettlingly creepy presence. And Phillip Van Zandt, often known for playing comic heavies, does well in a serious role as the Pindello brother. However, the female lead, Deannie Best, is very stilted and delivers her lines quite stiffly. She is attractive, but made only four known film appearances, this being her largest role, and her last movie. Ms. Best had quite a tumultuous life, being married five times. She stabbed her fifth husband, Willis Hunt, to death. He had been actress Carole Landis's second husband. Her daughter testified that the couple was arguing over disciplining her when Best slapped her, ripped the telephone out of the wall, then yelled at Hunt "I want to kill you!" Best's attorney claimed Hunt was "drunk and unstable."

The Shanghai Chest is another entertaining Charlie Chan mystery, with Roland Winters settling nicely into the role, and the importance of the Tommy and Birmingham characters was not overlooked. It had just the right amount of detective mystery and just enough comic relief. It was evenly structured, competently written, and well directed. While at this point the Charlie Chan films were low budget entertainment for double features or weekend matinees in neighborhood theaters, they still managed to turn in a profit for the studio.

Poster for *The Golden Eye*

The Golden Eye

Director: William Beaudine
Assistant Director: Wesley Barry
Original Screenplay: W. Scott Darling
Based on the character created by Earl Derr Biggers
Producer: James S. Burkett
Cinematography: William Sickner
Supervising Film Editor: Otho Lovering
Film Editor: Ace Herman

Cast:
Roland Winters: Charlie Chan
Wanda McKay: Evelyn Manning
Mantan Moreland: Birmingham Brown
Victor Sen Young: Tommy Chan
Bruce Kellogg: Talbot Bartlett
Tim Ryan: Lt. Mike Ruark
Evelyn Brent: Sister Teresa
Ralph Dunn: Jim Driscoll
Lois Austin: Mrs. Margaret Driscoll
Forrest Taylor: Manning
Lee "Lasses" White: Pete
Lee Tung Foo: Wong Fai
George Spaulding: Dr. Groves
Michael Gaddis: Pursuer
Geraldine Cobb: Girl in Riding Clothes
Mary Ann Hawkins, Aileen Babs Cox: Bathing Girls
Edmund Cobb, John Merton: Miners
Jack Gargan: Voice from Darkness

Sam Flint: Bit

Note: Research clams that Herman Cantor, Sam McDaniel, George L. Spaulding, Richard Loo, Barbara Jean Wong, and Tom Tyler are in the cast, but they do not appear in the film.

Shooting days: April 13-29 1948
Released August 22, 1948
Running Time: 69 minutes Black and White

Working title: *The Mystery of the Golden Eye*

This time W. Scott Darling wrote an original screenplay without an original story source, nor a previous film's script to draw from. The result is another solid, competent entry in the Charlie Chan series, with Winters continuing the explore what he can do with the role.

An Arizona mine owner named Manning is shot by an unknown assailant and Charlie Chan takes the case. Posing as a tourist, with Tommy Chan and Birmingham Brown accompanying him, Charlie checks into a dude ranch located near Manning's mine. They are met by police lieutenant Mike Ruark, who is working undercover for the government regarding the increase of gold ore descending upon the market. Manning is being investigated, as his mine has been producing massive quantities. However, when Manning is rendered unconscious by a mysterious fall in his mine, Chan and Ruark must continue their investigation without his input. They meet Manning's daughter Evelyn, his foreman Driscoll, and an assayer named Bartlett who had once known Charlie's number one son, Lee. The discovery of a criminal record, a fake nurse, and the illegal smuggling of gold out of Mexico leads Charlie to the identity of the criminals (see Appendix A).

Once again William Beaudine makes good use of darkness and the background music with his establishing scene of Manning being obviously followed. When he ducks into Wong's curio shop, the man peers at him through a window. The viewer is unaware as to what's going on and why. The expository portion of the narrative is revealed when Manning reveals to Wong about being followed in hopes that he can be connected to Charlie Chan. It is shortly after that when Manning is shot at by the assailant following him. The bullet is deflected and misses its target. Charlie Chan is then on the case.

The first scene with Birmingham Brown and Tommy Chan has them dressed up in cowboy gear, set for a vacation at the dude ranch. They go through some comic exploits trying to close a suitcase. "I think you have too many things in this suitcase," says Tommy. "No," insists Birmingham, "the suitcase is too small." It is amusing to see Birmingham and Tommy preparing to go into this new environment, and fun to see the film take the characters to a setting they haven't been seen in before.

The films then cuts to Lieutenant Ruark at the dude ranch, undercover, pretending to be a wealthy drunken tourist. When Charlie arrives

Mantan Moreland

and rests by the pool, he spots the detective who quickly lapses out of his drunken character and reveals to Charlie what he's doing. It is nicely done. The cop does not let on he notices Chan, just sits near him and quietly greets him.

Tim Ryan, who plays Ruark, a character that began in the previous movie and would remain to the end of the series, is given a lot of footage, balancing out with the other central figures. Ryan, who had at one time been teamed with his wife Irene (later Granny on TV's *The Beverly Hillbillies*) was a performer and writer at Monogram who was well respected at the studio. His presence in the Chan films might have been to bolster the Roland Winters character, as audiences were not always comfortable in accepting him after Sidney Toler's death.

Winters' approach to the Chan character expands in scope with each subsequent appearance. He has a lighter, more playful feel when engaged on a happier level with Tommy, Birmingham, or even Detective Ruark. His raised eyebrows often give an expression of bemusement at his level of control, rather than the introspection of Warner Oland's approach, or the suspicious look that Sidney Toler always displayed. Charlie Chan, as played by Roland Winters, enters their room after it had been ransacked, and reacts with amusement. He remains in control, but seems above being too dramatic about unfolding events. With each new movie, Winters was making the part his own as Oland and Toler each had. However, there are times Winters does not completely hold his own as well against all the side characters. Tim Ryan, for instance, steals his scenes Ruark, as his slipping seamlessly between investigator and the drunken undercover character was quite impressive.

As this is an original script, Birmingham and Tommy have been given more to do, often accompanying Charlie Chan as he investigates. The scene where the three explore Manning's mine gives Mantan Moreland the opportunity to do his scare bits in a dark setting. He sticks with Victor Sen Yung this time, and the two play off of each other in an amusing manner. So rather than Mantan's asides, he and Victor exchange in some funny dialog. And once again Tommy is able to come to the rescue when one of the culprits has the others at gunpoint. He sneaks up behind Driscoll, pretends to have a gun, and gets the upper hand. It is interesting that the Bartlett character is introduced as an old baseball teammate of number one son Lee Chan. In the next film, *The Feathered Serpent*, Keye Luke returned to the series in the role of Lee, the studio hoping it would further bolster box office success. The film concludes with Birmingham addressing the audience by looking straight into the camera and stating "if you think it ain't, then it is, and if you think it is, then it ain't" before bursting into his trademark giggles.

The cast of *The Golden Eye* includes Evelyn Brent as the phony nun Sister Teresa, who figures into the case.. Brent had been a leading lady during the 1920s, appearing in such classics as *Underworld* (1927) and *The Last Command* (1928), but once sound pictures came along her career declined. By the 1940s she was appearing in low budget movies like *Bowery Champs* (1944) with The East Side Kids, and this movie. After a 1960 appearance on TV's *Wagon Train*, Brent left acting. She lived until 1975.

Wanda McKay is very good as Evelyn Manning—she had a nice moment at the end where she took charge and helped take down the bad guy. Winters' Chan has an amusing aloofness that defines the Charlie Chan character in a new way, but there are times when he almost doesn't seem to take things seriously enough. This might not always be very appropriate to a story in which lives are depending on his solving the case.

The Golden Eye was still a good effort, and continued the series on a positive note, offering good, compact, B-level entertainment, and produced at a low enough budget to make a profit for the studio. But the series had apparently gone on too long, Roland Winters had not clicked with moviegoers as seamlessly as Sidney Toler had when Warner Oland died, and bookings became a bit more limited. Discovering that Keye Luke was again available, Monogram Pictures hired him to appear in the next Charlie Chan movie, *The Feathered Serpent* in hopes that the movie's box office success would increase. That film would be the only Charlie Chan movie in which both Keye Luke and Victor Sen Yung appeared together.

Lobby card for *The Feathered Serpent*, the only Charlie Chan film featuring number one and number two sons

The Feathered Serpent

Director: William Beaudine
Assistant Director: William Calihan
Story and Screenplay: Oliver Drake
Additional Dialog: Hal Collins
Based on the character created by Earl Derr Biggers
Producer: James S. Burkett
Cinematography: William Sickner
Film Editor: Ace Herman

Cast:
Roland Winters: Charlie Chan
Keye Luke: Lee Chan
Mantan Moreland: Birmingham Brown
Victor Sen Yung: Tommy Chan
Carol Forman: Sonia Cabot
Robert Livingston: Professor John Stanley
Nils Asther: Professor Paul Evans
Beverly Jons: Joan Farnsworth
Martin Garalaga: Pedro
George J. Lewis: Captain Juan Gonzalez
Leslie Dennison: Professor Henry Farnsworth
Jay Silverheels: Diego
Charles Stevens: Manuel
Milton Ross: Pete
Fred Cordova: Felipe
Erville Alderson: Professor Scott
Juan Duval: Dr. Castelar
Frank Leyva: Jose

Released December 19, 1948 by Monogram Pictures Corporation
Shooting days: September 25 to October 12, 1948
Running Time: 60 minutes Black and White

THE FEATHERED SERPENT IS SOMETHING of a milestone in that it is not only the one time the number one and two sons appear together in a movie, but it is also Victor Sen Yung's final Charlie Chan film. It is also penned by a screenwriter new to the series. Oliver Drake does what W. Scott Darling had initially done when he started writing Chan films. He dusted off an old script and adapted it for the series. The difference, however, is that Darling had used scripts from an old detective series he'd done where the lead character is also Chinese. Drake used a 1937 western he'd penned, *The Riders of Whistling Skull* and rewrote it as a Charlie Chan vehicle. The western featured Robert Livingston, and Mr. Livingston also appears in this movie, albeit in another role.

While headed to a vacation in Mexico with his two sons and Birmingham Brown, Charlie Chan comes upon a delirious explorer who had disappeared months earlier while on an expedition. He is taken to San Pablo, where he explains how his expedition with another man, named Farnsworth, found a lost Aztec temple where the two were held prisoner. Before he can elaborate further, Scott is murdered. The next day, Charlie Chan, his two sons, and Birmingham join the expedition, with Farnsworth's sister Joan, his fiancé Sonia and two archeologists – John Stanley and Paul Evans. They set out to find the still missing Farnsworth based on information Scott had given them. Stanley sneaks away from camp and goes to the temple where Farnsworth is being held. Birmingham spots an Indian leaving the camp, so Charlie Chan and Lee Chan follow him to the temple. Stanley orders them to be killed, but just as one of his henchman prepares to do so, he is shot dead by Pedro, the camp cook who turns out to be an undercover agent with the Mexican secret service. Another murder, further discoveries by the Chan sons and Birmingham, and the latter's capture, all lead to the capture of the killer (see Appendix A).

The opening scene of Lee ,Tommy, Charlie, and Birmingham all motoring to Mexico is immediately amusing. Beaudine keeps all four in the frame, with Tommy up front sporting a sombrero, strumming on a guitar, and singing "La Cucaracha" woefully off key as Lee, in the back seat, shakes his head disgustedly. It presents the dynamic between the Chan brothers perfectly and allows both to maintain the characters they had separately established. Lee is the more sober older brother, but is not above being admonished by his father. Tommy is the more comical one. Each are still intelligent enough to be helpful to Charlie, while Birmingham relates to each of them. When Tommy finishes singing, Birmingham asks, "Is everybody still in the car?"

As the film progresses, the setup has Tommy and Birmingham sticking together as usual, while Lee stays close to Charlie. When an intruder is seen in the window, Lee throws something at him, and the charges, almost capturing him by hand. These heroics had been a major part of this character in the earlier films. However, they also retained another aspect of the character. At one point early in the movie, Lee believes he has the entire case solved. Charlie states, "as detective, number one son is a very good airplane pilot."

Birmingham and Tommy stay back while Charlie and Lee investigate after Birmingham sees Manuel leave the camp. While the narrative's action centers on Charlie and Lee, director Beaudine thinks to include footage of Birmingham and Tommy back at the camp. Birmingham comes up and taps Tommy on the shoulder, who reacts by jumping up and raising his fist before realizing it is his friend. Birmingham reacts: "Tommy it's me, Birmingham! Everyone wants to fight around here!"

Unlike most of the Charlie Chan mysteries, there is really no mystery at all. It is quite evident by his actions that Stanley is the culprit, as this is revealed less than halfway through the movie. It is just the methods by which they eventually prove this and capture him that makes this movie enjoyable as well as the various twists (e.g. the jolly Manuel turning out to be an undercover agent). It's interesting that there isn't a twist at the end as there usually is, and that the film is less of a mystery and more of an adventure movie. Perhaps that's the result of the story being adapted from a script that wasn't initially intended for a detective series.

One of the most amusing sequences comes along when Tommy, Lee, and Birmingham join together to explore an area of the jungle while Charlie Chan and Manuel investigate elsewhere. It results in this exchange:

> Tommy: Just keep saying to yourself "I'm not afraid, I'm not afraid"
>
> Birmingham: I'm not afraid. I'm not afraid

Tommy: How do you feel now?

Birmingham: Like a liar!

Birmingham being captured allows Lee and Tommy to play the next few scenes together, and it allows us to see now effectively actors Keye Luke and Victor Sen Yung play off each other.

With its short running time, *The Feathered Serpent* seems even more compact than usual. But the return of Keye Luke, and the way this dynamic is offered, makes it interesting even if only for that reason. Despite it being drawn from older source material, the adaption works well here, as there are enough amusing scenes strewn throughout the feature to keeps the film's rhythm on pace.

But things were happening at Monogram Pictures. The transition to the headier Allied Artists was already being discussed, although it would not full take place for a few years. Thus, there was an interest in expanding the Charlie Chan series to something more prestigious and less at the B level. Now that Keye Luke was back, and since Roland Winters' interpretation of the Chan character was closer to Warner Oland than Sidney Toler, the studio considered returning to the more serious films as Luke and Oland had appeared in at Fox a decade earlier. This was not discussed with the actors, at least not yet, but the fact that Victor Sen Yung decided to leave the series made it a bit easier to more seriously consider such a transition.

Victor Sen Yung benefited well from appearing as Jimmy Chan in the Fox films with Sidney Toler, so when he returned to movies after serving his country overseas, there was a spot for him in the films after their move to Monogram. But Sen Yung enjoyed other opportunities outside of the series, playing small parts in as many as a half dozen or more movies each year. Television was also in its infancy, and Sen Yung wondered what sort of possibilities that smaller medium might have for him. Interested in branching out, Sen Yung left the Charlie Chan series after 18 films, more than any other actor except for Sidney Toler.

For their next film, the producers attempted to return to the dynamic as presented by Keye Luke and Warner Oland at Fox, but with Winters in the Chan role. Although a low budget film, *Sky Dragon* was one of the best Charlie Chan movies, as it promised a new direction.

The Sky Dragon

Director: Lesley Selander
Assistant Directors: Wesley Barry and Ed Morey, Jr.
Screenplay: Oliver Drake
Based on the character created by Earl Derr Biggers
Story: Clint Johnston
Producer: James S. Burkett
Cinematography: William Sickner
Film Editors: Roy Livingston and Ace Herman
Musical Direction: Edward J. Kay

Cast:
Roland Winters: Charlie Chan
Keye Luke: Lee Chan
Mantan Moreland: Birmingham Brown
Noel Neill: Jane Marshall
Tim Ryan: Lieutenant Mike Ruark
Iris Adrian: Wanda LaFern
Elena Verdugo: Marie
Milburn Stone: Captain Tim Norton
Lyle Talbot: Andy Barrett
Paul Maxey: John Anderson
Joel Marston: Don Blake
John Eldredge: William E. French
Eddie Parks: Jonathan Tibbetts
Louise Franklin: Lena Franklin
Lyle Latell: Ed Davidson
Gaylord Pendleton: Ben Edwards
Emmett Vogan: Doctor

Edna Holland: Old Maid
Joe Whitehead: Doorman
Lee Phelps: Plainclothesman
Charles Jordan: Assistant Stage Manager
Suzette Harbin: Second Maid
George Eldredge: Stacy
Bob Curtis: Watkins
Frank Cady: Clerk

Shooting days: December 6-22, 1948
Released April 27, 1949 by Monogram Pictures Corporation
Running Time: 64 minutes. Black and White

NOBODY REALIZED THAT *THE SKY DRAGON* would be the final Charlie Chan film of the series. In fact, it was considered something of a trial run before the series was updated and sent in another direction. A solid dynamic between Keye Luke and Roland Winters in their roles as Lee and Charlie Chan was tested in the previous movie *The Feathered Serpent* and was firmly established here. Along with being one of the better Charlie Chan films from the Roland Winters period, *The Sky Dragon* was also a promising look at the what was supposed to mark series' future.

Charlie Chan and his Number One Son Lee are flying on a commercial airline along with several others including two insurance couriers carrying a large sum of money, a detective named Anderson, a man named Andy Barrett, and follies performer Wanda LaFern. The stewardess, Marie Burke, is actually former racketeer Connie Barrett, a former acquaintance of Andy and Wanda, who accuse her of stealing money from them. She denies it and begs them not to reveal her identity. The passengers are served coffee and are all knocked out. When Lee Chan awakens, he sees that one of the couriers Ed Davidson, has been stabbed to death and the money has been stolen. He awakens Charlie Chan and points out the murder. Lee then goes to the cockpit where the pilot is knocked out and takes over the flying of the plane. The plane lands in San Francisco where it is met by Birmingham and Lieutenant Ruark. Ruark, Charlie and Lee Chan, and Birmingham Brown go to the theater where Wanda is performing and find pilot Don Blake unconscious with a fractured skull. Tim Norton, the other pilot, is caught

The Sky Dragon • 271

Noel Neill, Roland Winters, Elena Verdugo

while attempting to flee the scene. Later, Charlie Chan breaks into Andy Barrett's home. Barrett arrives with Marie and Charlie discusses what he knows about the case. When Chan returns home he is met by Norton's girlfriend, stewardess Jane Marshall, who insists he is innocent. Chan is receptive. Later, Barrett bursts into Charlie Chan's home and starts to give him important information, hoping to make a deal. But he is shot and killed by detective John Anderson, who had been trailing him. After Charlie and Lee, with Birmingham's help, do some research into the lives of the suspects, they are gathered onto the plane where the detective indicates that Blake has come to, and was able to identify the murderer. Lee comes onto the plane heavily bandaged to assume the role of Blake, and when one of the suspects prepares to shoot him, that suspect is shot by another. It is then that Charlie reveals the murderer and wraps up the case (see Appendix A).

The Sky Dragon was penned by Oliver Drake, who had done a nice job of adapting one of his old westerns into the previous Chan film, *The Feathered Serpent*. Drake appeared to understand the relationship between Lee and Charlie Chan despite the fact that the Monogram films offered a much different dynamic between Jimmy (or Tommy) and Charlie. Lee is enthusiastic and impulsive, but rarely bumbling, and has both skills and courage that are more supportive of Charlie Chan's investigation. Roland Winters and Keye Luke are allowed to play off each other. Birmingham is not on the plane, but does meet the Chans at the airport. While he is waiting, there is a delightful scene with him discovering an attractive woman who is giving him the eye. He starts to flirt with her and she says "you are a very impetuous man," whereupon Birmingham replies, "you're right, I should go on a diet."

Along with his connection to Charlie, the Lee Chan character also connects with Birmingham, and just as effectively as Jimmy (or Tommy) had in earlier films. Keye Luke is able to balance both aspects of his character – the comical and the serious – with equal aplomb. In one scene he is heroically flying an airplane to safety when the pilot is incapacitated, and in another he is joining Birmingham in enthusiastically spreading newspapers all over the apartment trying to help with the investigation, but is told to stay behind while Charlie ventures further by going to the theater. He and Birmingham sneak into the theater through a window despite Charlie's orders, entering from the alley. Of course Birmingham is his comically timid self, stating: "I got an idea! Let's go home!" Lee states, "I'll go in first." Birmingham says "and last." However, when they do get in, they discover the unconscious Marie. The script keeps them very much part of the investigation. They are not admonished by Charlie when he discovers they have arrived.

Charlie uses Lee much more than he would Jimmy (or Tommy). When he goes to meet with Barrett, it is revealed at the end of their meeting that Lee had been hiding in the closet with a gun pointed at the suspect. Lee is pure seriousness in this scene, and most effective.

The Sky Dragon is directed by Lesley Selander, a B movie specialist who worked effectively across many genres, especially westerns. It is perhaps this background that caused him to use loud musical flourishes in some scenes. In an otherwise quiet mystery, these moments can be jarring, but are still somehow effective. Not a stylist, Selander's main intent was to allow the narrative to progress. He does so effectively. Selander also makes good use of mystery movie clichés (hands creeping around doors, lights going out, et. al.).

The supporting cast is outstanding. Noel Neill, later Lois Lane on TV's *The Adventures of Superman*, and such noted veterans as Lyle Talbot, John Eldredge (who appeared in several Chan films), Tim Ryan (repeating his role as Ruark), and Iris Adrian add a great deal. Paul Maxey does a strong job playing against type. Elena Verdugo, according to her friend Jeffrey Roberts, enjoyed the experience:[1]

> She recalled it as being a happy set and she enjoyed Roland Winters as a fellow actor. She was pleased to be reunited with him on the *Meet Millie* sitcom of the 1950's. She spoke warmly of Roland Winters as a pleasure to work with and (I remember this specifically) as a better actor than he was given credit for. I do remember saying to her, "it's just cool you got to work with Charlie Chan!" Her reply was: "Well, after the Wolf Man, Bud & Lou, Jungle Jim, Bomba, Gene Autry and the rest - he fit right in! But Roland was a dear."

The Sky Dragon is a typically low budget movie, but does make use of several sets rather than a limited few. They do not expand the budget, but do expand the concept, adding more layers to the Lee Chan character and connecting him more to the case as something of a partner to Charlie Chan. That as the concept that would lead the studio into their next idea for the series, to film them on location in Europe. "We were supposed to make more pictures in Europe," Mantan Moreland recalled in a 1971 interview. "But I told them I couldn't go. Here in the states, I had movie jobs, I had stage work, a lot of things like that. In Europe I would just have the Charlie Chan job. But those pictures never did get made."

Keye Luke told Ken Hanke for his book *Charlie Chan at the Movies*:[2]

---

1. Social media message to the author, July 6, 2017
2. Hanke, Ken. *Charlie Chan at the Movies*. Jefferson, NC: McFarland, 2004

> *Sky Dragon* was the best thing we made at Monogram. They liked it so well they planned to make three more – one in London, one in Paris and one in Rome. *Sky Dragon* had a good story. I was in New York waiting to go over the Atlantic and got a call from them that said, 'Gee, we're sorry but Her Majesty's government devaluated the pound and our frozen funds have taken a dive.' So we never made them.

When one looks at *The Sky Dragon* as a harbinger for what the studio might do with a larger budget and location filmmaking, it is unfortunate that not one movie was made under these conditions.

If we imagine the Charlie Chan series entering the 1950s, the character would likely have adapted just as Depression era Charlie Chan adapted to wartime Charlie Chan. A change in the settings, in the stories, in the basic approach, but maintaining the essence of the established formula and the central actors. It appears, on paper, like it would have been a success. But, unfortunately, *The Sky Dragon* was the final movie in the Charlie Chan film series.

Charlie Chan After the Movies

THERE IS A SCENE on an episode of TV's *The Honeymooners* entitled "A Better Living Through TV" where, after Ralph Kramden and Ed Norton botch a live TV commercial, Norton looks at the camera and yells, "and now back to Charlie Chan." The joke here was that most of the major studios refused to put their movies on television, fearing the competition. If they can watch movies at home, then why go to the theater? The smaller studios like Monogram didn't have a problem with doing so, as they had now become the more prestigious Allied Artists and were glad to make some extra revenue from their older product. And, although they were a major studio, 20th Century Fox saw no harm in releasing some of their old B product to TV. Thus, beginning in the early 1950s, the Charlie Chan movies starting dotting the airwaves, and became a staple of afternoon programming for decades thereafter. When the *Honeymooners* episode aired in 1955, Charlie Chan films were already a major part of the TV schedule.

Television producers responded in 1957 by creating *The New Adventures of Charlie Chan*, a TV series featuring non-Asian actor J. Carroll Naish in the role of Chan (Naish had appeared in support of Warner Oland in *Charlie Chan at the Circus*), and James Hong, an American-born actor of Asian descent, as his son, Barry Chan. There were 39 episodes of this Chan series filmed, the first five in America and the rest in the United Kingdom. They followed the formula of the movies, with Charlie often denying a suspected killer is the actual culprit. However, the son in the TV series is more serious and helpful, and less bungling than often featured in the movies. The premise had Chan and his son traveling through Europe, and getting involved in murder cases along the way. Familiar character actors like Strother Martin and Hans Con-ried appeared in the various episodes, One episode features Phillip Ahn, who had also appeared with Sidney Toler in *Charlie Chan in Honolulu* and with Roland Winters in *The Chinese Ring*. Television seemed to be a natural fit for the Chan series. It had been a popular radio show almost for the entire duration of the movie series. But the series only lasted one season.

It wasn't until the seventies before another Charlie Chan TV series was produced, this time an animated cartoon for Saturday mornings. This was during a period when programming on Saturday morning was designed for youngsters, and in the Fall of 1972, *The Amazing Chan and the Chan Clan* was produced by Hanna-Barbera and telecast on CBS. Only 16 episodes were produced, and the series only ran new episodes from September 9 thru December 30. It continued in reruns until the summer of 1973, lasting one season. Despite its lack of any real success, this animated series is significant in that it hired former Number One Son of the movies Keye Luke to voice the character of Charlie Chan. This made Luke the first Asian actor to portray Charlie Chan since E.L. Park in 1929. This animated series had everything one might expect from a 1970s Hanna-Barbera cartoon, but that it continued the family dynamic established by the Chan films, and his kids got to play a large role in solving the cases.

In 1971, actor Ross Martin, best known for TV's *The Wild Wild West* had starred as Charlie Chan in a TV movie entitled *Happiness is a Warm Clue*, which was broadcast on British TV in 1973. The film did not play on American television, however, until 1979, where it was retitled *The Return of Charlie Chan*. In 1981, Clive Donner directed Peter Ustinov as Charlie Chan in the comedy *Charlie Chan and the Curse of the Dragon Queen*, which received a negative reaction from many Asian American moviegoers and flopped at the box office. In the early 2000's Lucy Liu was announced as planning to executive produce a new Charlie Chan film, in which she'd be cast as his granddaughter, but as of this writing, no such film has been produced.

In 2003, the Fox Movie Channel remastered their Charlie Chan films with Warner Oland and Sidney Toler, and planned to run a marathon on the cable station. After a few films had been broadcast, a protest from Asian American groups caused the marathon to be discontinued. The films were preceded by a panel discussion of Asian Americans (including actor George Takei) pointing out what they believed were negative interpretations in the Charlie Chan movies.

This was not the first time the films came under fire from groups who found them offensive. In a 1985 interview for TV Ontario in Canada, Keye Luke addressed the issue of the portrayal of Charlie Chan:

> I think that regardless of race, color, background, so on – if a man can create a character which you can believe, he is an artist and is entitled to the distinction of artistry, and I don't think race has a thing to do about it. Furthermore, at that time there were no Orientals around that could have possibly played that part, for one thing. They might have some today, but I don't know of any – that is, those that fit the Chan image - you know, that portly, genial sort of character.

Luke further stated, "my god, we had a Chinese hero!" Victor Sen Yung also defended the films, as did Layne Tom, jr.

However, despite the fact that all of the existing Charlie Chan movies from Fox and Monogram have been released to DVD, some Asian Americans continue to find the series offensive. In 2010 a 1968 documentary *The Great Charlie Chan* was discovered in the Warner Brothers vaults by Harvey Chertok, a vice president of the studio's publicity department, and its revival was met with the same sort of protests as had the films on cable TV. *The New York Times* stated:

> For many activists, Charlie Chan remains a symbol of Hollywood's failure to accurately portray Asians and Asian-Americans. The character was usually played by white actors who were made up to seem Asian and who spoke English with an exaggerated accent. But some Asian-Americans say that although Charlie Chan was an amalgam of stereotypes, he should be looked at in a broader context 80 years after he was created.

It should also be noted that, at the time the films were produced, the Chinese responded favorably to the Charlie Chan series coming from America. In *The Chinese Mirror: A Journal of Chinese Film History* an article on the Chan series stated:[1]

---

1. "Charlie Chan in China." *Chinese Mirror: A Journal of Chinese Film History* May, 2008

One of the reasons for this acceptance was this was the first time Chinese audiences saw a positive Chinese character in an American film, a sharp departure from the "sinister Oriental" stereotypes in earlier movies like *Thief of Baghdad* and *Welcome Danger*, which incited riots that shut down the Shanghai theater showing it. The popularity of the movies among the Chinese community extended beyond China itself: the greatest concentration of overseas Chinese in the 1930s was in southeast Asia, and a survey taken during that era showed that among all American motion pictures, the Chan films were by far the most popular. Warner Oland had an interest in China even before he assumed the Chan character, and had long wanted to visit. So after the Chan series made him famous there, Oland at last fulfilled this dream on March 22, 1936, when his travel party docked in Shanghai aboard the steamship, Asian Empress. His arrival electrified the city's news and movie communities, with every major Shanghai newspaper and film studio sending reporters to interview him. The typical headline on the story was, "Great Chinese Detective Arrives in Shanghai," the reports all referring to him as "Mr. Chan." Oland held a press conference at 5pm the day of his arrival, during which he tirelessly maintained his Charlie Chan persona while answering reporters' questions, even at one point referring to the goal of his China trip, not without humor, as being to "my ancestors." He expressed this again a few days later at a welcome banquet held for him by various Shanghai society and community leaders. He wore the familiar clothing the Chan character usually wore in the movies, stood up when the audience applauded him enthusiastically, and emotionally declared, "visiting the land of my ancestors makes me so happy." At that moment, Warner Oland and Charlie Chan had merged into one, becoming in the eyes of those present, one and the same Chinese person.

The article further states that in 1937 Chinese filmmakers began their own Charlie Chan series based on the American movies, with actor Xu

Xinyuan as Chan, operating his own private detective agency with the help of his daughter Man-na Chan, played by Gu Meijun.

As we conclude this text and its celebration of the Charlie Chan movies, respect must be given to those Asian Americans who remain offended by the series. The Charlie Chan films are a flawed but admirable attempt by Hollywood to bring a non-stereotypical Asian hero to the big screen. Unfortunately, some of the traits given to Chan—spouting Chinese proverbs, speaking broken English—ended up playing into those stereotypes (although Charlie did get to shoot down a racist remark directed toward him on occasion). And a lot of what we see as unsettling in the 21st century—namely, casting a white actor to play an Asian character—wasn't frowned upon as much back in the 1930s and 1940s. But the good things about the Chan character—his benevolence, intelligence, and sense of humor—seriously challenges anything that might be considered negative. It is important for any of us to approach ethnic portrayals with the understanding that nothing malicious was intended on the part of the actors and filmmakers involved, and that the movies remain fresh and enjoyable as late as the 21st century.

Appendix A
Revealing the Murderer In Each Movie

IN AN EFFORT TO AVOID SPOILERS in each chapter, with the understanding that there are some readers who have not seen every movie, we are listing all of the culprits in this Appendix. And, just to be more uniform, this includes all of the films for which there are chapters, even those that are lost at the time of this writing.

Charlie Chan Carries On
John Ross, a man with a limp

The Black Camel
Charlie Chan finds a piece of the diamond pin ein the heel of Anna's shoe, she confesses that she is Denny Mayo's wife and that she killed Shelah. Jessup the butler is the one who pulls a gun as Chan goes to arrest Anna, because he is in love with her. Jessop then confesses that he shot Smith and had thrown the knife at Charlie.

Charlie Chan's Chance
It is Dunwood who grabs Charlie Chan's gun without realizing it is unloaded, and confesses to Grey's murder.

Charlie Chan's Greatest Case
Harry Jennison, Dan Winterslip's lawyer, reveals himself as the murderer. Just as in the previous film, Jennison also picks up an unloaded gun in an attempt to escape.

Charlie Chan's Courage

An actor named Jerry Delaney poses as Madden, but is revealed as an imposter when he signs a document with his left hand (Madden is right handed). He is part of a crime ring, and it is Professor Gamble who is revealed to be the murderer of Louie Wong.

Charlie Chan in London

Charlie Chan announces to the suspects that the murderer's fingerprints are on the missing plans. Richmond then fires a gun at Chan, but it is filled with blanks – something Charlie arranged earlier. Richmond turns out to be a spy named Paul Frank. Meanwhile, Paul Gray is saved from execution and released from prison.

Charlie Chan in Paris

Xavier arrives and shoots at Charlie Chan and is captured by detectives. Detective Chan then removes a mask and it turns out Xaiver is Henri Latouche. He and Corday both used the disguise to create alibi for each other. Corday murdered Dufresne, and Latouche killed Nardi. Chan then tells the inspector that Yvette is his assistang, so she is released from custody.

Charlie Chan in Egypt

Charlie stops Thurston from stabbing Tom, and reveals that the bullets from Tom and Arnold were from a gun owned by Thurston, who is arrested by police.

Charlie Chan in Shanghai

Charlie pulls a gun on Andrews and accuses him of having been the gang leader all along. Lee arrives with a wire photo of the real Andrews, who was killed weeks earlier in California, proving Charlie's accusation to be correct.

Charlie Chan's Secret

The carbon remnants are revealed to be in the hand of Fred Gage.

Charlie Chan at the Circus

It is Tom Holt in the ape costume, who is killed. Nellie and her brother are arrested for having forged the marriage certificate after Kinney's death.

Charlie Chan at the Race Track

Lee creates a diversion, Charlie re-switches the horses, and is spotted by one of the crooks. When he is seen phoning the others, he is arrested. Charlie also deduced that one of the gamblers wrote a threatening note to himself to throw detectives off the track. He noticed that the man read the note without glasses, whereas otherwise he needed his glasses to read. It is because the first note he had written himself. The man behind everything is George Chester (Alan Dinehart).

Charlie Chan at the Opera

Chan shows that Gravelle's knife was not the murder weapon. Chan reveals that Anita was with Enrico and Lilli when they were unconscious, and was the only one who knew Gravelle was also there, allowing her to frame him. Anita confesses and is taken away.

Charlie Chan at the Olympics

Charlie shows that Cartwright made it look like Hopkins stole the device. And that it was Cartwright who murdered Hopkins and had earlier killed Miller in Hawaii.

Charlie Chan on Broadway

Charlie points out Speed as the murderer, indicating that his newspaper story pointed out that Billie had been shot in the back – something he would not have known had he not been the culprit.

Charlie Chan at Monte Carlo

Gordon is revealed as the murderer, tries to escape through a window, but he is hit by a car and killed

Charlie Chan in Honolulu

Charlie sets a trap to catch the killer, who turns out the lights but is caught by the flash of a camera that has been set up. The killer is revealed to be Captain Johnson, who had not been one of the immediate suspects during the narrative.

Charlie Chan in Reno

Vivien is revealed as the murderer, with Dr. Ainsley as her assistant when he is caught about to inject Mrs. Russell with a deadly poison.

Charlie Chan at Treasure Island
Rhadini is revelaed to be the real Zodiac. He had used his wand as a blowgun to kill Abdul, who posed as Zodiac, and wound himself, all as a ploy to keep detectives off the track.

City in Darkness
Petroff is revealed to be an enemy foreigh agent. Charlotte Ronnell is discovered to have been sending munitions to the enemy. Attempting to escape, she is killed in a high speed chase. Antoine admits to having killed Petroff after discovering he was a foreign agent.

Charlie Chan in Panama
The school marm is revealed to be Reiner when she pulls a gun. She attempts escape but is captured by police.

Charlie Chan's Murder Cruise
The killer attempts to murder Mrs. Pendelton and is revealed to be Professor Gordon

Charlie Chan at the Wax Museum
Tom Agnew is revealed to be Dagan.

Murder Over New York
Chan stops Fenton from drinking water given to him by Jeffrey, finds that it is poison, and declares Jeffrey is the culprit.

Dead Men Tell
The murderer is unmasked to reveal Jed Thomasson

Charlie Chan in Rio
Marana is revealed to be the brother to the murdered Manuel and confesses to murdering Lola, but Helen is revealed to be Barbara, his widow, and confesses to the murder. Marana was trying to spare her.

Castle in the Desert
Watson, the sculptor, is revealed to be Cesare, the killer

Charlie Chan in the Secret Service
Laska reappears as socialite Mrs. Winters tries to hurry away. She is

revealed to be the murderer, and that she is German spy Fraulein Maulich.

The Chinese Cat
Deacon was killed by Caitlin

Black Magic
Chardo is Paul Hamlin. Charlie reveals a spring gun concealed in a cigar used to kill Bonner.

The Jade Mask
The murders are done with a poison dart from a ventriloquist's dummy. Stella is the accomplice and Archer is the culprit, wearing a mask that disguises him as Walter, whose body is found later.

The Scarlet Clue
Mrs Marsh is revealed to be the killer and the leader of the spy ring. She is killed trying to escape.

The Shanghai Cobra
After Charlie reveals a bank guard is really Jan Van Horn, he also indicates that a bank officer is the gang leader and killer.

Red Dragon
Bradish is revealed as the killer.

Dark Alibi
Prison guard Kensey, chagrined that Harley opposed his marriage to June, frames Harley for a murder he committed.

Shadows Over Chinatown
Jeff Hay is revealed to be Winfield in disguise

Dangerous Money
The missionary and his wife turn out to be two men (one disguised as a woman) who committed the crimes

The Trap
The culprit who is involved in the car crash while fleeing is Mrs.

Thorn, who confesses and explains as she dies.

The Chinese Ring
Sergeant Davidson arrests Kelso, but Charlie Chan intervenes and explains how Armstrong stole Mei Ling's money and had plans to swindle Kelso and Kong out of ther take. He killed the maid and the mute boy.

Docks of New Orleans
Charlie reveals to police that Swendstrom is the murderer and that his wife was an accomplice.

The Shanghai Chest
It is the lawyer, Seward, whom Charlie Chan reveals to be the actual culprit.

The Golden Eye
Foreman Driscoll is outsmarted by Tommy Chan when entering the room and pulling out a gun. When he attempts to flee he is shot by Bartlett, who is revealed to be the actual head of the gold smuggling activities.

The Feathered Serpent
Stanley is the murderer in a film that reveals the murderer's identity early on.

The Sky Dragon
Connie pulls a gun on Lee, who is impersonating Blake, and is shot by Anderson, who is taken into custody.

Appendix B
Bibliography

BOOKS

Berlin, Howard. *Charlie Chan Film Encyclopedia* Jefferson, NC: McFarland, 2005
Berlin, Howard. *Charlie Chan's Words of Wisdom.* Washington DC: Wildside Press. 2003
Der Biggers, Earl. *Charlie Chan: Five Complete Novels: The House Without a Key; The Chinese Parrot; Behind That Curtain; The Black Camel; Keeper of the Keys.* Avenel, NJ: Avenel Books, 1981
Hanke, Ken. *Charlie Chan at the Movies.* Jefferson, NC: McFarland, 2004
Huang, Yunte. *Charlie Chan: The Untold Story of the Honorable Detective and his Rendezvous with American History* NY: WW Norton. 2010
Parish, James Robert. *The Great Movie Series.* NY: A.S. Barnes, 1971
Parish, James Robert and Michael Pitts. *The Great Detective Pictures* Lanham, MD: Scarecrow Press. 1990

ARTICLES

"Big Buildup Failed, Question is Why" *The Morning News* Wilmington, Delaware July 11, 1942
"Critical Focusing." *Movie Makers* January, 1936
Chan The Man. *The New Yorker.* August 20, 2010
"Charlie Chan in China." *Chinese Mirror: A Journal of Chinese Film History* May, 2008
"Charlie Chan Reveals" *Silver Screen* July, 1937
"Giving Charlie Chan a Second Chance" NPR book review

"Magnificent Charlie Chan is Making Great Comeback" *The Cincinnati Enquirer* September 17, 1943
"Script Notes Help Director to Relax" *Panama City Pilot* September 15, 1939
"Star Says Chan's Virtually Alive." *The Kane Republican* July 6, 1935
Studio News: At Fox's Western Avenue Studio. *Silver Screen*. October 1934
"35 Years' Obscure Success Finally over for Actor Toler" *Detroit Free Press* June 27, 1939

REVIEWS

"The Black Camel" *Motion Picture Herald* . May 16, 1931
"Charlie Chan at the Circus" *Modern Screen* June, 1936
"Charlie Chan at the Olympics" *Silver Screen* June, 1937
"Charlie Chan at the Opera" *Motion Picture Herald* October 17, 1936
"Charlie Chan at the Wax Museum" *Variety* October 2, 1940
"Charlie Chan Carries On" *Motion Picture Magazine.* July 31, 1931
"Charlie Chan in Honolulu" *Variety* December 21, 1938
"Charlie Chan in London." *Motion Picture Herald.* September 22, 1934
"Charlie Chan in Panama" *Motion Picture Herald* August 5, 1939
"Charlie Chan in Shanghai" *Motion Picture Herald.* September 14, 1935
"Charlie Chan on Broadway" *Box Office* August 7, 1937
"Charlie Chan on Broadway" *Variety* September 22, 1937
"Charlie Chan's Chance. *Variety.* January 26, 1932
"Charlie Chan's Secret" *Film Bulletin* February 5, 1936
"Charlie Chan's Secret" *Variety* January 22, 1936
"The Chinese Parrot." *Universal Weekly.* September 17, 1927
"City in Darkness" *Brooklyn Daily Eagle* December 18, 1939
"City in Darkness" *Variety* November 18, 1939
"Dead Men Tell" *Variety* March 26, 1941
"House Without a Key" review *Moving Picture World.* November 26, 1926
"The Jade Mask" *Film Daily* February 1, 1945

INTERVIEWS

Jeffrey Roberts – social media message to the author – July 6, 2017
Kay Linnaker in *Charlie Chan is Missing: The Last Days of Warner Oland* - 2005

Keye Luke interview conducted for Canadian television (TV Ontario) in
    Hollywood, California, circa 1985
Mantan Moreland – phone conversation with the author – 1971
Michael Blake – email to the author on July 3, 2017
Victor Sen Yung interview *St Louis Post Dispatch* November 4, 1971
Victor Sen Yung interview *The Lincoln Star* August 24, 1977

Index

A
Abbott, Bud 3, 163
Adrian Iris 273
A-Haunting We Will Go 167
Ahn, Phillip 119, 245, 276
Albright, Hardie 200
Aldrich, Katherine 167
All Quiet on the Western Front 124
Alyn, Kirk 238, 239
Allen, Gracie 5
Altman, Robert 38
Amazing Chan and the Chan Clan, The 276
Ames. Leon 100
Andiola, Alfred 120
Andrews, Stanley 252
Apana, Chang 3, 18, 19
Arbo, Manuel 9

B
Baldwin, Dick 110
Bank Dick, The 151
Bari, Lynn 110
Barrat, Robert 119
Barrie, Mona 38
Baxter, Warner 5
Beaudine, William 242, 244, 252, 254, 255, 256, 260, 266, 267
Beck, Thomas 45, 50, 51, 76, 84, 100

Behind That Curtain 5, 19, 21, 22, 84
Bellamy, Madge 38
Beddoe, Don 151
Bennet, Spencer Gordon 4
Bennett, Joan 147
Best, Deannie 257
Best, Willie 214, 215, 216, 230, 232, 244, 239
Big Noise, The 242
Biggers, Earl Derr 1, 3, 4, 5, 6, 8, 9, 14, 22, 23, 24, 28, 33, 38, 39, 62, 102, 139

Black Camel, The 3, 13-19, 26, 34, 36, 60, 76, 170, 173, 236
Black Magic 192-196, 198
Blake, Larry 238, 239
Blake, Michael 239
Blythe, Betty 191
Blystone, Stanley 157
Bogart, Humphrey 147
Bond Ward 110
Bonanova, Fortunio 216
Boteler, Wade 153
Bowery Boys, The 179
Bowery Champs 263
Boyd, Mildred 216
Brasno, George and Olive 67, 68, 70

Brent, Evelyn 263
Bretherton, Howard 236, 239
Brian, Mary 45
Bride of Frankenstein 80
Bridge, Al 200
Broken Blossoms 3
Brooks, Phyllis 119
Bromberg, J. Edward 100
Brown, Joe E. 124
Bryant, Jan 238
Buchanan, Elsa 38
Bufford, Daisy 190
Bullfighters, The 242
Burns, George 5

C

Cagney, James 45
Callahan, George 218
Calloway, Cab 5
Captain January 124
Captain Tugboat Annie 215
Carey, Harry 69
Carroll, Leo G. 151, 154
Carter, Ben 206, 216, 220, 221, 250
Castle in the Desert 175-178, 227
Cat and the Canary, The 5
Chan, Frances 193-198
Chandler, George 177, 211
Chandler, Jeff 216
Chandler Tanis 238
Charlie Chan and the Curse of the DragonQueen 276
Charlie Chan at Monte Carlo 102, 103-108, 176
Charlie Chan at the Circus 64, 65-70, 91, 163, 275
Charlie Chan at the Olympics 87-94
Charlie Chan at the Ringside see *Mr. Moto's Gamble*
Charlie Chan at the Opera 77, 78, 79-86, 88, 180, 242
Charlie Chan at the Race Track 71, 73-79, 91
Charlie Chan at the Wax Museum 154, 155-158
Charlie Chan at Treasure Island 127-134, 252
Charlie Chan Carries On 3, 7-11, 147, 150, 151
Charlie Chan in Honolulu 111, 113, 114, 115-120, 122, 172, 276
Charlie Chan in London 33-40, 96
Charlie Chan in Panama 133, 143-148, 153,
Charlie Chan in Paris 40-46, 50, 51, 58, 76, 173
Charlie Chan in Rio 169-174, 176
Charlie Chan in Reno 121-126, 172
Charlie Chan in the Secret Service 181, 183-186, 194
Charlie Chan is Missing: The Last Days of Warner Oland 104
Charlie Chan on Broadway 95-102, 104, 252
Charlie Chan's Chance 20, 21-25,
Charlie Chan's Greatest Case 24, 25-29, 196
Charlie Chan's Murder Cruise 11, 147, 149-154, 186, 221
Charlie Chan's Secret 58, 59-64, 66
Chertok, Harvey 277
Chinese Cat, The 187-194
Chinese Mirror: A Journal of Chinese Film History, A 277
Chinese Parrot, The 3, 4, 5, 29, 30
Chinese Ring, The 239, 241-246, 276
Chung, Bo 5
Churchill, Marguerite 11
City in Darkness 134, 135-142, 144, 145, 160

Clark, Dan 45
Clarke, Charles 167
Clyde, Andy 163, 232
Coffin, Tristam 257
Coghlan, Frank "Junior" 76
Cohan, George M. 3
Connolly, Walter 113
Conway, Morgan 125
Coogan, Jackie 4
Cortez, Ricardo 125, 162
Costello, Don 216
Costello, Lou 3, 163
Crosman, Henrietta 62, 63
Currie, Louise 245

D
Daddy 4
Dale, Virginia 252
Dangerous Money 229-234
Dante's Inferno 167
Dark Alibi 216, 217-222, 227
Darling, Scott 242, 248, 252, 253, 255, 260, 266
Darro, Frankie 76
Dead End Kids 163
Dead Men Tell 165-168
Deane, Shirely 68-69
Demarest, William 81
DeMille, Katherine 92
DeWitt, Jack 229, 232
Dickerson, Dudley 232
Dinehart, Alan 76
Dirty Harry 134
Docks of New Orleans 247-252
Dodd, Claire 119
Don Ricardo Returns 232
Donner, Clive 276
Down the Stretch 215
Dracula 17
Drake, Oliver 266, 272
Dumbrille, Douglas 177

E
East Side Kids, The 100, 179, 263
Eilers, Sally 14, 17, 18
Eldredge, George 222
Eldredge, John 219, 222, 273
Ellis, Robert 76, 138, 232
Eran Tece 9
Exhibitor's Herald World 4, 5

F
Fall of the House of Usher, The 157
Feathered Serpent, The 262, 263, 265-268
Fields, W.C. 5, 45, 100, 151, 163
Film Daily 46, 84, 147, 186, 200, 245
Fong, Benson 180, 183-196, 198, 201-222, 242, 272
Ford, Eugene 36, 102
Ford, Francis 69
Ford, John 69
Forman, Carol 252
Foster, Norman 124, 125, 128, 132, 145
Fowley, Douglas 100, 110, 131, 252
Foy, Bryan 178
Frankenstein 80
Frye, Dwight 17, 28

G
Gable, Clark 113
Garbo, Greta 46
Garrick, John 11
Gerard, Helen 239
Gladiator, The 124
Goetz, William 179
Golden Eye, The 259-264
Gordon, C. Henry 11, 13, 15, 140, 170
Gosford Park 38
Grable, Betty 156
Grace, Meyer 220

Granger, Dorothy 200
Grapes of Wrath, The 69
Grauman's Chinese Theater 210
Great Charlie Chan, The 277
Great Guns 167, 176
Green Archer, The 4
Griffies, Ethel 177
Griffith, D.W. 3
Griffith, Raymond 22

H
Hale, Jonathan 76, 92
Hamilton, John 110
Hands Up 22
Hanke, Ken 273
Hard to Handle 45
Harrigan, William 28
Harvey, Paul 119
Hayden, Harry 252
Henry, Charlotte 84
Hicks, Russell 222, 257
Holden, William 11
Honeymooners, The 153, 275
Hong, James 275
Hope, Bob 100, 215
Hoshelle, Marjorie 216
House Without a Key 3, 4, 24, 25, 26
How Green Was My Valley 69
Howard, Shemp 163
Huber, Harold 100, 105, 107, 1009, 110, 139, 140, 171
Hughes, Carol 216
Humberstone, H. Bruce 74, 82, 83, 88, 91, 92, 119
Hymer, Warren 11

I
Informer, The 69
International House 5
It's a Wonderful Life 22

J
Jade Mask, The 196, 197-202
Jazz Singer, The 10
Jitterbugs 177
Johnston, W. Ray 186
Jolson, Al 10
Jones, Haywood 250

K
Kansas City Confidential 210
Karloff, Boris 5, 6, 79-85, 134, 180, 205, 242
Karlson, Phil 210, 211, 212, 214, 216, 218, 219, 220, 221, 222, 224, 227
Keane, Robert Emmett 216
Keaton, Buster 17
Keeper of the Keys 3, 28
Kendall, Cy 113, 191
Kinnell, Murray 16, 32, 38, 170
Kissinger, Miriam 228
Kuwa, George 4

L
Lachman, Harry 68, 163, 167, 177
Lake, Arthur 69
Landis, Carole 257
Lane, Allan 92
Lane, Richard 119
Larkin, John 132-133
Larue, Jack 145
Last Command, The 263
Laurel and Hardy 64, 113, 163, 167, 176, 177, 243, 256
Lawrence, Marc 100, 119
Lawrence, Rosina 64
Leeds, Herbert 141
Leni, Paul 5
Leyton, Drue 32, 37, 38, 67
Linaker, Kay 104
Ling, Bo 5
Littlefield, Lucien 177

Liu, Lucy 276
Livingston, Robert 266
Logan, Helen 76, 138, 232
Lorre, Peter 51, 85, 100, 108, 109, 110, 134, 178
Lowery, Robert 125, 151, 163
Lost Weekend, The 38
Love Insurance 3
Lowe, Edward T. 76
Lugosi, Bela 5, 12-18, 170
Luke, Edwin 196, 198
Luke, Keye 1, 41,42, 46, 51-113, 116, 117, 120, 131, 134, 152, 180,184, 196, 198, 201, 262, 268, 270, 272, 273, 276, 277

M
MacBride, Donald 131, 162
MacFadden, Hamilton 14, 15, 19, 45, 173
Major, Robert W. 201
Maltese Falcon, The 125
Man Called Horse, A 232
Man on the Flying Trapeze 45
Man Who Shot Liberty Valance, The 69
Marsh, Joan 100
Martin, Ross 1, 276
Maxey, Paul 273
McCabe, John 64
McKay, Wanda 263
Meet Millie 273
Meeting at Midnight (see: *Black Magic*)
Meijun, Gu 279
Miljan, John 45
Milland, Ray 38
Miller, Walter 4
Millionaires in Prison 163
Mr. Moto's Gamble 108, 109-114
Mr. Moto's Last Warning 113
Mr. Wong Detective 248

Mr. Wong in Chinatown 242, 244
Modern Screen 69
Moore, Pauline 92, 132
Moran, Lois 5
Moran of the Lady Letty 4
Moreland, Mantan 180-227, 230, 232, 235-269, 273
Morse, Terry 222, 224, 228, 230, 232
Motion Picture Daily 84, 125, 186, 201, 206
Motion Picture Herald 19, 28, 39, 46, 58, 84, 111, 133, 147, 177, 206, 245
Motion Picture Magazine 9
Moving Picture World 4
Mowbray, Alan 38
Mudie, Leonard 152
Mundin, Herbert 62, 64
Murder Over New York 158, 159-164, 173
Mysterious Dr. Fu Manchu, The 10

N
Nagel, Anne 238
Naish, J. Carrol 1, 65,68, 275
Nash, Mary 145
Neill, Noel 273
Network 11
New Adventures of Charlie Chan, The 275-276
Newman, Samuel 254
Nixon, Marian 23
Norton, Jack 206
Nothing But The Truth 215

O
Oland Warner I, 6-109, 111-113, 119, 120, 125, 131, 145, 147, 150, 153, 154, 163, 176, 178, 196, 222, 239, 242, 249, 275, 278

One Night in the Tropics 3
Osborne, Ted 157
Our Relations 163
Owens, Jesse 92

P
Painted Veil, The 46
Palmer, Ernest 45
Park, E.L. 5, 276
Parry, Harvey 146-147
Parsons, Milton 167, 177
Perry Mason 254
Peterson, Ruth 46
Phantom of Chinatown 180
Phenix City Story, The 210
Pinn-Martin, Chris 145
Pitts, ZaSu 124
Poe, Edgar Allen 157
Post, William, jr. 16
Powell, William 113

Q
Qualen, John 46
Quigley, Charles 64
Quigley, Rita 239
Quillan, Eddie 132

R
Raft, George 147
Ray, Allene 4
Red Dragon, The 212, 213-216, 238
Reeves, George 167
Return of Charlie Chan, The 276
Revier, Dorothy 14, 15, 17, 18
Reynolds, Marjorie 245
Richmond, Kane 145, 162
Riders of Whistling Skull, The 266
Roberts, Jeffrey 273
Robinson, Dewey 191
Rogers, Jean 145
Rogers, Roy 132
Romero, Cesar 131

Rooney, Mickey 215
Rogers, Jean 167
Rogers, Will 76
Rosen, Phil 180, 185, 188, 190, 199, 200, 204, 210 212, 214
Rosenbloom, Maxie 110
Rozelle, Rita 16
Ryan, Irene 262
Ryan, Sheila 167, 173
Ryan, Tim 220, 257, 262, 273

S
Sanders, George 178
Saturday Evening Post 4, 8, 14
Scarlet Clue, The 203-20
Schrock, Raymond 227
Shadows Over Chinatown 222, 223-228, 232, 233
Shanghai Cobra, The 208-212
Searchers, The 69
Seiler, Lewis 45
Sen Yung, Victor 113, 115-175, 180, 181, 184, 194, 198, 206, 222, 225-268, 277
Sennett, Mack 124
Scott, Randolph 17
Selander, LeRoy 272-273
Seven Keys to Baldpate 3
Shanghai Chest, The 222, 253-258
Shanghai Express 10
She Wouldn't Say Yes 215
Sheik of Araby, The 22
Shores, Lynn 157, 179
Showman's Trade Review 125
Silver Screen 75
Singleton, Penny 69
Skouras, Spyros 156
Sky Dragon, The 269-274
Spider, The 215
Spy Smasher 125
Stalag 17 11
Stone, George E. 110

Summerville, Slim 124
Sunset Boulevard 11
Superman 124

T
Takei, George 276
Talbot, Lyle 273
Three Stooges 11, 163, 232
Toler, Sidney 1, 91, 113-239, 242, 245, 249, 250, 252, 262, 263, 268, 276
Tom, Layne jr. 89, 91, 92, 119, 153, 277
Trap, The 229, 232, 233, 234-240
Tilbury, Zeffie 11
Tracy, Spencer 17
Turpin, Ben 22

U
Underworld 263
Ustinov, Peter 1, 276

V
Valentino, Rudolph 4, 76
Van Zandt, Phillip 257
Varconi, Victor 16
Variety 46, 62, 100, 112, 119, 133, 139, 147, 153, 154, 158, 167, 177, 186, 201
Vallee, Rudy 5
Verdugo, Elena 273
Vernon, Wally 132

W
Wagon Train 263
Walking Tall 212
Walton, Douglas 38
Warner, H.B. 23
Warren, Janet 201
Watkins, Pierre 257
Watson, Minor 45
Way Out West 64

Weaver, Marjorie 151, 162
Welles, Orson 196
Werewolf of London 10
Whelan, Arlene 177-178
White, Marjorie 11
Williams, Tudor 83
Winters, Roland 1, 239-273, 276
Witherspoon, Cora 151
Withers, Grant 245
Withers, Jane 179
Witherspoon Cora 151
Woman Haters 11
Wong, Iris 125, 171, 172
Wong, Barbara Jean 216, 238, 260 (aka Jean Wong)
Woodbury, Joan 191
Woods, Donald 32, 100
Wylie, Phillip 124

X
Xinyuan, Xu 278-279

Y
Yamaoka, Otto 16, 18
Yarbrough, Barton 216

Z
Zanuck, Darryl 45, 46, 83, 156
Zodiac 134
Zucco, George 117. 118

www.ingramcontent.com/pod-product-compliance
Lightning Source LLC
Chambersburg PA
CBHW060111170426
43198CB00010B/846